Debating the Eighth

Edited by

Conor O'Riordan

DEBATING THE EIGHTH

Repeal or Retain?

Edited by

Conor O'Riordan

ORPEN PRESS

Published by
Orpen Press
Upper Floor, Unit K9
Greenogue Business Park
Rathcoole
Co. Dublin
Ireland

email: info@orpenpress.com
www.orpenpress.com

Paperback ISBN 978-1-78605-050-2
ePub ISBN 978-1-78605-051-9

Printed in Dublin by SPRINTprint Ltd

To my wife, Maryanne O'Riordan, for her support and understanding the importance of this subject

ACKNOWLEDGEMENTS

I would like to acknowledge my friend Derick Parsons for the advice he has provided throughout the process of putting this book together.

About the Contributors

Ursula Barry is an associate professor with University College Dublin responsible for the MA in Gender Studies and the author of a wide range of research reports and articles on gender, inequality and public policy in Ireland, including 'Discourses on Foetal Rights and Women's Embodiment' in *Abortion Papers Ireland*, Volume 2, and 'Gender and Economic Inequality in Ireland' (with Dr Maggie Feeley) in *Cherishing All Equally 2016*.

Róisín Bradley is a Trinity College Dublin law graduate. Róisín comes from County Donegal and is 21 years of age. She is currently studying for a Masters in Law in Trinity and will be pursuing a career as a barrister in the near future. Róisín is a member of the Ard Chomhairle of Fianna Fáil.

Catherine Connolly is an Independent Teachta Dála for Galway West/South Mayo. Catherine sits on the Public Accounts Committee and is Chair of the Committee on the Irish Language, the Gaeltacht and the Islands. Prior to her election to Dáil Éireann in 2016, Catherine was a city councillor for seventeen years, having been first elected to Galway City Council in the West local electoral area in June 1999 and subsequently re-elected in the South local electoral area in 2004. In that same year Catherine was elected Mayor of Galway.

Eóin de Bháldraithe is a priest in Bolton Abbey, Moone, Co. Kildare.

Mark Fitzpatrick was born in 1968 and raised in a Roman Catholic home. In 1985 he was converted to the Evangelical faith. He has been involved in church leadership for the past 25 years and is currently the pastor of Arann Reformed Baptist Church, which meets in Rathfarnham, Dublin.

Karen Gaffney is the president of a non-profit organisation dedicated to championing the journey to full inclusion in families, schools, the workplace and the community for people with developmental disabilities. She does this by creating awareness and calling attention to the tremendous capabilities of people with disabilities, delivering presentations and workshops to audiences worldwide. In addition to her non-profit work, Karen also works part-time at the Oregon Health Sciences University in their Institute on Development and Disability and in the Down Syndrome Clinic at OHSU.

Declan Ganley is a Galway-based businessman and political activist, and the Chairman and Chief Executive Officer of Rivada Networks. He is well-known for campaigning for a more democratic and accountable European Union, and led the successful campaign against the Lisbon Treaty in 2008. Declan lives near Tuam, Co. Galway, with his wife, Delia, and their four children.

Bernadette Goulding is the director of Rachael's Ireland and co-founder of womenhurt.ie.

Tracy Harkin is mum to Kathleen Rose, who is living with the life-limiting condition Trisomy 13. Tracy and her husband, Tom, are members of the parent support group everylifecounts. She resides with her family in County Down where she heads up the Iona Institute NI.

Kevin Keane is the President of Trinity College Dublin Students' Union. Previously, he studied law in Trinity and was very deeply involved in lobbying government on behalf of the students' union, and activism more generally in the college. His particular focus had been on education rights in developing countries, as well as refugee rights in Ireland.

Dr Anthony McCarthy is an ethicist based in London at the Society for the Protection of Unborn Children, having previously held the post of Research Fellow at the Linacre Centre, now the Anscombe Bioethics Centre. He holds degrees in Philosophy from King's College London, University College London and the University of Surrey, and lectures on bioethics and sexual ethics, including as a visiting scholar at the International Theological Institute in Trumau, Austria. He is the author of *Ethical Sex: Sexual Choices and their Nature and Meaning* and *Abortion Matters* (in press) in addition to articles on bioethical and other topics, both for an academic and a wider readership.

Kate O'Connell is a Fine Gael TD for Dublin Bay South. Originally from rural Westmeath, she is a qualified pharmacist with a Masters in Primary Care and Business. She is married to Morgan and they have three children, aged seven, five and two years. Since elected she has focused much of her energy on health, campaigning for improvements in the areas of women's health, drug strategy and cancer.

Jan O'Sullivan's involvement in politics began with the establishment of the first family planning clinic in Limerick in connection with the late Jim Kemmy in 1982. She was first elected to Dáil Éireann in the March 1998 by-election following the death of Jim Kemmy. Jan O'Sullivan has been re-elected at every election and she has served as Minister for Education & Skills, Minister of State for Housing & Planning, and Minister of State for Trade & Development in the thirty-first Dáil. She was first elected to Limerick City Council in 1985 as a member of the Democratic Socialist Party and served as a Senator and leader of the Labour Party in the Seanad between 1993 and 1997. She is married to Paul O'Sullivan and has two adult children, Paddy and Emily.

Bríd Smith is the People Before Profit TD for Dublin South Central and lives in the constituency. She has been a long-time socialist and feminist and has been active in building the movement to repeal the Eighth Amendment. Bríd is the only TD to have spoken publicly about her own personal experience of abortion. She is a member of the Joint Oireachtas Committee on the Eighth Amendment.

Valerie Tarico is Chair of the Board of Advocates for Planned Parenthood of the Great Northwest USA, and a psychologist and writer with a passion for personal and social evolution. Her articles have appeared on sites including the *Huffington Post, Jezebel, Salon, AlterNet*, and the *Institute for Ethics and Emerging Technologies*, and are available at *ValerieTarico.com*. As a social commentator, she tackles issues ranging from religious fundamentalism to gender roles, reproductive rights and technologies. A primary focus is on improving access to top-tier contraceptive technologies. To that end, in 2015 she co-founded Resilient Generation, a family-planning advocacy hub based in Seattle, Washington. She serves on the board of Advocates for Youth, a D.C.-based non-profit with wide-ranging programmes related to reproductive health and justice, and is a Senior Writing Fellow at Sightline Institute, a think-tank focused on sustainable prosperity.

Niamh Uí Bhriain is a pro-life activist and a spokeswoman for the Life Institute. She is also a director of the Save the Eighth campaign, which seeks to retain the constitutional protection afforded to both mother and baby in the Eighth Amendment.

Table of Contents

Table of Contents

Introduction

Conor O'Riordan

Most of us have had the experience of listening to, or joining in, heated debates on the issues of the day. In the Irish media, RTE's *The Late Late Show*, in tackling a range of subjects over the years, has many times successfully reproduced scenes of debate and discussion from our own colleges, living rooms and pubs.

Sometimes voices are raised and the passion and sincerity of those speaking are evident in the expressions and body language of the guests. As we approach the time of the vote on the Eighth Amendment of the Irish Constitution, I look forward to watching and listening to the debates which accompany it.

Media discussions on TV and radio, however, don't always allow for arguments to be properly examined. Similarly, internet discussions, while they can be helpful, often shed far more heat than light. In a world of 'instant responses', it is easy for debates to obscure rather than clarify the issues, particularly on an exceptionally fraught and sensitive issue such as abortion legislation.

The subject of abortion raises strong feelings; in many ways, it would be odd if it did not. The stakes are high, to say nothing of personal experiences in this area which can ground particularly strong emotions. A good and productive debate need not exclude emotion and should very often include it. However, for a good debate, we need of course more than emotion: we need rational arguments too.

What I, and I believe many others, want is to get a proper handle on what each side is trying to assert without time constraints or people talking over each other. I want to know what the arguments are and whether they establish what they purport to.

This book, I believe, gives us the arguments 'unvarnished' by affording to each contributor an equal platform to state their case at reasonable length as to why they believe we should repeal or retain the Eighth Amendment.

I believe you will be more informed having read this book as to the various perspectives and in a better position to decide where you stand and which position you will take in the referendum and in later political debates. Even for those who have firmly made up their minds, I would venture to say that this book will leave you enlightened and better informed. I have certainly learned myself from these contributions.

In these pages you will hear from politicians, academics, full-time campaigners, two members of the clergy (from different denominations), and those representing a younger voice from both perspectives. One contributor makes mention of her personal experience with abortion from the repeal perspective, counter-balanced by a campaigner from the retain position who will outline her own personal story. We often hear debated the ethics of abortion in the case of Down syndrome but rarely hear an opinion on that issue from someone *with* Down syndrome. In this book, you will hear precisely that. While the great majority of contributors are Irish, some contributors come from beyond these shores, and I hope that the international perspective offered helps to enrich the book as well.

I am most grateful to Orpen Press for allowing this book to go forward and for their professionalism throughout the process. This is such a divisive subject that there were some who advised me that this book would never come about. There would be too many terms, conditions and demands from both sides which would be impossible to resolve. I am happy to say that there were no such difficulties and wish to thank the authors for embracing this project and simply going about the business of writing without any fuss.

Of course, the very fact that there were such fears is telling in itself. Very few subjects arouse passions in quite the same way. A subject which embraces life and death, autonomy, privacy, feminism and sex equality, parenthood, dependency and independence, human nature and human embodiment brings many underlying issues to the surface when discussed. In a political context, when we consider the nature of the state and individual rights a subject like abortion takes us to the heart of the matter.

In these pages you will find political, legal and philosophical arguments, but also attempts to bring to the fore particular aspects of the abortion debate through real-life stories as well as rigorous arguments about the principles at stake. In finding an array of writers from different disciplines and with different life experiences it is my hope that we will get beyond the clichés that surround the debate and allow people to be truly informed before the referendum.

In the context of medicine we often hear about the need for informed consent. Similarly, when it comes to voting on what both sides regard as a momentous issue, we need to be informed. And by informed I do not just mean informed about legal or medical or scientific facts, but also about ethical principles and how our choices shape the society we live in. By informing ourselves in the deepest way about what is at stake we will not only be acting as good citizens but also as reflective people who have learnt something about who we are and who we want to be.

Voting on the Eighth Amendment will be a significant event in our lives. Not all votes are like that, but this one certainly will be. I hope that this book, which brings together very different voices, will also prove to be significant at this time in Ireland's history. What you choose at this referendum matters, and I hope that this book, at the very least, gives some sense of just how much it matters.

Finally, as these issues will not, of course, go away following the referendum – whatever the outcome may be – I hope that the book's usefulness as a resource and reference point will long outlast the referendum, and help Irish people in many future debates and personal reflections too.

Conor O'Riordan
Dublin
10 November 2017

Ireland on the Frontline: Challenging Foetal Rights Ideologies

Ursula Barry

In 2013 I wrote about the rise in foetal rights ideology and the consequences for women in Ireland and globally.[1] I looked at developments in both the US and Ireland and used the example of judgments from the Canadian Supreme Court as a reference point for the kind of debate that is needed in Ireland. I view Ireland as on the global frontline in the battle over women's reproductive rights and the fight for reproductive justice. Many things have changed since I wrote the chapter for *The Abortion Papers in Ireland*, Volume 2[2] and not much for the better. Ireland is among the few countries across the globe with the most restrictive abortion laws, together with a highly controversial clause establishing foetal rights in the constitution. The full weight of criminal law penalties is used to create nervousness and fear among women and potential health service providers. A pregnant woman who accesses abortion, or anyone who assists or facilitates her in accessing abortion, other than when her life is in danger (under strict conditions of verification) face a penalty of fourteen years in prison.

Compulsory pregnancy continues to be the norm in Ireland for women who cannot travel, or who cannot afford to travel to another country (mainly the UK), including women with severe health conditions, women asylum seekers, women and girls in state care, and women subject to violence and abuse. Women who travel for abortions are isolated and shamed in a system that treats them as criminals for accessing a health service that is fully lawful across Europe.[3] Ireland is caught in a struggle over reproductive justice that is worldwide, and is being used as a frontline state by Christian fundamentalists, alongside Malta, El Salvador, the Philippines, Poland and Guatemala.

In the post-Trump era in the US, foetal rights have gained traction in the most dangerous of ways, reflected in the undermining of contraceptive access and support services, and the attack on Obamacare, as well as escalating hostility towards abortion services and providers. One of the significant consequences of the Trump victory is a greater capacity by the Republican right to determine the shape of the US Supreme Court, an objective they have pursued since the liberalisation of abortion access based on the *Roe v Wade* judgment in 1973. And in Ireland, while some things have improved, new battle lines are been drawn in the lead-in to the promised referendum on the Eighth Amendment in 2018.

In 2013 I highlighted the danger in the move from foetal rights ideology that aims to designate the foetus as one of two *equal patients* – which has been the key to the impact of the Eighth Amendment in Ireland. The foetus as *equal citizen* is the ultimate implication of foetal rights ideologies. This is the most immediate danger of the rise of new forms of foetal rights ideology in the US which provide legal precedents for new restrictions on pregnant women and new powers to states to intervene in pregnancy or to prevent health-based interventions in the interests of women's health. The power of foetal rights ideology in the US has always had implications for Ireland. Historically, while the foetus has never been recognised as a person with full legal rights in Ireland, the Eighth Amendment to the Irish Constitution establishes the foetus as having equal rights with a pregnant woman. Consequently, detection of a foetal heartbeat is enough to deny women urgent medical attention, as was evident in the Savita Halappanavar case.

Other legal systems across the world treat the foetus as an integral, rather than separate, part of a pregnant woman. The term 'foetal rights' came into wide usage following the *Roe v Wade* case, in which the US Supreme Court ruled that a woman has a constitutionally guaranteed unqualified right to abortion in the first trimester of her pregnancy and a more limited right in the second trimester. The conservative right, represented by the Trump administration in the US, would dearly like to change this judgment, which determined that the foetus is 'not a person' under the US Constitution, and looks to Ireland as one of a small number of countries that have integrated foetal rights into statute and constitutional law, and that could influence future decisions in an altered US Supreme Court. This is why everyone concerned with reproductive justice will have their eyes on Ireland in 2018. There is much at stake in Ireland and globally.

To explore a counterview, it is worth recalling the statement by the Canadian Supreme Court following a hotly contested case in relation to a pregnant woman with serious drug addiction issues. A landmark judgment was delivered in October 1988 by the Supreme Court of Canada which ruled by a seven-to-two majority that nobody has the right to interfere with a woman's pregnancy against her will, even if her behaviour threatens the health of the foetus, in *R. v Morgentaler*. Madam Justice Beverley McLachlin wrote the decision for the majority. She stated: 'The only law recognized is that of the born person. Any right or interest the foetus may have remains inchoate and incomplete until the birth of the child.'[4]

She concluded that any attempt to forcibly treat a pregnant woman would violate:

> ... the most sacred sphere of personal liberty – the right of every person to live and move in freedom. ... A pregnant woman and her unborn child are one .... To make orders protecting foetuses would radically impinge on the fundamental liberties of the mother – both as to lifestyle choices and as to where she chooses to live.[5]

She expressed concern that if the state were found to have a right to interfere with a pregnancy then women who smoke cigarettes or who exercise strenuously might be next to be taken into custody. This could cause the problem to be driven underground: pregnant women might refuse counselling and medical help out of fear of being confined; some might even resort to having an abortion in order to continue their addiction. She concludes, 'In the end, orders made to protect a foetus's health could ultimately result in its destruction.'[6]

This is interesting in the light of the High Court decision in Ireland on 2 November 2016 which refused to force a pregnant woman to have a Caesarean section against her will, determining that 'it was a "step too far" to order a forced CS [Caesarean section] even if that increased the risk to both mother and child'.[7] The case was brought by the Health Service Executive (HSE) against the pregnant woman and demonstrates the potential far-reaching negative implications of the Eighth Amendment – we will not know what a Supreme Court decision would have been if the HSE had appealed. In the event, the woman herself elected for a C-section after her waters broke.[8]

The US Center for Reproductive Rights (CRR) documents reproductive rights issues globally, and identifies what it analyses as 'an emerging trend to extend a right to life before birth, and in particular from conception [which] poses a significant threat to women's human rights, in theory and in practice'.[9] In its view, these efforts are often 'rooted in ideological and religious motivations and are part of a deliberate attempt to deny women the full range of reproductive health services that are essential to safeguarding women's fundamental rights to life, health, dignity, equality, and autonomy, among others'.[10]

The core strategy of Christian right-wing fundamentalists is to establish recognition of a right to life before birth, and a range of legal processes based on constitutional and statute law, and legal and medical regulations, on a country-by-country or state-by-state basis, are being used to achieve this aim. The

CRR documents a wide range of constitutional and legislative changes across different countries that attempt to grant a right to life before birth – recognition of a prenatal legal personhood which aims to outlaw any procedure that terminates a pregnancy and sometimes make certain forms of contraception and in vitro fertilisation illegal. Examples include:

- Explicit recognition of a constitutional right to life before birth, as in the national constitutions of Guatemala and Chile
- Constitutional protections that confer equal protection for the life of both the pregnant woman and the 'unborn', as in the national constitutions of Ireland and the Philippines
- Legislation establishing that the right to life is subject to prenatal protection, as in Poland
- A new constitution adopted in the Dominican Republic in 2010 which recognised a right to life from conception
- Amendments by sixteen Mexican states since 2008 to their constitutions to protect the right to life from either fertilisation or conception
- The new *Protection of Life in Pregnancy Act* 2013 in Ireland, which enshrines for the first time a definition of the foetus in law as 'a potential human being from the point of implantation in the womb' and allows restrictive abortion only when the life of a pregnant woman is at risk and also in which an abortion would alleviate that risk
- In a major move which will likely have life-threatening consequences for women around the world, US President Trump has expanded the Global Gag Rule, which virtually restricts all global health assistance provided by the US federal government. Trump's new guidelines cut back global health programmes by up to $8.8 billion in funding and is a '... a major assault on those who serve the world's poorest and most vulnerable women. This policy does not protect life. It jeopardizes the lives of countless women by withholding critical information and access to the full range of reproductive health care'.[11]

But some positive changes have also taken place which are highly relevant:

- In 2008 and 2010 the US state of Colorado and in 2011 the US state of Mississippi rejected initiatives to amend the constitutions of these states to recognise that 'life begins at conception' and that from the moment of fertilisation zygotes, embryos and foetuses are people with all the rights guaranteed to persons under their state constitutions.

4

- In 2015 the US Supreme Court denied pharmacists in Washington State the right not to comply with a state ruling making it compulsory to stock and distribute contraceptives.
- In 2007 the Slovak Constitutional Court found that granting the right to life to a foetus would directly contradict women's constitutional rights to health and privacy and upheld the constitutionality of their abortion law.
- The CRR submitted a complaint on 10 October 2017 in federal court in the District of Columbia challenging rules introduced by the Trump administration that threaten to curtail access to birth control coverage for thousands of women.[12]
- The Nepal Supreme Court in 2009 concluded that '[a] fetus is able to exist only because of the mother; if we grant the fetus rights that go against the mother's health or well-being it could create a conflict between the interests of the mother and the fetus, and even compel us to recognize the superiority of the fetus, a situation that would be against the mother. It is not possible to put the mother's life at risk to protect the fetus'.[13]
- In the summer of 2017 Chile's Constitutional Tribunal voted six to four to pass an abortion bill allowing women, from January 2018, to access safe and legal abortion services in cases of life-threatening conditions.
- The Colombian Constitutional Court in 2008 ruled that Colombia's restrictive abortion law must be expanded to permit abortion in certain circumstances. The court held the law to be unconstitutional because it 'entails the complete pre-eminence of the life of the fetus and the absolute sacrifice of the pregnant woman's fundamental rights.' The Court further explained that '[this law] extinguishes the woman's fundamental rights, and thereby violates her dignity by reducing her to a mere receptacle for the fetus, without rights or interests of constitutional relevance worthy of protection'.[14]
- In 2012, Motion 312 was introduced into the Canadian parliament calling for a House of Commons Committee to determine when human life begins – this motion was defeated by 203 votes to 91.
- Abortion was included as part of the Inter-Provincial Billing Agreement in Canada in 2015. This was a significant change and brought abortion care in line with the *Canada Health Act*, which ensures that coverage must be maintained when a person travels outside of their home province. In 2015, the abortion drug mifepristone was also approved by Health Canada.
- A federal district court judge issued a temporary restraining order blocking a 2017 Texas measure banning the safest and most common form of medicated abortion. A state district court permanently blocks Oklahoma's restrictions on women's access to medication for abortion.

In new and serious developments in October 2017, the US House of Representatives passed a nationwide ban on abortion after 20 weeks, prohibiting abortion
without regard to the health of the woman – a move many have deemed unconstitutional. And President Trump's administration issued a new regulation that
enabled employers to opt out of providing contraceptive coverage as a part of
their healthcare plan 'if they claim a religious or moral objection to doing so'.[15]
But this discussion of so-called religious freedom denies a critical reality. While
Trump's new policies might be protecting the religious ideologies of fundamentalist Christian corporation owners, they are directly infringing on the religious
rights of others. Rolling back contraceptive provisions under Obamacare undermines important protections for women's health and in one strong statement it
is argued that these measures are in direct contradiction to Jewish women's religious practices in particular: 'In cases where a life is in danger, Jewish law not
only allows birth control, but mandates it. Abortion, for instance, is mandated if
the mother's life is in danger.'[16]

One of the most shocking cases of foetal rights laws being used against a
pregnant woman was that of Purvi Patel, an Indian-American woman and
imprisoned in South Bend, Indiana after a successful prosecution convicted her
of causing the death of her foetus by attempting to terminate the pregnancy
(crime of taking illegal abortion drugs) and *at the same time* of causing the
death of her baby (crime of foeticide and neglect of a dependent). Patel was
convicted and received a twenty-year sentence – a truly bizarre and horrific situation – which was thankfully overturned on appeal in July 2016. "'The verdict
makes Patel the first woman in the U.S. to be charged, convicted and sentenced
for 'feticide' for ending her own pregnancy", according to the group National
Advocates for Pregnant Women (NAPW).'[17] Though Patel said she had had a
miscarriage, she was found guilty of taking 'illegal abortion drugs'. The Indiana
statute under which Patel was convicted bans 'knowingly or intentionally termi-
nat[ing] a human pregnancy' with any intention other than producing a live
birth, removing a dead foetus or performing a legal abortion. NAPW Executive
Director Lynn Paltrow expressed deep disappointment at the extreme sentence:

> While no woman should face criminal charges for having an abortion or
> experiencing a pregnancy loss, the cruel length of this sentence confirms
> that feticide and other measures promoted by anti-abortion organiza-
> tions are intended to punish not protect women. Ms. Patel is not the
> first woman in the U.S. to have been arrested and charged with a crime
> for terminating her own pregnancy or based on allegations that she had
> attempted to do so. This case, however, is the first time any woman has

been charged, convicted, and sentenced for the crime of feticide for having attempted to end her own pregnancy.[18]

All of the recent rulings are being challenged in the US courts and while that is a hugely positive development, it does mean that women's bodily integrity in Ireland, the US and elsewhere is constantly subjected to definition and dissection by patriarchal legal systems. What these various judgments make clear is that recognising foetal rights in law inevitably sets up a situation of conflict of rights between foetus and pregnant woman. The UN CEDAW (United Nations Convention on the Elimination of Discrimination Against Women) Committee has concluded that any measures a state takes to protect prenatal interests must recognise the fundamental rights of pregnant women and not perpetuate discrimination – one of the founding principles of human rights law. CEDAW has noted that 'the proposition that protection of the foetus should prevail over the health of the mother is grounded in stereotyped roles for women and constitutes gender-based discrimination in violation of a woman's rights'.[19] It is important to note that this conclusion prioritises the health of the mother and is not restricted to her life, and in this sense Ireland's Eighth Amendment to the Constitution and the *Protection of Life During Pregnancy Act* 2013 are both in direct contravention of women's human rights as recognised by the UN.

It is not surprising, in this context, that the United Nations Human Rights Committee Chair (and former UN Special Rapporteur on Torture), Nigel Rodney, in 2015 concluded that Ireland's abortion laws treat pregnant women as 'vessels and nothing more'[20] and argued that Irish laws are urgently in need of change. In a June 2016 conclusion from the UN Commission on Human Rights, Ireland's abortion law was defined as 'cruel and inhumane'[21] and the Commission recommended that abortion be made available in Ireland in circumstances where pregnancy is a result of rape, in cases of fatal foetal abnormality and where a women's health is endangered by proceeding with the pregnancy. The Citizens' Assembly in Ireland that explored the issue of abortion came to similar conclusions in 2017[22] and in addition argued the abortion should be available up twelve weeks with no restrictions and that socioeconomic circumstances should be deemed grounds for an abortion. These conclusions are strongly supported by the Irish Human Rights and Equality Commission (IHREC) and it is worth reading closely their statement in September 2017 to the Oireachtas (Parliamentary) Committee on the Repeal of the Eighth Amendment to the Constitution:

[I]n the view of the Irish Human Rights and Equality Commission, the State should approach reforms on access to abortion in Ireland primarily as a matter of healthcare policy, and that to do so would be in keeping with its obligations under international human rights law. ...

Concerns about the barriers placed by the existing legal framework on women's right to the highest attainable standard of health, the right to privacy, to equality before the law, to non-discrimination and to freedom from inhuman and degrading treatment, as well as the State's special obligations towards minors (in particular the girl child), have been raised by several international human rights bodies. ...

The UN Committee on Economic, Social and Cultural Rights has made clear that the 'realisation of women's right to health requires the removal of all barriers interfering with access to health services ... including in the area of sexual and reproductive health'. It has identified 'criminalisation of abortion' and 'restrictive abortion laws' as among these barriers.

The Committee has also specifically expressed its concern on the discriminatory impact on women who cannot afford to travel abroad to access abortion services, or access the necessary information. ...

The Commission is of the view that the key areas that require attention by this Committee include the development of a legislative and regulatory framework that provides for access to abortion for reasons of:
- Risk to life and health
- Socio economic or family circumstances
- Pregnancy as a result of rape or incest
- Fatal foetal abnormality

...

The Commission has also raised concerns about the barriers that assessment and certification requirements place before women with restricted access to medical practitioners or health information, such as women from poorer socio-economic backgrounds, women from ethnic minority groups, or women with intellectual disabilities.

A reformed framework for access to abortion services under a wider set of circumstances should avoid the creation of new processes where vulnerable women and girls may be subject to trauma, re-victimisation, delays in treatment or other harms.

The Commission is of the view that a new framework for access to abortion should place the decision-making process primarily in the hands of the pregnant woman in consultation with her physician. ...

As has been highlighted at the Citizens' Assembly and in other fora, the criminalisation of abortion constitutes a potentially serious chilling factor for women seeking medical care, and for health care staff providing such care. The Commission, therefore, is of the view that, notwithstanding limitations that may be placed on access to abortion by legislation and regulation, the State should decriminalise abortion in all circumstances, as required by the UN Committee on the Rights of the Child in its Concluding Observations on Ireland adopted in 2016.

Finally, the Commission and others have highlighted serious shortcomings in Ireland's sexual and reproductive health education system. In parallel to a reformed legislative and regulatory framework for access to abortion in Ireland, it is crucial the State develop a comprehensive, scientifically objective, sexual and reproductive health education policy.[23]

CANADA: FALLING ABORTION RATES AND EARLY-STAGE ABORTION

The debate concerning the Eighth Amendment and abortion law in Ireland needs to be informed by practices in other countries. A key country is Canada, a country that has successfully taken abortion completely out of constitutional and criminal law and placed it in the context of women-centred health regulations. This is a huge achievement and creates a whole new context within which the provision of abortion should be framed, a context that Ireland should follow.

Canada has achieved hugely positive outcomes by establishing a crime-free, woman's- health-centred approach to abortion:

- Without legal obstacles, access and travel delays, most abortions are done at a very early stage.
- Numbers of abortions in Canada have been decreasing since abortion was decriminalised in 1998.
- This falling abortion rate is linked to greater access to contraception and sex education.

Dramatic Change in Abortion Access

In 2015 Canada celebrated the twenty-fifth anniversary of when regulation of abortion was taken entirely out of criminal law and placed within the healthcare system. It currently is limited to the *Canada Health Act*. The Canadian *Criminal Law Amendment Act* 1968–1969 was introduced shortly after the British abortion legislation of 1967. This Act – similar to the British Act – legalised abortion subject to a committee of doctors signing off that abortion was necessary for the physical or mental wellbeing of the pregnant woman.

This 1969 law was interpreted differently by different doctors and hospitals, leading to very uneven access to abortion in rural areas and also in certain provinces which had low levels of access. The principle set down in the legislation was the 'physical or mental well-being of the pregnant woman' and the decision on access to abortion was to be decided by each individual hospital's Therapeutic Abortion Committee (TAC). However, there was no requirement for every hospital to have a TAC or for it to meet, and in practice only about one-third of hospitals had one.

In defiance of the law, Doctor Henry Morgentaler began performing abortions at his clinic without the approval of a TAC and in contravention of the law. In 1973, Morgentaler stated publicly that he had performed 5,000 abortions without the permission of a TAC, even going so far as to videotape himself performing operations. Morgentaler's actions prompted a nationwide movement to reform Canada's abortion laws and in 1970, as part of what was called the Abortion Caravan, thirty-five women chained themselves to the parliamentary gallery of the House of Commons, closing Parliament for the first time in Canadian history.

The Quebec government took Morgentaler to court three times, and each time juries refused to convict him despite his outright admission that he had performed many abortions, as he stated, in contravention of the law. In 1988, in a dramatic ruling, the Supreme Court of Canada, in the case of *R. v Morgentaler*, ruled that existing abortion laws were unconstitutional and the 1968–1969 law was struck down. In this landmark decision, the Supreme Court declared that the entirety of the country's abortion law were unconstitutional. The court ruled that the existing law was essentially a breach of the woman's right to security of the person, which is guaranteed under Canada's Charter of Rights and Freedoms and concluded that:

> … forcing a woman, by threat of criminal sanction, to carry a foetus to term under a law that asserts that the woman's capacity to reproduce is to be subject, not to her own control, but to that of the state is a breach of the Charter.[24]

The majority of the Court emphasised the unfairness of unequal access, the Supreme Court highlighted barriers that included all-male TACs, doctors who did not wish to refer matters to TACs, and geographical and financial differentials in access to treatment by women faced with an unwanted pregnancy. Just two years later, in June 1990, a teenager from Ontario was injured during a botched abortion performed in a man's home and just several days later a

Toronto woman died from a self-induced, coat-hanger abortion. Reporting of these cases created widespread opposition to proposed new criminal legislation and the intense controversy arising from these tragic deaths resulted in a situation in which no subsequent government has re-visited criminal law proposals.

This has been the historical context that has led to the unique situation of Canada having no criminal or constitutional law on abortion. Abortion is now treated like any other medical procedure, governed by health regulations. Canada is the only country in the world that has *no* criminal law restricting abortion at all. Canada continues to have problems trying to deliver accessible abortion services to women. Access is hampered by its sheer size – the second largest country in the world after Russia and by far the least populated for its size – and that makes it much harder to deliver accessible abortion services to all Canadian women. Also, many clinic abortions are not funded in Canada, which forces women to go to hospitals instead which are varied in their support for women needing abortions. A second problem is anti-choice harassment and violence. Three Canadian doctors have been shot in the last five years.[25]

Access to health services is guaranteed by health legislation in Canada and abortion is considered a safe, legal, insured and funded service. Abortions in Canada are funded by Medicare but just one-third of hospitals perform abortions, and these perform two-thirds of abortions in the country. The remaining abortions are performed by public (not-for-profit) and private (for-profit) clinics. Regulations and accessibility still varies between provinces and non-legal obstacles exist that are mainly financial. Access to abortion care is mostly provided in large urban centres. Women in small communities or in rural areas still have to travel to the major centres providing care. With the approval of mifepristone, access will likely improve as physicians incorporate medical abortion into their family practice.[26]

IRELAND: WHAT NEEDS TO HAPPEN?

In Ireland, we need to fully recognise that abortion is a reality in women's lives and that our heavily restrictive laws criminalise and harm women, particularly vulnerable women (women with poor health; women on low incomes; undocumented women; women subject to violent and sexual abuse). To achieve the kind of positive results that are evident in Canada, based on a women's-health-centred approach two things need to happen:

- The Eighth Amendment to the Constitution needs to be repealed.
- The *Protection of Life During Pregnancy Act* 2013 needs to be repealed.

Women who may have abortions and those who may assist them would then no longer be treated as criminals under the law. Abortion would be taken out of the Constitution and decriminalised. Women's physical and mental health would move centre stage and women-centred health regulations would set down key principles for the provision of abortion services in Ireland.

The experience in Ireland of extending a right to life before birth has posed a significant threat to women's human rights, in theory and in practice. At a global level, this is part of a deliberate attempt to deny women the full range of reproductive health services that are essential to safeguarding women's fundamental rights to life, health, dignity, equality, and autonomy. These attempts to grant citizenship before birth – and therefore recognise prenatal legal personhood – seek to bestow rights that undermine the rights of pregnant women.

The ideology of foetal rights has now been debated over decades through the courts and legal systems of different countries. In many cases, these measures aim to outlaw any procedure that terminates a pregnancy. In other cases, restrictions have been sought on access to in vitro fertilisation and contraception. Across the board, these strategies attempt to deny women the right to make autonomous decisions regarding their fertility and consequently mean a disregard for women's basic human rights. The contested arena of foetal rights is more about the regulation and control of the bodies of pregnant women than about the specific issue of access to abortion.

REFERENCES

Adkins, Laura E. (2017) 'How Trump's Birth Control Policy Tramples Jewish Women's Religious Liberty', *Forward*, 11 October, http://forward.com/opinion/384774/how-trumps-birth-control-policytramples-jewish-womens-religious-liberty/.

Amnesty International (2015) *She Is Not a Criminal: The Impact of Ireland's Abortion Law*, www.amnesty.org.uk/files/she_is_not_a_criminal_report_-_embargoed_09_june.pdf.

Barry, Ursula (2013) 'Discourses on Foetal Rights and Women's Embodiment' in A. Quilty, C. Conlon and S. Murphy (eds), *Abortion Papers in Ireland*, Volume 2, Cork: Cork University Press.

Carolan, Mary (2016) 'Judge Refused to Order Woman to Undergo Caesarean Section', *Irish Times*, 2 November, www.irishtimes.com/news/crime-and-law/judge-refused-to-order-woman-to-undergo-caesarean-section-1.2852130.

Center for Reproductive Rights (2009) 'Landmark Decision by Colombia's Highest Court Liberalizes One of the World's Most Restrictive Abortion Laws', *Center for Reproductive Rights*, 11 May, www.reproductiverights.org/press-room/landmark-decision-by-colombias-highest-court-liberalizes-one-of-the-worlds-most-restricti.

Center for Reproductive Rights (2011) 'Nepal Supreme Court: Abortion Is a Right', *Center for Reproductive Rights*, 1 March, www.reproductiverights.org/feature/nepal-supreme-court-abortion-is-a-right.

Center for Reproductive Rights (2014) *Whose Right to Life? Women's Rights and Prenatal Protections under Human Rights and Comparative Law*, www.reproductiverights.org/sites/crr.civicactions.net/files/documents/RTL_3%2014%2012.pdf.

Center for Reproductive Rights (2017a) 'Expanded Global Gag Rule More Dangerous Than Ever', *Center for Reproductive Rights*, 12 June, www.reproductiverights.org/feature/expanded-global-gag-rule-is-more-dangerous-than-ever.

Center for Reproductive Rights (2017b) 'Center for Reproductive Rights Announces Challenge to Trump Administration's Contraceptive Coverage Rules', *Center for Reproductive Rights*, 10 October, www.reproductiverights.org/press-room/center-for-reproductive-rights-announces-challenge-to-trump-Contraceptive-Coverage-Rules.

Citizens' Assembly (2017) *First Report and Recommendations of the Citizens' Assembly: The Eighth Amendment of the Constitution*, www.citizensassembly.ie/en/The-Eighth-Amendment-of-the-Constitution/Final-Report-on-the-Eighth-Amendment-of-the-Constitution/Final-Report-incl-Appendix-A-D.pdf.

Cullen, Paul (2017) 'Irish Abortion Law Violated Woman's Human Rights, UN Says', *Irish Times*, 13 June, www.irishtimes.com/news/health/irish-abortion-law-violated-woman-s-human-rights-un-says-1.3118145.

Grant, Kelly (2017) 'Long Awaited Abortion Pill Mifegymiso makes Canadian Debut', *Globe and Mail*, 20 January, www.theglobeandmail.com/news/national/long-awaited-abortion-pill-mifegymiso-rolls-out-in-canada/article33695167/.

Irish Family Planning Association (2014) 'UN Urges Reform of Irish Abortion Law', *IFPA Newsletter*, September, www.ifpa.ie/node/580.

Irish Human Rights and Equality Commission (2017) *Submission by the IHREC to the Joint Oireachtas Committee on the Eighth Amendment*, www.oireachtas.ie/parliament/media/committees/eighthamendmentoftheconstitution/Opening-Statements-by-Ms.-Emily-Logan-and-Prof.-Siobh%C3%A1n-Mullally,-IHREC-0410.17.pdf.

Kaplan, Sarah (2015) 'Indiana Woman Jailed for "Feticide". It's Never Happened Before', *Washington Post*, 1 April, www.washingtonpost.com/news/morning-mix/wp/2015/04/01/indiana-woman-jailed-for-feticide-its-never-happened-before/.

National Advocates for Pregnant Women (2015) 'National Advocates for Pregnant Women Decries Purvi Patel's Sentence of 41 Years', *National Advocates for Pregnant Women*, http://advocatesforpregnantwomen.org/blog/2015/04/napw_decries_purvi_patels_sent.php.

Quilty, A., C. Conlon and S. Murphy (eds), *Abortion Papers in Ireland*, Volume 2, Cork: Cork University Press.

R. v Morgentaler (1988) SCC Cases (Lexum), https://scc-csc.lexum.com/scc-csc/scc-csc/en/item/288/index.do.

Richer, Karina (2008) *Abortion in Canada: 20 Years after* R v Morgentaler, Library of Parliament, PRB 08-22E, https://lop.parl.ca/content/lop/ResearchPublications/prb0822-e.pdf.

United Nations Convention on the Elimination of Discrimination against Women (CEDAW) (2011) *LC v Peru* CEDAW Committee Communication No 22/2009 15.15 U.N. Doc CEDAW/C/50/D/22/2009, Section 8.15 www2.ohchr.org/english/law/docs/CEDAW-C-50-D-22-2009_en.pdf.

ENDNOTES

1. Barry (2013).
2. Quilty et al. (2013).
3. Amnesty International (2015).
4. *R. v Mortenhaler*, 1988.
5. *Ibid.*
6. *Ibid.*
7. Carolan (2016).
8. *Ibid.*
9. Center for Reproductive Rights (2014), p. 1.
10. *Ibid.*
11. Center for Reproductive Rights (2017a).
12. Center for Reproductive Rights (2017b).
13. Center for Reproductive Rights (2014). See also Center for Reproductive Rights (2011).
14. Center for Reproductive Rights (2014). See also Center for Reproductive Rights (2009).
15. Center for Reproductive Rights (2017b).
16. Adkins, 2017.
17. Kaplan (2015).
18. National Advocates for Pregnant Women (2015).
19. United Nations Convention on the Elimination of Discrimination against Women (CEDAW) (2011).
20. Irish Family Planning Association (2014).
21. Cullen (2017).
22. Citizens' Assembly (2017).
23. Irish Human Rights and Equality Commission (2017).
24. *R. v Morgentaler*, 1988.
25. Richer (2008).
26. Grant (2017).

Abortion and Reason

Anthony McCarthy

Introduction

There are many arguments made in favour of liberalising abortion laws. One thing they all have in common, with few exceptions, is that they regard abortion as morally justified, at least in many circumstances.

Of course, someone can believe that certain kinds of act are morally wrong and even absolutely wrong (adultery would be one example) without thinking it would be good to criminalise those acts (for example because enforcing them would involve unacceptable invasions of privacy). But if abortion is, in fact, as pro-life people believe, a form of homicide of the innocent, it is not going to be the kind of act the law should tolerate, insofar as this is precisely the kind of moral wrong states are morally obliged to prohibit in accordance with basic justice.

Who exactly each law targets and what penalties should be attracted and what mitigating circumstances should be recognised are, of course, further questions for each jurisdiction to determine as best it can. But if abortion truly is homicide and a serious violation of human rights, it won't be an argument in favour of legalising it to say that abortion will still take place to some extent, regardless of the law. Do we say this of honour killings, for example, or female genital mutilation? Would we legalise these too, perhaps carrying them out in state facilities, to stop them being done covertly or exported abroad?

Moreover, there are many things a society can do to support those under very real pressure to break the law, who may do something seriously harmful to others and themselves. Even today in Ireland, many women with crisis pregnancies do not have abortions but rather have their babies, whether because of the deterrent effect of having to travel for abortion or break the law or simply because they become reconciled to having the baby, perhaps finding positive support close to home. Many young people are alive and well today, loved and accepted by proud parents, who would almost certainly have lost their lives if Ireland's abortion law had not been what it is.

In short, if there are no good arguments to justify abortion morally, there can be no serious case for repealing Ireland's Eighth Amendment.

So, what are the arguments used to justify abortion? Below I will lay out and examine the central pro-choice arguments. In the public square such arguments are rarely heard in detail and much of the debate is reduced to slogans carrying all sorts of unexamined assumptions. The 'right to choose/choose to control my body' is one example: how can 'choice' be a right irrespective of what is chosen?

SEX EQUALITY

Before looking at arguments based specifically on bodily autonomy, it is worth examining the argument from equality which has gained popularity in recent times. The argument goes like this:

> Pregnancy and motherhood are in themselves burdensome and deprive women of the opportunity to participate as fully equal citizens in the marketplace and civic life. Men do not get pregnant nor in the very early years is there anything like the same social expectation that they be involved as intimately as the woman is with her baby. Therefore, basic justice requires that abortion be readily available for all pregnant women who wish to access it. And that requirement does not merely protect 'private' choices from state intervention, but encapsulates the more radical idea that the state has a *positive duty* to provide abortion.

Note that this argument holds that abortion is absolutely necessary as a means of securing sex equality. The question of the moral status or 'personhood' of the foetus – a question I will discuss below – is here rendered irrelevant. Indeed, the feminist writer Catharine MacKinnon plainly states:

> Separate fetal status in a male-dominated legal system in which women have been controlled (inter alia) through the control of their procreative capacity, risks further entrenchment of women's inequality .... Fetal rights as such are thus in direct tension with women's sex equality rights.[1]

However, as Kate Greasley, herself a prominent academic advocate of abortion rights, has acutely noted, such arguments:

... correctly point out that it is not chiefly pregnancy but *childrearing* [emphasis in original] which threatens to socially disadvantage women and curtail their independence from men. Thus, laws which prohibit infanticide of born children up to any age at which they are still significantly dependent *also* impede sex equality, if women would otherwise choose to liberate themselves that way. Women could probably secure better equality with men if they could have their born children exterminated at any time. But it is unthinkable that the sex equality interest could ever be strong enough to justify that .... Consequently, if the fetus is presumed to be a person, the sex equality interest is not sufficient to show that abortion is morally justified.[2]

BURDENS OF PREGNANCY

We will return later to abortion seen as the right to escape the burdens of parenthood and childrearing, and not merely those of pregnancy. Clearly, pregnancy, like childrearing, can be burdensome – even very burdensome – but, like childrearing, pregnancy is so much more than simply a burdensome experience.

To begin with, pregnancy is an entirely natural condition: the very opposite of something pathological. A normal pregnancy is a sign of healthy functioning: the woman's body is oriented not just towards conception but toward reception of an embryo, moving that embryo into the womb, and nurturing the embryo and foetus through to birth. The sheer number of physiological changes which take place in the woman in very early pregnancy geared towards the protection of her embryo give us an insight into the nature of reproductive health. If these changes do not take place, that is a sign that something is 'wrong': the woman's health is affected and she may be at risk of miscarriage.

The very notion of health can only be understood in terms of the harmonious functioning of the human body and its ability to achieve its natural ends. Gestating a new human being is an expression of health, no less than any other, and a perfectly natural condition for a woman to be in, even if not all women wish to be mothers or to express in this way their reproductive powers.

Of course, some conversely present abortion as *serving* reproductive health, such that the destruction of the unborn through one or other invasive or disruptive method is seen as something that restores the woman's health – despite the fact that pregnancy is not a disease.

However, the Hippocratic oath itself, the founding document of the medical profession, rejects abortion, presenting it as incompatible with the ethical practice of medicine. And indeed, a 'quasi-medical' act which aims explicitly at ending a new human life in nearly all cases also aims at the termination of healthy reproductive functioning on the part of the woman. As regards psychological health, there is no evidence that abortion benefits women psychologically in the long term, as compared to giving birth.[3] And even if abortion *did* benefit women's health, medicine does not normally take one human life to benefit another: a 'solution' that would normally be rejected with horror if seriously proposed.

Aside from these considerations, however, the view of pregnancy made explicit in the 'sex equality' argument is entirely negative. As Erika Bachiochi has observed:

> Pregnancy, with all its risks and demands, is seen primarily as a burden when viewed from the perspective of the unencumbered, autonomous male. Seen from the perspective of most women, and the men who love them, childbearing is a great gift – a gift that has been recognized as such in many preindustrialized countries both historically and today .... Because men are not so designed, our industrialized, highly technical, produce-and-consume culture rates the life-giving power of women well beneath whatever products and feats the unencumbered, wombless male can produce and achieve. But women, unlike men, are gifted with the capacity to do both.[4]

The clear and fundamental biological difference between men and women is something given and not chosen.[5] As far as pregnancy is concerned, the difference is conclusive, for men and women are, to use a legal phrase, 'not similarly situated' with regard to sex equality.[6] To claim that women are somehow disadvantaged by their very biology seems to assume that the biology of the man is inherently 'superior' and that the male biological nature should be the paradigm against which the woman's biological nature is to be measured. But there is no reason to think that. And while unjust discrimination in civic life can and does occur, there is no reason to view pregnancy itself, a natural state and an expression of a woman's reproductive health, as inherently, intolerably burdensome simply because it involves a unique kind of bodily support which is female in kind and non-transferable.

BODILY AUTONOMY AND BODILY DETACHMENT

I will now turn from arguments seeking to justify abortion on the wider ground of sex equality to arguments focusing more specifically on *bodily* autonomy. The slogan 'my body, my choice' encapsulates this approach.

As before, such arguments do not focus on the humanity or status of the unborn but explore the scope of bodily rights as far as the woman is concerned. After all, even assuming that the unborn are people, we do not normally expect people to support other people with their bodies in quite such a direct way. It is claimed that just as a woman has a right not to have her bodily organs co-opted to support a born human being, so she has a similar right to 'detach' herself from the foetus she is carrying (an example sometimes used is that of someone awaking to find an unconscious stranger attached to her via tubes who will need to stay attached and use her kidneys for nine months in order to survive).[7]

What can we say about such an argument? Firstly, abortion does not involve mere 'detachment', but rather involves a deliberate, violent and lethal bodily assault on the unborn. With some abortion methods this is particularly obvious, since the foetal body is visibly broken up by the abortionist, but other methods too assault the unborn by violently expelling it before it can live outside the womb, breaking up foetal tissues such as the amniotic sac as they do so. These are targeted assaults on the baby itself, and, in this way, quite different from procedures that target therapeutically the mother's body alone (removing a cancerous womb or damaged fallopian tube are two classic examples).

Secondly, society clearly does not and never can recognise a 'right' on anyone's part to absolute bodily autonomy regardless of the impact of one's choices on others – or even on oneself. We may not move our limbs in ways that injure others simply because we wish to move them, still less with the *aim* of inflicting undeserved harm.

It may be objected that the right to bodily autonomy particularly concerns what happens inside one's body. However, in the context of pregnancy, an 'absolute right' to bodily autonomy – i.e. a literal right to decide on *everything* that happens inside one's body – would presumably also have to allow a pregnant woman (say, as part of an experiment on foetal pain) to consent to someone inflicting maximal pain on the late-term foetus she was carrying. However unlikely it is that women would agree to such an unconscionable intervention, if some particular woman *did* agree to it, it is ludicrous to suggest she would have a perfect right to do so as part of her right to control her body. There is clearly no absolute right of bodily autonomy in the sense the slogan 'my body, my choice' seems to imply.

The law rightly takes a particularly adverse view of deliberate as opposed to negligent acts against the lives and health and well-being of others. That said, even negligent acts are sometimes prohibited in law or via medical regulation: the medical use of thalidomide during pregnancy has long been discontinued, and a doctor who used thalidomide on a pregnant patient these days could be struck off for doing so. Of course, this is not to deny that a pregnant woman may have a legitimate need of medication or surgery which may harm or even kill the foetus as a side effect (as with the cancer treatment mentioned earlier).[8] Still less is it to deny that a woman has guardianship of her unborn child and has the right to *refuse* medical interventions which she deems inappropriate as well as making day-to-day decisions on possible risks, such as risks of certain foods which may perhaps harm her unborn child.

In short, pregnancy is nothing like being medically attached to a stranger who is using your bodily organs. It is not a high-tech form of medical support, much less some pathological state. It involves a mother who stands in a unique relationship to her own human offspring, whose guardian she is in a very special way. That offspring is not a parasite but a fellow human at the earliest stage of development. Whether living in the womb or being transported towards it by the mother, the unborn is exactly where it should be.

PROCREATIVE CONTROL

In any case, even if we were to concede that a woman has a right to detach herself from the unborn, this would not establish what is often sought in abortion: the specific right to end the life of the unborn so that no child will survive – even a child whom others will be looking after. This aim is very clear in relation to post-viability abortions where the foetus is lethally injected to prevent it surviving, including where intensive care could help it survive even in the long term.

In the future, the time of viability-with-support may be pushed back considerably via the perfecting of 'artificial wombs'. If an unborn child can exist in isolation from the mother at earlier and earlier stages, then again, abortion defenders have to supply us with an *additional* justification for ending the life of the unborn when that life could continue outside the woman's body.

Some claim that the more significant interest protected by 'abortion rights' is the interest in 'procreative control' – that is, the right to decide if one will become a parent.[9] But then, why couldn't such a right justify ending the life of one's newborn – or even that of an older child? If it is objected that the newborn is already one's child, such that it is too late to decide if one will 'become a parent', why is that not also true of the unborn?

PARENTHOOD, HARM AND SUPPORT

It is sometimes objected that the unborn – perhaps even the newborn – is not the child of the woman unless she has *chosen* it to be her child. However, being a parent, like being a son or daughter or sibling, need not involve a choice to be one. After all, in the case of fathers, society rightly holds them responsible for the support of their offspring even when they never chose to become fathers. The mere fact that they stand in a unique biological relation to their child generates a presumptive moral and legal responsibility for that child.

Appeal to procreative control also raises another question: can a father legitimately demand that his offspring be destroyed if he decides not to be a father, overriding the objections of the woman with whom he achieved conception? Clearly not if the offspring is in her womb, as this would involve a forced abortion, violating the woman's right to freedom from coercive bodily invasions. However, in the United Kingdom, a man with embryo offspring in the freezer can prevent the mother of those offspring (or anyone else) from bringing them to term. So, could a father perhaps insist on having a foetus in an artificial womb – even a nine-month-old foetus – destroyed, if he does not want to be a father? There seems to be no compelling answer as to why not if we take the idea of 'procreative control' as seriously as pro-choice advocates seem to.

There is no right not to be a parent of one's already existing child. A man or a woman cannot deliberately kill a newborn, by act or omission, on the grounds they have no wish to be a parent. Talk of every child being a 'wanted' child does not change this. As the philosopher David Oderberg has asked, 'Does "every child a wanted child" entail "every unwanted child should be killed"? What is the logic behind the entailment?'[10]

HOMICIDE

Without taking a position on the metaphysical and moral status of the unborn, some abortion defenders argue that even if it can be shown that the foetus has basic human rights this does not necessarily mean that abortion is morally unjustified. For it seems that most societies do allow for killing in certain circumstances. Killing in pursuit of a just war or in self-defence is generally accepted as morally legitimate, with capital punishment also accepted by many as not always morally wrong. So why is abortion different?

First of all, killing in a just war does not extend to the deliberate killing of non-combatants, which is generally condemned as a war crime. Yet in abortion the unborn child is specifically targeted – almost always, to be deliberately killed. Similarly, justifications for capital punishment, whatever one may think of them, never apply to those innocent of any crime but only to the guilty.

Executing an innocent person is a miscarriage of justice. Yet a foetus cannot be guilty of any crime. So-called legitimate forms of killing, if they are in fact

justified, can only be so on grounds which have nothing at all to do with what is at stake in abortion. Indeed, in the cases of just war and capital punishment, killing of the innocent is explicitly excluded from the justification for each.

In the case of individual self-defence, the justification for killing is ordinarily that sufficient force may be used against aggressors. Such force may, as a side effect, result in the death of the aggressor but this is not to be intended (one is not permitted to kill an aggressor one has disabled through use of sufficient force). Again, this has no application to abortion as the foetus is in no way performing an aggressive act, to say nothing of the intention to kill that is typically present in abortion, though not in the case of legitimate self-defence.

It seems especially wrong to harm your child deliberately simply to avoid having to support that child, including in various bodily ways (holding, changing, breast- or bottle-feeding and so on). Not only is such support reasonable to expect from parents, we normally expect it even of strangers who find a child on their doorstep and need to support the child until someone else is found to do so. Certainly, to end the child's life to avoid its demands for physical support seems a very clear moral wrong.

IDENTITY AND PERSONHOOD

Thus far we have looked at pro-choice arguments which don't of themselves take a position on the personhood of the unborn. We come now to what is generally regarded as the central argument of the abortion debate. Firstly, am I the same living being as the unborn and, secondly, did I always have my current moral right not to be deliberately killed?

The philosopher Alexander Pruss, in a detailed paper on this question, argues that:

> I was once a fetus and before that I was an embryo ... it would be at least as wrong to have killed me before I was born as it would be to kill me now ... if you kill me earlier, the victim is the same but the harm is greater since I am deprived of more the earlier I die.[11]

At the moment of my conception a sperm from my father fertilised an ovum of my mother.[12] Although containing DNA from both my mother and father, the new living being was genetically distinct and not a part of either parent, still less a part of both. Nor did it behave like a part of either parent, but behaved like what it was: an entirely new living entity whose functioning was directed toward its own welfare and survival, interacting harmoniously with the support provided by my mother until it was old enough to be born. If we watch the development of that living being or organism, gradually forming into a foetus, neonate, toddler, adolescent and adult we see a continuous development. There are no sudden breaks. Now apply a simple metaphysical principle – 'If an organism that once existed has never died, then this organism still exists.'[13] Let's call the original organism HERE.

We know that HERE did not die (if the organism died when would that death have taken place?) But if HERE has not died, where has HERE gone? To quote Pruss:

> ... surely there is no mystery .... Every part of [HERE] ... developed continuously into a part of me, and every part of me has developed ultimately out a part of [HERE]. It is thus quite futile to look for [HERE] outside of me. If [HERE] is anywhere he is right here, where I am .... [HERE] can't be a mere *part* of my body, because *all* of my body has continuously come from [HERE'S] body. So where is [HERE]. The answer is simple: *Here. I am [HERE].*'[14]

Now it seems that the only serious way to object to this argument is to say that I and my living body are two separate things – so the foetus who grew up to be my living body was not me because my living body is not what I am. But this is plainly absurd. I am not a mere disembodied spirit. I am sitting here, right now, tapping at my laptop as an embodied human being. When I last made love it was not 'my body' which made love while my 'real self' stayed in the background. My body is not mere property[15] I own. If you talk to me, smile at me or hit me, it is me you connect with, not a separate human body.

Reflecting on these questions, some philosophers talk in terms of 'persons' and claim that while perhaps we are indeed human beings from conception, we were not always persons – and it is only persons who mustn't be unjustly killed. By 'person' is normally meant not just 'being with a right to life' or 'being of a rational kind' but 'being with current psychological abilities' – such as the ability to think, choose and so on.

The philosopher Bernard Williams, although no pro-lifer, pointed out some of the central problems with such personhood arguments and his thoughts are worth quoting at length:

> ... if the foetus is not yet a person, then neither is the newborn baby; nor again, if the requirements of personhood are made sophisticated enough, will small children be persons. What is more, the senile, and other adults

in defective condition, will be, on this sort of showing, ex-persons or sub-persons … if failure to qualify in the person stakes is enough, as this argument would have it, to eliminate restrictions on killing the foetus, it is presumably enough to remove restrictions on killing those other non-persons as well, and the results of taking this line are wide-ranging indeed. There is a deep fault with the notion of a person, as used in these connections. It sounds like an all-or-nothing matter whether a given creature displays, to some extent – it seems, an arbitrary extent – some psychological and social characteristics which lie on a sliding scale.[16]

Of course, if the decision as to who counts as a person is arbitrary it will very likely be made by whoever is most powerful in a given society. The weak and the young and vulnerable have no intrinsic protections in such a context.

In summary, a human being or living human 'whole' is present right from fertilisation through pregnancy to birth, infancy and beyond.[17] We begin at fertilisation (except for identical twins[18]) and never cease to be the same living human being we were then. If it is wrong to kill me now, it was also wrong to kill me at a younger age. For the same core reasons that killing older human beings is wrong, so is killing human beings at an earlier stage of life. And just as it is absolutely wrong deliberately to kill an innocent born human being so it is wrong to kill that same human being earlier in his or her trajectory. No amount of obfuscation is going to change that fundamental moral and meta-physical truth.

More Counterarguments

In light of the above, let us look very briefly at some further counterarguments. I will say very little on the case of rape as I know others in this book will have covered that issue. I limit myself to saying here that the manner in which a new human life is conceived has no bearing on the value and dignity of that life – so a child conceived through rape has no less right not to be killed than any other child, even if his or her mother, as the victim of a terrible crime, is likely to need much more support.

Oaks and Acorns

Two common examples used by pro-choice advocates in recent abortion debates are as follows. It is pointed out that there is every difference in the world between a mighty oak tree and the mere acorn from which it grows. Just as we are not bothered about the destruction of acorns, as we don't see them as valuable in the way that oak trees are, cannot we say something similar about the early embryo and foetus and the fully grown human being?

But the argument fails on a number of levels. Firstly, a mere acorn is more like an unfertilised ovum than it is like an embryo – whereas an activated, *germinating* acorn is biologically a new oak organism, just like the oak sapling and the grown tree. The grown 'tree' is simply an older version of the same 'oak', just as a grown 'man' or 'woman' is simply an older version of the same 'human being'.

Secondly, we value a great oak largely instrumentally for what it gives us in terms of beauty, shade and so on. But humans possess a supreme intrinsic value in virtue of their humanity and rational nature which is not dependent upon whatever instrumental value they may have for other humans.

Fire in the Lab

Another argument runs as follows. If I were in a lab and a fire broke out and I could only save a five-year-old child or 10 or even 1,000 IVF embryos, whom would I save? Most people, whatever their views on the right to life of embryos, would in practice save the five-year-old. But if that is so, doesn't it tell us something important about how we value the lives of born human beings way above those of embryos?

Note, however, that the argument says absolutely nothing about whether it could be justifiable to *kill* the embryos. It is set up in such a way as to avoid the central question surrounding abortion, namely the moral question as to the rightness of intentionally killing new human beings.

What it posits is a priority question. But if I choose to feed my own child with limited resources and not a stranger's children – even many more children – that in no way implies a) that it is ok to deliberately kill those children or b) that they have lives of any less value than my own child's. We all have special moral roles and limited resources, but that is completely compatible with valuing all human lives to the extent of not believing it is ever acceptable to end such lives deliberately and unjustly. If we would, in this example, tend to favour the five-year-old, it is likely to be for the kinds of reason medical charities prioritise the healthcare of certain categories of patients above others – and nothing to do with thinking it's OK to kill the unrescued group.

There is much more to say about this case – for example, about our tendency to prioritise those we can see over those we cannot see (including those unconscious and locked away in hospital wards) – but the general response should be clear. We are equal, *not* in having an equal right to be rescued – not everyone can be rescued in conflict situations – but in our basic right not to be deliberately killed or attacked when we have done nothing to deserve that. This also applies if we are deciding whom to save of a pregnant and a non-pregnant woman: if we choose to save the pregnant woman, together with her baby, we are hardly intending the non-pregnant woman die, or saying she has less moral worth.

CONCLUSION

You will not, I believe, find any refutation of any of the pro-life arguments laid out above either in this book or in any of the debates surrounding the Eighth Amendment. Not one of the pro-choice arguments we have looked at can stand up to rational analysis. Why, then, do pro-choice advocates continue not only to repeat these arguments, but to seek to impose abortion on the Irish people, whether born or unborn?

The powerful of this world, if they wish to increase their power – even by deciding who lives and who dies – have every reason to dehumanise the vulnerable. There are many among those lucky enough to be born who are themselves vulnerable in some way. Among them are many who feel guilt and confusion as they contemplate this whole debate, whether because of a painful experience in their past or out of fears for a future in which they may 'need' an abortion. But in the end, there is nothing to fear from reality, which is not whatever the powerful say it is, but something 'out there' to which we can always choose to respond. We have reason as our ally, for we are rational creatures, and if we use our reason we can recover just what it is to be human and recognise the humanity of the entire human family, never excluding from that family the unborn members we once were.

REFERENCES

Bachiochi, Erika (2011) 'Embodied Equality: Debunking Equal Rights Protection Arguments for Abortion Rights', *Harvard Journal of Law & Public Policy*, Vol. 34, No. 3, pp. 889–950.

Braine, David (1994) *The Human Person: Animal and Spirit*, Notre Dame, IN: Notre Dame University Press.

Fergusson, David M., L. John Horwood and Joseph M. Boden (2008) 'Abortion and Mental Health Disorders: Evidence from a 30-Year Longitudinal Study', *British Journal of Psychiatry*, Vol. 193, No. 6, pp. 444–451.

Fergusson, David M., L. John Horwood and Joseph M. Boden (2013) 'Does Abortion Reduce the Mental Health Risks of Unwanted or Unintended Pregnancy? A

Re-Appraisal of the Evidence', *Australian & New Zealand Journal of Psychiatry*, Vol. 47, No. 9, pp. 819–827.

Garcia, J.L.A. (1997) 'Intentions in Medical Ethics' in David S. Oderberg and Jacqueline A. Laing (eds), *Human Lives: Critical Essays on Consequentialist Bioethics*, pp. 161–181, London: MacMillan.

Greasley, Kate (2017) *Arguments About Abortion: Personhood, Morality and Law*, Oxford: Oxford University Press.

Jarvis Thomson, Judith (1971) 'A Defense of Abortion', *Philosophy and Public Affairs*, Vol. 1, No. 1, pp. 47–66.

MacKinnon, Catharine A. (2005) *Women's Lives, Men's Laws*, London: Harvard University Press.

McCarthy, Anthony (2017) 'Forget Not the Body: Reflections on Artificial Wombs', *The Public Discourse*, 21 June, www.thepublicdiscourse.com/2017/06/19532.

Moore, Keith L., T.V.N. Persaud and Mark G. Torchia (2013) *Before We Are Born: Essentials of Embryology*, eighth edition, Philadelphia, PA: Saunders.

National Collaborating Centre for Mental Health (2011) *Induced Abortion and Mental Health: A Systematic Review of Outcomes of Induced Abortion, Including Their Prevalence and Associated Factors*, London: Academy of Medical Royal Colleges.

Oderberg, David S. (2000) *Applied Ethics: A Non-Consequentialist Approach*, Oxford: Blackwell.

Pruss, Alexander (2002) 'I Was Once A Fetus: That Is Why Abortion is Wrong', *Life and Learning*, Vol. 12, pp. 169–182, http://uffl.org/vol12/pruss12.pdf.

Watt, Helen (2016) *The Ethics of Pregnancy, Abortion and Childbirth: Exploring Moral Choices in Childbearing*, New York, NY and Abingdon: Routledge.

Williams, Bernard (2014) 'The Logic of Abortion', in Bernard Wiliams (ed.), *Essays and Reviews 1959–2002*, pp. 146–152, Oxford: Princeton University Press.

ENDNOTES

[1] MacKinnon (2005), pp. 139–140.

[2] Greasley (2017), p. 99.

[3] See, for example, Fergusson, Horwood and Boden (2008); Fergusson, Horwood and Boden (2013); Academy of Medical Royal Colleges (2011).

[4] Bachiochi (2011), p. 941.

[5] For more on this see Braine (1994).

[6] Certain kinds of rape can only be carried out by a male, yet it is no argument against laws outlawing such acts to say that they in some way discriminate against men on account of their biology.

[7] See Jarvis Thomson (1971).

[8] On double effect see Garcia (1997). For a detailed examination of maternal–foetal conflicts, see Watt (2016).

[9] See McCarthy (2017).

[10] Oderberg (2000), p. 47.

[11] See Pruss (2002), p. 169. The following section owes much to this article.

[12] Note however that not all embryos are created from egg and sperm: in the case of identical twinning or cloning an embryo can arise from the cell or cells of a precursor embryo. This does not in any way affect the argument below.

[13] *Ibid*, p. 171.

[14] *Ibid*, p. 172. Of course foetal organs like the placenta will cease to be part of the organism but every unshed part will have developed continuously into me.

[15] Note that rape is the crime it is precisely because it immediately involves the person, not just a 'body' the person 'owns'.

[16] Williams (2014), p. 148.

[17] With regard to when an embryo becomes a human being, human embryologists generally are clear in affirming that 'The scientific answer is that the embryo is a human being from the time of fertilization because of its human chromosomal constitution. The zygote is the beginning of the developing human': Moore, Persaud and Torchia (2013), p. 327.

[18] See note 12.

THE TIMES THEY ARE A-CHANGING:
THE SOCIALIST CASE FOR REPEAL

Bríd Smith

I was 25 when the Eighth Amendment was introduced into our constitution in 1983. I campaigned against it then and I have been campaigning against it ever since – all my adult life. I am delighted to say that now, thanks to profound changes in Irish society and the emergence of a new generation of young Irish women (and men) who will not accept the old restrictions and hypocrisy, we have a real chance of repealing this reactionary amendment which has no place in our constitution.

I, myself, will do everything in my power to make sure this happens through action within the Dáil where I am sitting on the Oireachtas Committee charged with making recommendations to the parliament on the planned referendum, and on the streets by building a movement of mass people power, which I believe is always key to change. And as a People Before Profit TD I am proud of the fact that I have the full support of my party in this. Unlike many other parties, People Before Profit (and Solidarity, our Dáil ally) is not divided on this question. All our TDs and elected representatives, and the very large majority of our members, are unequivocally pro-choice and are campaigning vigorously for repeal.

On behalf of my party I moved the *Protection of Life During Pregnancy (Amendment) Bill* 2017 in March 2017. If passed, this would have reduced the penalty for the 'offence' of having an abortion, or helping someone else to have one (by getting the abortion pill, for instance), from fourteen years' imprisonment to a €1 fine. Of course it would have been preferable to eliminate *any* charge, but as a short-term measure to support the estimated ten women a day leaving our shores to terminate a pregnancy, this would have had an immediate impact. The Bill was defeated, shamefully, with many of those who now proclaim their 'pro-choice' credentials voting against the measure.

The reason repeal is so essential is simply that the Eighth Amendment, by making the life of the foetus equal in law to the life of the pregnant woman, treats abortion in almost all circumstances as equal to murder and so makes impossible any progressive, humane or even mildly liberal stance on this issue. It leaves Ireland in the absurd and dreadful position of having an unenforceable but monstrous fourteen-year sentence on the books for taking the abortion pill, of treating abortion as a worse crime, subject to more draconian sentencing, than rape or child abuse (remember the two-and-a-half years for Tom Humphries?) and of being repeatedly condemned by the United Nations and others for violating the human rights of women forced to travel abroad to access abortion.

When I recently stated in public that I had had an abortion in the 1980s, I was the first public representative to do so. I have no doubt that I am not alone among my peers in having had an abortion, but such is the power of dominant ideas in society that such an experience is still deemed, if not 'shameful', then at least best left unmentioned. Thus the culture of silence and guilt goes unchallenged, in the same way that the culture of 'putting up' with sexism and abuse of women has persisted for so long; the avalanche of pain and outrage following the Weinstein revelations in Hollywood demonstrates how pervasive this is. I think it's important that we continue to challenge the culture of silence about what is unacceptable in society. It's the least we owe the next generation of young women.

But if the issue of repeal is currently the key battleground it is nonetheless only one episode in a very long struggle over women's reproductive rights in Ireland and the positions taken by most public representatives and spokespersons on this derive, by and large, from where they stand on the wider issue of a woman's right to choose. In this chapter I want first to survey, briefly, the spectrum of the debate in Ireland, including explaining my own underlying conviction; second, to locate this debate in Irish history; and then, third, to make some comments on the current situation.

THE SPECTRUM

At one end of the spectrum there are those who are completely and utterly opposed to abortion in virtually all circumstances and are therefore intransigent defenders of the Eighth. At the heart of this group, its ideological and organisational drivers, are what might be called Christian conservatives or Christian fundamentalists. Fundamentally, their position derives from religious doctrine – either from scripture (as they interpret it) or church teaching, or a combination of the two.

It is important to understand this because this group, which has considerable economic resources, possesses trained representatives and advocates who do their best to present their case in terms of 'rational', 'scientific' and 'medical' arguments. They have no shortage of so-called 'experts' who are able to quote scientific papers and refer to medical research. But this is essentially a smoke-screen. In reality their position is based on religious dogma, teaching or faith, call it what you will. So they cite research when it suits them, but really would hold their absolutist position whatever the medical research showed. I am not saying here that the medical research doesn't matter – indeed in so far as abortion is a medical procedure it matters a great deal – but it doesn't really matter to the Christian right whose views, fundamentally, are faith- not evidence-based. One of the clearest indications of this is that many of these Christian fundamentalists are against not only to abortion but also contraception, which from a medical or social, as opposed to doctrinal, point of view is clearly absurd. This needs stressing, I believe, because at the heart of this whole debate lies an attempt to impose their particular religious beliefs – to which they are entitled – on the rest of us, on society as a whole, by means of the constitution. That they are *not* entitled to do.

Another key characteristic of this group is that they invariably describe themselves as 'pro-life'. What is galling about this for activists like myself is that these 'pro-lifers'' concern for human life never seems to extend beyond the moment of birth. In many years of campaigning I have *never* seen the organisations who have often put thousands of people on the streets of Dublin to oppose choice mobilise to oppose cuts in child benefit or lone parents' allowance or welfare cuts or cuts to SNAs or anything that actually affects the quality of life of children. The draconian cutbacks that followed the bank bailouts, and subsequent austerity Budgets, disproportionately affect the most vulnerable children in Irish society – the children of the poor. And the scandal of literally thousands of homeless children being reared in emergency accommodation, or miserable direct provision centres for asylum seekers – these shameful features of Irish society seem to elicit little condemnation, and less action, by the devotees of the 'unborn'. The anti-choice organisations like to style themselves as the champions of the disabled, claiming that abortion targets people with disabilities. Yet for the last nine years the Irish state has refused to ratify the rights of disabled people as per the UN Convention on the Rights of Persons with Disabilities (UNCRPD), and cuts to benefits for disabled people were among the first implemented during the recession years. The silence of the 'pro-life' lobby in this regard has been deafening. They say that human life is 'sacred', that 'the right to life' is absolute and that 'only God' can decide when to end life. But if this were really their view and they were in any way consistent, they would have to oppose all war as a matter of principle – war, let us remember, is organised killing. In fact, these 'pro-life' organisations have never lifted a finger to oppose wars or, for example, Ireland's complicity in US wars via the military use of Shannon. Indeed many of them actually support the death penalty, which totally contradicts any notion of the sacredness of human life. This is why on our side of the debate we reject the label 'pro-life' and say that in fact they are just anti-choice.

We should also note that this religious fundamentalist opposition to abortion exists in most countries and the struggle over women's reproductive rights is global.[1] It is striking, for example, that on this question the Protestant fundamentalists in Northern Ireland – the Paisleyites who thought the Pope was the Antichrist and always raised the bogey of 'Rome rule' – stand united with their Catholic counterparts in the South. Nevertheless, the Christian fundamentalist position has a particular role and influence here in Ireland because of the historic role and hegemony of the Catholic Church. This is a matter to which I'll return.

At the other end of the spectrum – the end I'm coming from – there are the feminist and socialist left who believe strongly in free, safe and legal abortion for all. The anti-choice lobby always refers to this as 'abortion on demand' because language is very important in this debate and abortion on demand sounds both aggressive and casual – like water on tap – but we call it a woman's right to choose and a woman's right to bodily autonomy. This matters for reasons that go beyond PR and spin. First, because it is wrong and deeply misogynistic to imagine or suggest that women have abortions lightly or 'casually'. Second, because when we speak of choice and bodily autonomy this is part of a package which includes the right to have children along with the material and social resources to make that a viable option (housing, healthcare, an income above poverty levels, etc.). And here in Ireland we can't help recalling that many of the forces most vehemently opposed to abortion rights were the same forces that shamed and persecuted single parents and brought us the Magdalene laundries and Tuam.

This brings me to my own position as a feminist and socialist and for me those two things go together. For me a woman's right to choose is both a crucial right in itself and an integral part, actually a precondition, of women's equality and emancipation. Without control over their own bodies, including and especially their reproductive faculties, women cannot have control over their lives, let alone achieve full social, economic and political equality with men. It is just as vital, if not more so, as the right to equal pay, the right to equal job opportunities and the right to freedom from sexual harassment, domestic abuse and male violence. These rights go together and without them the thousands of years of second-class citizenship endured by women will continue regardless of the declarations and aspirational words of politicians.

It is a fact not widely recognised but a fact nonetheless that radical socialists, such as People Before Profit and Solidarity today, have *always* stood for women's emancipation. Marx and Engels both wrote about it, Engels especially in his famous book *The Origin of the Family, Private Property, and the State.*

Ireland's greatest socialist, James Connolly, was a strong supporter of women's rights and the women's suffrage movement of the day, as were many of the women in the Irish Citizen Army, such as Kathleen Lynn, Rosie Hackett and Helena Moloney. The Russian Revolution legislated from the outset for women's equality, including establishing the right to abortion as early as 1920. Socialist feminists played a leading role in the birth of the women's liberation movement in the late 1960s/early 1970s (sometimes called 'second wave feminism') and in Ireland were involved in the struggle for women's right to choose from its inception.

Socialism is about equality – full social, economic and political equality – and that obviously must involve equality for women. That's why every serious socialist also has to be a feminist. In contrast, capitalism generates and depends on inequality of all kinds: first and foremost massive inequality between the classes, between rich and poor. But in order to sustain that central inequality it encourages and thrives on all sorts of ethnic, national and gender inequalities that help keep ordinary people divided. In particular, many capitalists benefit from having a section of the workforce to whom they can pay lower wages and the capitalist system as a whole benefits from having a layer of the population obliged to work unpaid in the home and rearing children.

That is why we say 'There can be no women's liberation without socialism and no socialism without women's liberation.' But women's liberation as a whole and the equal participation of women in politics and the movement is impossible without bodily autonomy, without full reproductive rights. That is why my position on repeal and on women's right to choose fits in completely with my socialism.

Between the two poles of outright opposition to all abortion rights and clear advocacy of free, safe and legal abortion without restrictions lies the so-called 'middle ground' who favour a compromise, an intermediate solution of legalised abortion but only within more or less narrow limits. Before discussing the actual nature of this middle ground I first want to challenge the assumption widespread in much of the media discourse on this question that the middle or 'moderate' position between 'the two extremes' must somehow always be right. Some examples: Copernicus and Galileo said the Earth went round the sun, while the Church said the sun went round the Earth – the truth was not halfway between the two; some say Hitler murdered six million Jews in the Holocaust, others deny it happened at all – the truth is not somewhere in the middle; some people were pro-slavery, others were for abolition – was the answer semi-slavery? Indeed I think it would be more true to say that when it comes to human rights, and women's rights are human rights of course, a compromise half-way position is generally not justified or viable.

As to the actual 'middle ground' on this issue now in Ireland, we are again talking about a spectrum which ranges from a minimal reform of existing law to allow for abortion in the case of fatal foetal abnormalities, rape and incest only, to the kind of major reforms suggested by the Citizens' Assembly, allowing abortion up to twelve weeks on grounds of the woman's health and on socioeconomic grounds.

It should be said that the first, most conservative, option is not really the middle ground at all but an extremely minor and inadequate concession. For the overwhelming majority of women who need abortions the situation would not change and for the minority it would cover it would raise the additional very time-consuming and traumatic difficulty of proving the pregnancy was the result of rape or incest. Imagine a woman presenting to her doctor or clinic and knowing she was pregnant through rape or incest only to be asked 'Where is your proof?' and knowing that getting that proof might take months or years or be impossible.

In essence the 'middle ground' boils down to the question of the extent of the restrictions being put in place. Here it is necessary to remember that abortion is, and always has been, a class question as well as a gender question. Rich women, women of the upper classes, have always been able to obtain abortions regardless of the law. The current law which bans abortion in Ireland but allows women to travel abroad discriminates against those – the young, the poor, asylum-seekers, etc. – who lack the resources or ability to travel. The truth is that every restriction that is established will disproportionately affect working-class and poor women.

It is also necessary to understand that the 'middle ground' consists of two distinct groups of people: on the one hand, many ordinary people who are in the process of thinking the issue through; on the other, a layer of establishment politicians and media people who are sticking their fingers in the air to see which way the wind is blowing before committing themselves.

The instincts of this latter group have been and remain very cautious and conservative, which is why we waited so long for any response to the X Case judgment and why it has taken such determined campaigning to force this issue onto the agenda. The leaderships of Ireland's two main parties, Fine Gael and Fianna Fáil, both know that their parties depend in part on the support of 'unreconstructed' and 'traditional' forces in more conservative rural areas whom they wish to appease. Their response is therefore essentially opportunistic. If the battle for public opinion were won they would be happy to proclaim themselves as 'modern' and 'liberal', but they will not fight to win that battle. It was the same over LGBT rights and marriage equality. The establishment figures did not move until after the heavy lifting had been done by courageous activists on the ground and they knew it was 'safe'. Taoiseach Leo Varadkar epitomises this position.

But the majority of ordinary people are in flux. They have moved and are continuing to move from total opposition in the past in the direction of a pro-choice position. Why and how this happened I will explore in the next section, but it is clear from the Citizens' Assembly and the opinion polls that they are already way ahead of the politicians, and this is especially true of young people. (Witness the recent large vote by UCD students to impeach their anti-choice President for removing abortion information from the Student Handbook.) This means the 'middle ground' is there for the winning, not by timid and unprincipled compromise but by determined grassroots campaigning.

THE HISTORICAL MOMENT

The struggle over women's reproductive rights is now global – it is being waged as far apart as the US, Poland and South Korea – but in this international war the island of Ireland is one of the key frontlines – both in the southern Republic and in the still British-ruled six counties of the North. Why this is so is a product of the peculiarity of Irish historical development.

For nearly 150 years the Catholic Church held a grip on Irish society: it was Catholicism at its most conservative and the grip was cruel. It brought with it mother and baby homes run by religious orders where so-called 'illegitimate' children were taken from their mothers, sold off to America or allowed to die through neglect; it brought Magdalene laundries where 'fallen' women were treated as slaves for decades and industrial schools where the children of the poor and the working classes were beaten and abused.

This was not always so. It was not 'age-old' or in the Irish DNA. Yes, the majority of Irish people were Catholic but the Church did not establish this fierce hold until after the terrible trauma of the Irish Famine, the Great Hunger, of the 1840s, which claimed more than a million lives by direct starvation and forced millions more into emigration, cutting the Irish population almost in half (from 8 million in 1841 to 4.5 million in 1861).[2] The Famine altered the structure of the Irish family, establishing a pattern of late marriage, based on middle-aged and older men marrying younger women after extended celibacy. The Church assumed the role of policing the sexual repression on which this rested. In 1840 the ratio of priests to Catholic laity was 1:3,023; by 1911 it had risen to 1:210.[3] The number of nuns in Ireland increased *eightfold* between 1841 and 1901. In 1926 2 per cent of all single males aged 45–54 were priests and monks and 4.9 per cent of single women of that age were nuns and lay sisters.[4]

The stranglehold exercised by the Catholic hierarchy was reinforced by the counter-revolution that followed the Irish Revolution of 1916–1922. This revolution was part of the international wave that included the Russian Revolution of 1917, the German Revolution of 1918–1923 and the Italian Red Years of 1919–1920. It began with the Easter Rising of 1916, led by the socialist James Connolly and Irish nationalist Pádraig Pearse, and continued with mass strikes, workers' occupations, formation of local soviets and the mass revolutionary War of Independence, involving 100,000 people joining the Irish Republican Army. This struggle won partial independence from Britain for the 26-county 'Free State' in the South, but the counter-revolution led by Michael Collins, with the support of British imperialism, defeated the anti-Treaty IRA, and enforced the partition of Ireland, establishing two reactionary states – one Protestant, British and dominated by conservative Unionism, the other conservative, capitalist and Catholic.

The alliance of the Southern Irish capitalist class and the Catholic Church was personified in the association between two men: Taoiseach (later President) Éamon de Valera and Archbishop John Charles McQuaid, who between them ruled Irish society in the 1930s and 1940s and wrote our highly religious constitution.

The Church dominated almost every aspect of civic society in the Republic: above all education and hospitals. Central to its ideology and practice was denial, hatred and repression of sex in general and women's sexuality in particular. At the heart of this was total opposition to abortion. The persistence and strength of the Church's hold is symbolised by the fact that only in 1978 was there even limited legalisation of contraception and divorce remained illegal until 1995.

Northern Unionism and Orangism was rabid in its sectarian opposition to 'Rome Rule', i.e. Irish unification, but on one thing it was always totally in accord with 'Rome': its conservative attitude to sex and therefore to abortion.

Ireland remained economically backward, poor and Church-dominated right into the 1980s but the combination of economic development from the 1990s onwards and persistent struggle has brought fundamental change. The spectacular economic boom of the Celtic Tiger, in the 1990s and early 2000s, transformed the country. It brought massive urbanisation, undermining the rural social structures on which Catholic Ireland rested; it brought large-scale immigration, turning Ireland into a multi-cultural society; crucially, it femi-nised the workforce. By 1996 there were 488,000 women at work – an increase of 213,000 since 1971. This compares with a growth of just 23,000 in male employ-ment over the same period. In 1996 half the female workforce was married – 241,400 married women were working outside the home, an increase of more than 600 per cent since 1971.[5] All this produced new generations of women and men unwilling to accept the old stifling restrictions and oppression.

But, of course, change did not come by itself – mass struggle on the streets played a crucial role. In early 1992, nine years after the passing of the anti-choice Eighth Amendment, there came the X Case. On 6 February the Attorney General obtained an interim injunction restraining Miss X, a fourteen-year-old girl, pregnant as a result of rape and reportedly suicidal, from travelling to Britain to obtain an abortion. Up and down the country there was an explosion of anger. Thousands of mainly young women and men poured onto the streets to say 'Let her go.' Day after day and night after night thousands of women and men took to the streets. In Dublin there were several semi-spontaneous marches of up to 10,000 people – the equivalent population-wise of over 100,000 in London. These numbers were matched proportionately in Cork, Waterford, Galway and smaller towns too. The country was convulsed. And, crucially, the Government and the High Court, terrified by this explosion, backed down.

This was a massive breakthrough and in the new climate the deep hypocrisy of the Catholic hierarchy started to be exposed. Ireland's best-known bishop, Eamonn Casey, was revealed by his partner to have fathered a child, Another well-known priest, famous for preaching chastity, was shown to have had two sons by his 'housekeeper'. This gave courage to people who had been abused physically and sexually by priests and nuns under the old repressive regime. As they started to talk, news came almost weekly of priests being arrested. Between 1993 and 1997 priests from all over the country were convicted of sexual abuse, including rape, of children as young as eight years old. And it emerged that Church officials, having been made aware of the allegations, had typically acted not to protect the children and bring the culprit to book but to protect the church and let the guilty go free – often to abuse elsewhere. The moral authority of the Church never recovered.

The dramatic change in attitudes that has taken place is shown in the fact that in 2015 more than one in three births were outside marriage[6] and the number of children born to co-habiting couples increased by 32 per cent within a year.[7] And above all in the resounding majority for marriage equality in the 2015 referendum – 62.07 per cent to 37.93 per cent, with over 80 per cent in favour in the Dublin working-class areas radicalised by the water charges struggle.

The battle is far from over however. Ireland's two main establishment political parties, Fine Gael and Fianna Fáil, still depend on their base among conservative rural farmers and businesspeople who remain unreconstructed. Moreover, the Church retains both a lot of institutional power (it still runs most schools and many hospitals) and considerable ability to mobilise its supporters.

For these conservative forces the issue of abortion is their line in the sand and they will fight tooth and nail to keep the Eighth Amendment: On 1 July 2017, in a demonstration backed by almost every Catholic parish church in the country, the so-called pro-lifers (i.e. anti-choice) put at least 30,000 people on the streets of Dublin.

But, of course, there is an even more vibrant movement for repeal. On 8 March 2017, International Women's Day, thousands of mainly young women and men occupied O'Connell Bridge and held it for several hours. Then in the evening of the same day about 30,000 marched to the Dáil demanding an immediate referendum. The 2017 March for Choice on 30 September was huge, upwards of 40,000–50,000 people. The following week saw the biggest ever pro-choice demonstration on the streets of Belfast – estimated at 2,000–3,000 (mainly young) people. Clearly the movement for choice, in its multiple manifestations, has won the minds of the young and stands on the right side of history.

WHERE WE ARE NOW

At the time of writing the Joint Oireachtas Committee on the Eighth Amendment has recently voted by fifteen votes to three, with two abstentions, against the retention in full of the Eighth Amendment. This means there is almost certainly going to be a referendum in 2018. Numerous opinion polls suggest that a large majority of the Irish people, something around 75 per cent, favour at least limited legalisation of abortion and would therefore be likely to vote for repeal. Only 10 per cent are opposed to abortion in all circumstances, with about 18 per cent favouring a regime similar to that in the UK (close to the pro-choice position).[8] Consequently, two immediate questions arise:

1. When will the referendum be held?
2. What question will it ask?

The date makes a difference. Two months have been mentioned – May and June – but in June large numbers of young people, especially students, are off travelling or looking for work. These are the cohort most affected by this issue and who will likely have to live with the consequences of the referendum for years to come. They have never before in the lives had a chance to vote on the matter. Basic democracy and natural justice require that they are given the chance now. That means the referendum should be in May.

The question the referendum will ask also matters a lot. I believe it should be simple and straightforward: *for* or *against* repeal of the Eighth Amendment. Then, if repeal is passed, it will be over to the Oireachtas to legislate, which is its job. I think any attempt to ask multiple questions or two questions in one (as in 'Do you want to repeal the Eighth and replace it with X or Y?') will create confusion and difficulty for all concerned. Much better a clear question and a clear decision – one that will hopefully take this matter of women's health out of the Constitution, where it never belonged in the first place.

But in this referendum, when it is called, the battle will be for the hearts and minds of the Irish people. To win that battle for freedom, women's rights and a better future for Ireland in which the dark days of oppression are put behind us we will need a mass popular campaign. The voices of opposition to change, of conservatism and religious bigotry, will be loud, organised, and well-funded, but we will have people power on our side. We must use it. We will need groups of women and men to organise themselves in every community, every estate, every workplace and every college to own the streets, the bridges, the squares, and to canvass every house possible.

This is our time. Let's make it happen.

REFERENCES

Central Statistics Office (2017a) *Vital Statistics Annual Report 2015*, www.cso.ie/en/releasesandpublications/ep/p-vsar/vitalstatisticsannualreport2015/.

Central Statistics Office (2017b) *Chapter 4: Households and Families*, www.cso.ie/en/media/csoie/releasespublications/documents/population/2017/Chapter_4_Households_and_families.pdf.

Horgan, Goretti (2001) 'Changing Women's Lives in Ireland', *International Socialism Journal*, No. 91, http://pubs.socialistreviewindex.org.uk/isj91/horgan.htm.

Leahy, Pat (2017) 'Poll: Voters Would Pass Limited Abortion But Block Full Liberalisation', *Irish Times*, 6 October, www.irishtimes.com/news/politics/poll-voters-would-pass-limited-abortion-but-block-full-liberalisation-1.3246138.

Orr, Judith (2017) *Abortion Wars: The Fight for Reproductive Rights*, London: Policy Press.

ENDNOTES

1   Orr (2017).
2   Horgan (2001), p. 56.
3   *Ibid*, p. 56.
4   *Ibid*.
5   *Ibid*.
6   Central Statistics Office (2017a).
7   Central Statistics Office (2017b), p. 41.
8   See, for example, the Ipsos MRBI poll in Leahy (2017).

I Will Not Remain Silent

Bernadette Goulding

I cannot remain silent.

I had an abortion after a life-altering decision. Truly, by exercising my 'right to choose', my baby's heart stopped, and my heart was broken.

I was born and raised in the south of Ireland. I went to live and work in England when I was nineteen years old. I worked in an office in London and loved my job. I enjoyed the social scene and began to experiment with alcohol and became sexually active; as a result I became pregnant. I felt very much afraid and alone. I did not want to burden my family with being an unmarried mother, and the shame it would bring on them. I suffered with constant nausea and couldn't even go to work. I knew that if I carried this pregnancy to term that I would have to give up my job and this I was not prepared to do.

I eventually ended up in a hospital in London suffering from dehydration. The doctor examined me and for the first time my pregnancy was confirmed. I was admitted to hospital and a doctor came to speak with me. I told him that I did not want to be pregnant and that I would kill myself. He told me that he could do a termination. He said that there was nothing there, just a bunch of cells. He assured me that I would be just fine afterwards. There was no mention of any risks to my physical or mental health. The word 'baby' was never mentioned and I didn't allow myself to think that there was a baby there. It was just a big problem for me, and soon it would be over and no one would ever know. I was raised to respect doctors, and I felt that they knew best. I was assured that all would be well, which fed into my denial.

THE JOURNEY

You hear a lot of talk today of the stress the women endure who have to travel to England for their abortions. I didn't have to travel very far for my abortion as the hospital was just a short distance from where I lived at that time. Perhaps if

I had to travel from Ireland to the UK it would have given me the time I needed to think more about my situation and I would have given life to my child.

AFTER THE ABORTION

Initially I felt relief, but that was short-lived. The pregnancy was gone, and yet I felt so empty, like there was something missing. What was to follow was more like a nightmare than reality. I began to have nightmares about my aborted baby. I would see this beautiful baby and would try to reach out and take him into my arms but he was always just out of my reach and I would wake up screaming. I began to drink heavily. I felt like I had a big 'A' on my forehead (A for abortion) I felt like everyone could see through me and knew my big secret.

DENIAL

No woman is proud of having had an abortion. After the abortion, and because the experience is so horrible, many women go into denial. This can provide some short-term relief. Eventually, however, the emotional and spiritual pain is so severe that the women believe that they deserve to suffer for what they have done, and find many ways to punish themselves. To cope and somehow get on with my life I had to go into denial. Denial involves convincing yourself that nothing bad really happened. I tried to convince myself that I had no choice but to abort. That my child was better off. That I would have been a hopeless mother. I built a wall of denial around myself which helped me to cope. But every time I heard a baby cry I would be overwhelmed with grief. Seeing pregnant women was a trigger which would make me feel so guilty. I would go in and out of denial.

GUILT

The guilt I experienced was unbelievable. It was my constant companion. I began to believe that being guilty helped me to constantly remember my lost child. It has been suggested to me on several occasions that my guilt was because I was a Catholic, but having heard the stories of Catholics, Protestants, Baptists, atheists and agnostics, the tears of regret and shame and loss are all the same.

I would think about my baby. No one told me that at 21 days my baby's heart was beating. No one told me that I would long to have my baby back, and that I would forever wonder what my baby would look like. No one told me that I would suffer from depression, especially on the anniversary of the abortion. One day I went into a toy shop and I bought a small doll. Every time I moved this doll it would cry like a baby. I carried it around in my handbag. It was a symbol of my lost child and it was a constant reminder of what I had done.

No one told me that on the special events of my living children's lives – birthdays, first words, first steps, and first day at school – I would forever remember the one who would never celebrate a birthday, never speak a first word, and never have a first day at school. There is a space in my family that can never be filled. I had flashbacks, suicidal thoughts, self-hatred, panic attacks, anger and no self-esteem.

With abortion there is no focus for your grief. There is no body to bury, no family and friends to help you grieve your loss, no graveside to visit, no flowers, no sympathy cards. Just emptiness, isolation and grief, which a woman must face all alone. Every event in my life was shadowed by this secret sadness.

Abortion is chosen by many women for many different reasons. Most women abort out of fear that carrying an unexpected pregnancy to term will deprive them of a wanted relationship, the approval of others, their education, a career, or some other desired goal. Even if abortion helps you to achieve some desired goal in life, many women, as I did, discover that the goal they have achieved has lost its meaning.

ANGER

I suffered from a lot of anger after the abortion. Anger at myself for having had the abortion. Anger at my parents because I felt at the time that I could not tell them about my pregnancy and ask for their help, which I now realise they would have given. Anger that the doctor lied to me by telling me that there was nothing in my womb but cells. Anger that the doctor did not warn me of the possibility of risks to my mental and physical health. The best witnesses to the humanity of unborn children are mothers and fathers who weep for their lost children. We are not grieving over a bunch of cells or products of conception. We are grieving for our dead children.

When I realised that at 21 days there is a heartbeat, and that at the time of my abortion my baby's little heart was beating under my heart, I was overwhelmed with grief. I believed all the lies, that there is nothing there. I now know that life begins at the beginning. Something non-human doesn't become human by getting older and bigger. Whatever is human is human from the beginning. My baby had his own DNA, his own functioning heart separate from mine. Abortion ends the life of your unborn child and takes away your peace, your joy. You feel like you have no right to be happy. I sacrificed my child on the altar of pride and selfishness. I denied my child life, and the with realisation that my aborted child represented a branch of my family tree, not just my child's life but the possibility of generations to come had ended. All my child's life experiences were taken away because of a choice. My choice. My abortion was supposed to be a quick fix for my problems. No one told me that there was no quick fix for regret.

SILENCED BY SHAME

The shame I felt was huge. My shame told me that what I had done was really bad and that I was bad. Later on I met the man who would be my future husband. I was so ashamed and fearful of telling him that I had an abortion. When I told him about the abortion he just encouraged me to forget about it and move on with my life. Pregnant with my first child, I was so happy and managed to push down all the fear and anxiety and memories of the abortion. When my child was born and someone asked me, 'Is this your first child?' it was like a knife being twisted around in my heart. I knew that it was not my first child.

THE BIG SECRET

I was terrified of someone finding out my big secret. The power of the secret keeps you in a prison of fear and anxiety. Fear of someone finding out, fear of being judged. It takes a lot of energy to keep those feelings in check. I would have nightmares about someone in my workplace finding out about my abortion. As a general rule, women simply don't talk about their abortions as readily as they talk about other pregnancies. It simply does not lend itself to casual conversation.

One woman had this to say after her abortion:

> After the abortion I was led into a 'recovery room'. I ended sitting up sitting next to the same women I had been with when we were all still pregnant. Nobody was happy. A great heaviness hung over all of us. As we talked, between tears, I made the remark that I was about 12 weeks pregnant. The woman next to me looked at me and said, 'You were ....' That's when it really hit me. My baby was gone – forever. On my way out I had to walk through the recovery room of brand new 'patients' who were no longer pregnant. My eyes met one of them and I gave her a salute. She returned the gesture. We never spoke. We didn't have to. We were now sisters in a secret society of women who had done something they didn't want to do, but saw no other way out.[1]

My husband and I decided to move back to Ireland. God blessed me with three more children. I was so fearful that something bad would happen to my children and that I didn't deserve them. I became very friendly with a lady in my parish and she was always applauding me for helping with different groups in the parish. I felt such a fraud when she would praise me. One day I decided to challenge her friendship and to share with her the story of my abortion. I remember I closed my eyes and just let it come tumbling out. I was reluctant to open my eyes as I dreaded the look of condemnation which I expected to see in her eyes. When I opened my eyes she was crying. She said, 'Don't waste your suffering, and use it for good.'

The freedom I felt was unbelievable. I had begun to dismantle the secret, and my friend did not judge me. I had been stuck in a guilt trap. This was the first step on a long and difficult road to healing. It wasn't God or religion that had kept me there. It was myself. I now realise that the guilt was the only way I had of keeping the memory of my baby alive. Under that guilt was a huge need to grieve for my baby. I had exercised my right to choose, and I believed that I had forfeited my right to grieve. What right had I to grieve for a child I didn't want? What right had I to grieve for a child whose life I had ended?

We have all heard the isolating rhetoric: 'Abortion is a personal and private decision.' But the reality is that we are human beings – social beings who need and rely on our connections to others. Abortion encourages isolation and secrecy. The secrecy kept me in a prison for many years, and now I had escaped from that prison of secrecy and isolation by sharing my story with my friend. Abortion is a death experience. I had to face my life with honesty. I had to acknowledge that the abortion ended the life of my unborn child.

It is easier to have an abortion if you convince yourself that there is nothing there. Those who are pro-abortion are often hesitant to recognise the reality of post-abortion grief because they fear that this means that they have to recognise the death of a baby, which may somehow undermine the political argument for abortion.

Breaking the silence is a major step in healing. Just as I carried my shame in silence for a long time, I carried my healing the same – hidden. There is an element of perceived safety in silence. There was still the fear of condemnation from others. We are silenced by shame. In my way of thinking, carrying my healing in silence protected it from being stolen from me. I later learned that breaking the silence is a major step in healing.

POST-ABORTION SUPPORT GROUP

I had spent so many years feeling so isolated and feeling that I was the only one who felt so bad after the abortion. I began to speak out about my experience and many women and men would contact me and tell me their stories of loss and grief and regret. I then realised that there was no help out there for women like myself who deeply regretted their abortions. I heard about a psychotherapist in the United States, Dr Theresa Burke, who has founded a beautiful weekend programme for women and men who have been deeply damaged by their abortions. I contacted her and our first weekend was held in Cork in October 2003. It is an amazing weekend. It is a very gentle but emotionally intensive therapeutic process that combines both psychological and spiritual elements. It offers women and men an opportunity to examine their abortion experience, identify the ways the loss has affected them, and acknowledge whatever pain is there. The programme helps them deal with repressed grief, guilt, anger, feelings of abandonment, pressure and ambivalent attachments to their aborted children.

I began to realise that there were many women suffering after abortion and I decided to speak out publicly about my abortion experience. It was a difficult decision. Before I could go public I had to tell my children about the abortion. This was a very difficult thing for me to do, but I knew that I felt so strongly about this and that I could not go forward until I had shared the secret with my children. They had also experienced a loss even though they never knew their sibling. Their feelings needed to be sorted out. They now support me fully in the work I do with post-abortive women and men.

THE RIGHT TO REMAIN SILENT

Who are the women who choose abortion? They are our daughters, partners, wives, sisters, relatives, friends and members of our parish communities. Very often they carry a secret wound in their hearts that is re-opened every time they hear a baby cry or see a pregnant woman. The pain is so deep that sometimes they cannot even say the word 'abortion' without suffering huge distress. These women suffer in silence and isolation because of guilt and fear of disclosure. I pray for the day when women and men from all walks of life will be able to publicly confess their guilt over past abortions and proclaim their healing to others.

Another aspect of post-abortion healing which should not be missed is its impact on family members. Many people remain silent about abortion in general because they do not want to hurt loved ones whom they know have had abortions. For every woman who has had an abortion, there are numerous people who remain neutral on abortion, or hide their pro-life sympathies, out of deference to her feelings.

One of the myths I have come across is that only pro-abortion women have abortions. The truth is that pro-life Christian women also have abortions. It is easy to stand on one's principles when one is not faced with a crisis pregnancy. It is easy to say 'I would never have an abortion' until you are actually faced with that situation yourself. The tears of the Catholic, Protestant, Evangelical, atheist or agnostic are all the same.

To date I have facilitated over 180 healing weekends in countries such as England, Scotland, Malta, Faroe Islands, South Korea, Lebanon, Hungary, Croatia, Slovenia and South Africa. These are countries where abortion is legal and freely available and yet the suffering is the same. It is a universal experience. I have listened to the varied stories of the women who shared how they were coerced into unwanted abortions through threats, pressure, emotional blackmail and even violence. Many told of being misinformed and mistreated at abortion facilities and of being dismissed after the abortions, shamed into silence and told to get on with their lives.

I hear it so often in these times from 'professional medical personnel' who say that women are not affected by abortion. They say that the women must have had pre-existing health problems. This is so offensive to women who suffer deep regret and grief after abortion.

RESEARCH ON MENTAL HEALTH ISSUES AFTER ABORTION

A study in New Zealand that tracked approximately 500 women from birth to 25 years of age has confirmed that young women who have abortions subsequently experience elevated rates of suicidal behaviours, depression, substance abuse, anxiety and other mental health problems.[2]

Dr Julius Fogel, a psychiatrist and obstetrician in the US who has been a long-time advocate of abortion and has personally performed over 20,000 abortions, insists:

> Every woman – whatever her age or background – has a trauma at destroying a pregnancy. A level of humanness is touched. This is a part of her own life. When she destroys a pregnancy, she is destroying herself. There is no way it can be innocuous. One is dealing with the life force. It is totally beside the point whether or not you think a life is there. You cannot deny that something is being created and that this creation is physically happening .... Often the trauma may sink into the unconscious and never surface in the woman's lifetime. But it is not as harmless

and casual an event as many in the pro-abortion crowd insists. A psychological price is paid. It may be alienation; it may be a pushing away from human warmth, perhaps a hardening of the maternal instinct. Something happens on the deeper levels of a woman's consciousness when she destroys a pregnancy. I know that as a psychiatrist.[3]

ABORTION: A WOMAN'S ISSUE

We hear so often that abortion is a woman's issue, yet in my experience I have met so many men who are deeply damaged by abortion. I have heard the stories of men who have suffered from depression, anxiety, self-hatred and shame, and of the broken relationships and marriages. This is what one of the many men that have come to me seeking healing has said:

> The day of the abortion was the day that something inside of me died. I felt dead inside for 20 years. When we returned home after the abortion I struggled to understand myself as husband and provider. I knew deep down that I had rejected my child and I felt such a hypocrite. Like a lot of men, I dealt with this wound by not dealing with it. I stuffed it down deep, and put all my energy into my work. I felt that my identity was taken from me and I did not feel whole. I was successful in my career, but I had this nagging sense that disaster was just around the corner and couldn't enjoy or trust anything good in my life. Abortion stole my peace, affected our relationship. It was a great big wound in our marriage.

The following letter was written to his aborted son by a man who participated in one of my weekends:

> Dear Son,
>
> Today instead of preparing to go and watch a football match together, I am in the depths of depression and trying to make sense of my life. Your mother and I were still getting to know each other when you were conceived. She fought hard to keep you, but I was immature, unsettled and living a life that was not mine. I was filled with fear. I am so very sorry my son. I know that I cannot change the past, but I believe that you are watching and guiding me from heaven. Since your termination my life has completely changed. I was a person full of dreams, adventures,

aspirations, and a simple life dedicated to help other people. After you were gone I became mostly dumb, existing but not living. Thoughts are always far away, and when I try to socialise I always feel that my mind is far away, in a could have been world. I have lost all the motivation that I once had. Sometimes I try to wonder how life would have been if you were here with us. How you would play with my nephew and be cuddled by your grandmother. Please find it in your heart to forgive me for aborting you.

Love Dad.

Today, more men than ever are coming forward as part of a growing multitude of those who have been wounded by abortion. They talk about the anger that comes from abortions they could not stop and the overwhelming despair they feel because of the abortions they insisted upon and financially supported. They have learned how even abortions in which they had no participation at all have had the power to alter their lives

I must also mention the women who suffered rape and who decide on abortion, and are now being used by pro-abortionists to further their agenda. The grief that those women feel is a double trauma: the trauma of the rape and the trauma of the abortion. The following are the experiences of two women. One woman aborted after being raped and the other woman gave birth to her child.

I soon discovered that the aftermath of my abortion continued a long time after the memory of my rape had faded. I felt empty and horrible. Nobody told me about the pain I would feel deep within, causing night-mares and deep depressions. They had all told me that after the abortion I could continue my life as if nothing had happened. I grieve the loss of my child.[4]

The following is the testimony of a woman who was raped and decided to give life to her child:

I, having lived through rape, and also having raised a child 'conceived in rape', feel personally assaulted and insulted every time I hear that abortion should be legal because of rape and incest. I feel that we're being used by pro-abortionists to further the abortion issue, even though we've not been asked to tell our side of the story.[5]

THE EIGHTH AMENDMENT HAS SAVED MANY LIVES

The current debate to legalise abortion on the grounds of the child's disability sends a dreadful message to our disabled friends and family members. We are actually saying that their life is not worth living. I have had numerous women participate in one of my weekends who were given this diagnosis and decided on abortion. The suffering and grief of those women was painful to watch. We can do better than abortion for mothers and babies with a challenging pregnancy.

You have only to look at the situation in Britain where 90 per cent of babies diagnosed with Down syndrome are aborted. What a betrayal of those babies who have so much to offer the world. Life doesn't have to be perfect to be beautiful.

I know that the abortion issue can be difficult to speak about. We have a responsibility to be sensitive in the language that we use so as not to add to the anguish and pain of those most personally affected by this issue. But we cannot sweep the truth under the carpet. That would be the ultimate betrayal of women and their unborn children.

No country is perfect but we have every reason to be proud of Ireland's pro-life laws. The abortion debate presents us with two radically different visions of human rights. In the end, we cannot sanction abortion and also claim to defend human life. We need to make life better, not take it away.

I have shared the most painful chapter of my life with you. I have done so because my decision to exercise 'my right to choose' stopped my baby's heart, and broke my own. I will continue to share my story as long as other women, my sisters, in similar situations, make the same life-altering and life-shattering decision that I made. If I can help prevent one woman from making the same mistake, or help one who has, to find peace and healing, my little effort to open my heart to you will have been worthwhile.

I have shared with you my painful experience of repetitive nightmares. Now I want to proclaim for the entire world to hear, that I have a dream, yes, I have a dream: that in my lifetime, my sisters all around the world suffering after an abortion will stand as one, break their silence, insist that their stories be heard, and their pain be acknowledged.

Many people are alive today because of the Eighth Amendment to our Constitution. I know now that if I had been living in Ireland when I was pregnant back then, and had that precious time to reflect, it would have made all the difference to my situation and my child could be alive today.

REFERENCES

Burke, Theresa (2002) *Forbidden Grief: The Unspoken Pain of Abortion*, Luton: Acorn Books.

Fergusson, David M., L. John Horwood and Elizabeth M. Ridder (2006) 'Abortion in Young Women and Subsequent Mental Health', *Journal of Child Psychology and Psychiatry*, Vol. 47, No. 1, pp. 16–24.

Reardon, David C., Julie Makimaa and Amy Sobi (eds) (2000) *Victims and Victors: Speaking Out about Their Pregnancies, Abortions, and Children Resulting from Sexual Assault*, Luton: Acorn Books.

ENDNOTES

1   Burke (2002), p. 35.
2   Fergusson, Norwood and Ridder (2006).
3   Burke (2002), p. 33.
4   Reardon, Makimaa and Sobi (eds) (2000).
5   *Ibid.*

Repealing the Eighth Amendment Means More Flourishing Families

Valerie Tarico

How many of the women you know and love have chosen to end a mistimed or unhealthy pregnancy? Whatever answer came to mind is probably wrong, because laws that force women out of the country for abortion care – laws that are coupled with stigma and shame – also force them into silence afterwards, sometimes for decades; sometimes for a lifetime. I once sat in a small gathering at a retirement home and listened as elderly women shared with each other their childbearing decisions, including abortions that some had never even told a husband or daughter.

When Ireland votes on the Eighth Amendment, the outcome will be felt around the world by women, especially those for whom the price of staying true to themselves and their values has been silence. But the ability to end an ill-conceived pregnancy or one gone terribly awry doesn't affect just women. When prospective parents can prepare and then time their pregnancies –when they can build up physical health, social support, education, and financial security before adding a child to their family – everyone does better: women, yes, but also men and older children and children not yet born, and grandparents and aunties, and the broader communities that surround them. When it comes to stacking the odds in favour of human flourishing, family planning is one of the most powerful tools ever invented. And when family planning fails, or pregnancy goes wrong, abortion offers the mercy of a fresh start. This creates a profound moral argument in support of abortion access.

For many people from many different religions and cultures, ethics and morality are about reducing suffering or increasing well-being for humans (and sometimes for other sentient beings). And despite our differences, we broadly recognise what that means. We all want health and security, love and autonomy, and aesthetic beauty. We want to experience what life has to offer in the form of pleasure and to be free from too much pain. We want these things, especially for our family and friends and our children – but we recognise that others want them too. That is why, when it comes to how we should treat other conscious beings like ourselves, humanity's shared moral core converges somewhere around the Golden Rule: *Do unto others as you would have them do unto you* or – since we can imagine that not everyone wants exactly the same thing – the Platinum Rule: *Do unto others as they would have you do unto them.*

So we have this shared moral core, but for each of us, moral decisions – including family decisions – are a matter of our own deepest values and highest aspirations – our hopes for the future and how we make meaning of our lives. Many people call this the spiritual dimension of life, including some of us who are wholly secular. Religion offers a set of traditional agreements about this dimension of life, a set of answers carefully handed down from our ancestors about what is real and what is good and how we should then live. But even among those who are religious, even those who share the same tradition and largely accept these answers, values differ from person to person. Whether religious or not, we form our moral and spiritual core based on culture, reasoning, thoughtful inquiry, human biology, and lived experience – our own experience and that of those around us.

Artist Favianna Rodriguez is a rising star who uses her bold gripping graphics to drive conversation about an array of social issues and to inspire change. When she got pregnant as a young art student, she looked back on all that her immigrant parents had done to create opportunity for their children and she looked forward at the creative endeavours that were just becoming possible, and, to her, the choices were clear. Like millions of other women, Favianna's decision to abort her pregnancy was grounded in her family values and dreams.

My friend Judy's abortion decision was driven by her deep commitment to being a loving parent. Judy says, 'I believe that parenting begins before conception.' This belief compelled Judy and her husband, Peter, to terminate a malformed twin rather than bringing a newborn into the world to suffocate at birth. Their decision combined love with foresight, courage and compassion. It was a powerful expression of Judy and Peter's most deeply-held values.

In a 2012 case, now famous, 31-year-old dentist Savita Halappanavar died from septic miscarriage after being denied abortion care at University Hospital Galway. Halappanavar was Hindu, and her doctor's refusal to end her pregnancy-gone-awry had nothing to do with her own religious beliefs or spiritual values. She wanted to live and have another chance at motherhood, and she repeatedly asked for the abortion that could have saved her life. These were her values as a Hindu, but the same might be true for a native-born Irish Catholic. In the US, a group called Catholics for Choice speaks for committed Catholics who believe that the greater good lies in letting individual couples make decisions about the beginnings and endings of life.

Because of our differences, imposing a set of rules derived from one specific subset of one specific religion, as in the current Irish abortion prohibition, can almost never reflect the moral and spiritual priorities of a whole country of people. We each see the world through a lens that is unique when it comes to the most important decisions that shape our lives – whom we love, whom we marry, what callings we pursue, whether we have children and with whom, whether we feel compelled to carry forward or end an ill-conceived pregnancy. Consequently, every society is left in the end with the question of who decides. My husband and I, in forming our family, have been grateful that we could make these decisions for ourselves.

OUR ABORTION BABY, BRYNN

My elder daughter, Brynn, took her first steps in Ireland, during a trip I made with my husband, Brian, almost 22 years ago. And on the same trip, my body announced that our second daughter, Marley, was on the way – I mean announced it with an ocean of fatigue and nausea that had me ordering potato soup at every meal, including breakfast when I could get it. Brynn and Marley are our first and second daughters, but they weren't our first and second pregnancies. The first one we aborted and without that abortion Brynn would not exist and likely Marley wouldn't either.

Five years into our marriage, Brian and I embarked on a shared dream. He quit his job and I temporarily closed my psychology practice. We turned savings into traveler's cheques, packed our backpacks for a year of Lonely Planet travel, and boarded a flight for Mexico City. In the coming months, we rode standing-room-only buses with chickens at our elbows, and 'luxury' buses where violent, lurid Hollywood movies made the kilometres seem eternal, and one narrow-gauge train with lace-edged linens in the hard sleeper. We stayed sometimes in sweet guest houses, but more often in bare cement rooms with spiders or mice.

Knitted into this simple and sometimes difficult mode of travel we encountered the bountiful kindness of shared humanity, even in the midst of poverty, and the beauty of this one precious planet. We once slept on the dirt floor of a kind Cancún worker who picked up two foreign hitchhikers in his decrepit Ford truck. We paused to volunteer briefly in a small rural clinic. We swam in travertine pools and hiked in the dark to watch the sun rise over a live volcanic crater. We marvelled at the tenacity of a small eco-collective and dairy surrounded by rainforest, and we humbly shared the home of a Salvadorian mother whose labour organiser husband had been 'disappeared'.

Without work to focus on, my biological alarm clock went off and scarcely a month into the trip I announced that I wanted to get pregnant. Brian was a bit surprised, but (in contrast to me) he had always known he wanted to be a parent. Besides which, he's an adaptable person and he recognised a window of opportunity, so he set to work wrapping his mind around the idea. We were in southern Costa Rica at the time, about to crew our way through the Panama Canal to a new continent and, I figured, the next phase of life.

Then we got news that my father had died in a mountaineering accident while on a work trip to Switzerland. We flew back to the States for a month, where I comforted myself by putting our garden back in order – pruning and weeding, only mildly annoyed by the neighbourhood cats who had been loosening the soil so it would be easier for them to bury their business. It was while we were at home that I got pregnant. Somehow in my mind, the new life that was growing inside me made it seem like Dad wasn't completely gone. His death, my pregnancy and the tenacious weeds eddied together in a soothing reminder of the flow of life.

We hit the road again, this time flying east to Jakarta, and after more three months of bumpy bus rides where violent films and loud music fused with all-day-long 'morning sickness', I was so ready to have that baby!

We landed in Singapore at the trailing edge of first trimester and got a gorgeous ultrasound picture of the foetus we had nicknamed 'Gecko'. To celebrate, we splurged at a little French bistro with crusty bread and gorgonzola pasta and a wee bit of wine, with the picture on the table between us. And then, the next day, we got test results showing that I had acute toxoplasmosis, a disease transmitted by cats – in my case probably the cats who had been digging in the garden back home, or the scrawny feral cats that are a constant presence in much of Indonesia. Probably not a big deal, right? We trucked ourselves over to the university library to find out. It turns out acute toxoplasmosis can affect the developing brain much like Zika virus.

It seemed like a nightmare. We both wanted a baby. But it also felt irresponsible to gamble. Not only would we be taking a chance on the quality of life of our first child, but potentially committing any future children to a life of caretaking that they had no option to choose or reject. We would be risking our own ability to give to the community around us – and possibly creating a situation in which our small family needed to suck more out of society than we could put back into it. As painful as the decision felt, our moral values were clear, and we scheduled to terminate the pregnancy.

The loss felt enormous, in part because that pregnancy was so tied up with my father's death. I was still letting him go – dreaming that I was in Switzerland rather than Costa Rica when he fell, kneeling and scooping the bright red snow while a helicopter flew his body away. Or talking to him at his desk and telling him I wouldn't see him again. Or reliving my mother's middle-of-the night screams when, not knowing what to do with the blood-soaked clothes that the Swiss government had mistakenly shipped to Arizona, she put them in the washing machine and a piece of Dad's skull fell out of the wet heap.

But three months later, before that first pregnancy would have come to term, we were able to conceive again, and so began the pregnancy that would develop into our daughter Brynn. Even then, I felt the loss of that first imagined child, but when Brynn came into the world and I looked into her eyes, I knew that I couldn't possibly wish for any child other than the one in front of me. I didn't want some alternate reality in which someone else existed instead of her, a reality in which she *couldn't* exist; I wanted her.

Today, instead of a hypothetical potential child who might spend a (short or long) lifetime struggling to be and do the things we all cherish most, we have two real daughters who are loving and generous and playful and strong and way smarter and more disciplined than their mama will ever be. Had Brynn or Marley – or some other genetic bundle – come into our family less perfect, or even with the same defects at risk in that first pregnancy, we would have loved them fiercely and done everything in our power for them to flourish. Mercifully, we never faced that situation, because a kind and competent doctor gave us the choice to end that infected pregnancy and start over.

I tell our story because it illustrates something important that is rarely talked about in the back-and-forth about abortion. Most people who choose an abortion also chose to have a child or children who *would not exist* if they carried through that earlier pregnancy. The future is always in motion and all manner of decisions and non-decisions, small and large, change the flow of history. If a woman coughs or rolls over after sex, a different sperm reaches an egg and a different person comes into the world. Abortion and birth control don't create a tragic world of 'missing people' as some opponents like to argue. On the contrary, all around us are people who exist only because their parents had the mercy of a fresh start, or the freedom to delay a pregnancy till the time and partnership felt right – like my daughters, Brynn and Marley.

WHY I AM PRO-ABORTION

In 2015, I wrote an article titled 'I Am Pro-Abortion, Not just Pro-Choice'.[1] The title was provocative, as it was meant to be; another author had said, almost casually, 'nobody is pro-abortion' and I thought, *that simply isn't true*. Mind you, I wish abortion were obsolete. Surgical abortion is an expensive, invasive medical procedure that can be emotionally complicated even when a woman (or couple) feels clear that it is the best choice in a difficult situation. And medical abortion is no cakewalk either. Like chemotherapy or orthopaedic surgery or antibiotic therapy, abortion is a costly harm-reduction strategy, and I wish nobody needed any of these. That's why preventing cancer and accidents and infections when we can – and preventing mistimed or unwanted or unhealthy pregnancies – makes so much sense. Reducing harm is a positive social good, but why mitigate harm if you can simply prevent it?

We now have the means to prevent most of the mistimed and unwanted pregnancies that lead to abortions. For the price of an early abortion a woman can obtain a state-of-the-art long-acting contraceptive that drops her risk of a mistimed pregnancy below 1 in 500 annually, and lasts for years or until she feels ready to have a child. Long-acting contraceptives toggle the fertility switch to *OFF* until a person wants it *ON*. And when these tools – modern IUDs and implants – get used broadly, abortion rates plummet. People who oppose abortion would do well to lobby for better access to better birth control.

Someday, implanted slow-release contraceptives will be the norm, and men too will have excellent means to manage their fertility – and the need for abortion will be limited to cases like Savita's and mine. But in the meantime, abortion care is a critical part of family planning services – a much-needed back-up when all else fails. That is why many of the kinds of good that come from abortion are the same kinds of good that come from family planning:

- *Abortion is a positive social good because well-timed pregnancies give children a healthier start in life.* We now have ample evidence that babies do best when women are able to space their pregnancies and get both pre-natal and pre-conception care. The specific nutrients we ingest in the weeks before we get pregnant can have a lifelong effect on the well-being of our offspring. Rapid repeat pregnancies increase the risk of low birthweight babies and other complications. Wanted babies are more likely to have their toes kissed, to be welcomed into families that are financially and emotionally ready to receive them, and to get preventive medical care during childhood and the kinds of loving engagement that helps young brains to develop.
- *Abortion is a positive social good because parenthood is worth doing well.* Most female bodies can incubate a baby; and thanks to antibiotics, Caesareans and anti-haemorrhage drugs, most of us are able to survive pushing a baby out into the world. But parenting is a lot of work; and doing it well takes twenty dedicated years of focus, attention, patience, persistence, social

support, mental health, money and a whole lot more. This is the biggest, most life-transforming thing most of us will ever do. The idea that women should simply go with it when they find themselves pregnant after a one night stand, or a rape or a broken condom completely trivialises parenthood.

- *Abortion is a positive social good because being able to delay and limit childbearing is fundamental to female empowerment and equality.* A woman who lacks the means to manage her fertility lacks the means to manage her life. Any plans, dreams, aspirations, responsibilities or commitments – no matter how important – have a great big contingency clause built in: 'until or unless I get pregnant, in which case all bets are off'. Think of any professional woman you know. She wouldn't be in that role if she hadn't been able to time and limit her childbearing. Think of any girl you know who imagines becoming a professional woman. She won't get there unless she has effective, reliable means to manage her fertility. In generations past, nursing care was provided by nuns and teachers who were spinsters, because avoiding sexual intimacy was the only way women could avoid unpredictable childbearing and so be freed up to serve their communities in other capacities. But if you think that abstinence should be our model for modern fertility management, consider the little graves that get found every so often under old nunneries and homes for unwed mothers.

- *Abortion is a positive social good because **intentional childbearing helps couples, families and communities to get out of poverty.*** Decades of research in countries ranging from the US to Bangladesh[2] show that reproductive policy is economic policy. It is no coincidence that the Western middle class rose along with the ability of couples to plan their families, starting at the beginning of the last century. Having two or three kids instead of eight or ten was critical to prospering in the modern industrial economy. By contrast, early unsought childbearing nukes economic opportunity and contributes to multi-generational poverty. Strong, determined girls and women sometimes beat the odds, but their stories inspire us precisely because they are the exception to the rule.

All of these are reasons that everyone, not just a privileged few, should have access to the very best contraceptive technologies, family planning services and information about their own bodies. These are the reasons why people who care about flourishing children and families and communities should invest in modern family options, and especially better options for young men, who are forced to rely on a technology – the condom – that is nearly a century old.

- *Contraceptives are imperfect and people are imperfect too.* Each year, one in six couples relying on condoms, or about 18 per cent, will find themselves facing a surprise pregnancy – better than the 85 per cent who would face a pregnancy in the absence of contraception, or the 75 per cent who would face a pregnancy if using traditional strategies like the rhythm method or pulling out – but still far from ideal. The high failure rate is due in part to condoms breaking, but mostly it's because in the heat of the moment ordinary people make poor decisions and mistakes.

  The Pill is somewhat better, but not nearly as effective in real life as most people think. In the real world, 1 in 11 women relying on the Pill, or about 9 per cent, gets pregnant each year.[3] Again, sometimes pills themselves fail. But also, it's just really hard for most people to take a pill at the same time every day for years on end. Young and poor women – those whose lives are least predictable and most vulnerable to being thrown off course – are also those who have the most difficulty taking pills consistently. Pill technology most fails those who need it most, which makes abortion access a matter not only of compassion but of justice.

  State-of-the-art IUDs and implants radically change this equation, largely because they take human error out of the picture for years on end, or until a woman wants a baby. And despite the deliberate misinformation being spread by opponents, these methods are genuine contraceptives, not abortifacients. Depending on the method chosen, they disable sperm or block their path, or prevent an egg from being released. And, as I said, once settled into place, an IUD or implant drops the annual pregnancy rate below 1 in 500.

  But even if we totally modernised reproductive healthcare by making sure that all women have same-day, no-cost access to the birth control method of their choice – and even if we developed highly effective modern contraceptive options for men – the need for abortion wouldn't go away entirely.

- *Reproduction is a highly imperfect process.* Genetic recombination is a complicated progression with flaws and false starts at every step along the way. To compensate, in every known species, including humans, reproduction operates as a big funnel. Many more eggs and sperm are produced than will ever meet; more combine into embryos than will ever implant; and more implant than will grow into babies. This systematic culling makes God or nature the world's biggest abortion provider: nature's way of producing healthy kids essentially requires every woman to have an abortion mill built into her own body. In humans, an estimated 60–80 per cent of fertilised eggs self-destruct before becoming babies, which is why the people who kill the most embryos are those who try to maximise their number of pregnancies or who simply 'let go and let God' manage their fertility.

But the weeding-out process is also highly imperfect. Sometimes perfectly viable combinations boot themselves out; sometimes horrible defects slip through. A woman's body may be less fertile when she is stressed or ill or malnourished, but as pictures of skeletal moms and babies show, some women conceive even under devastating circumstances. Like any other medical procedure, therapeutic contraception and abortion complement natural processes designed to help us survive and thrive.

People fail, contraceptives fail, and reproduction itself fails. Nothing is perfect in this world, and that is where abortion comes in.

- *Do you believe in mercy, grace, compassion, and the power of fresh starts?* Many years ago, my friend Chip was driving his family on vacation when his kids started squabbling. His wife, Marla, undid her seatbelt to help them, and as Chip looked over at her their top-heavy minivan veered onto the shoulder and then rolled, and Marla died. Sometimes people make mistakes or have accidents that they pay for for the rest of their lives. But I myself have swerved onto the shoulder and simply swerved back. The price we pay for a lapse in attention or judgement, or an accident of any kind, isn't proportional to the error we made. Who among us hasn't had unprotected sex when the time or situation or partnership wasn't quite right for bringing a new life into the world? Most of the time we get lucky; sometimes we don't. And in those situations, we rely on the mercy, compassion and generosity of others.

In this regard, an unsought pregnancy is like any other accident. I can walk today only because surgeons reassembled my lower leg after it was crushed between the front of a car and a bicycle frame when I was a teen. And I can walk today (and run and jump) because another team of surgeons re-assembled my knee joint after I fell off a ladder. And I can walk today (and bicycle with my family) because a third team of surgeons repaired my other knee after I pulled a whirring brush mower onto myself, cutting clear through bone. Three accidents, all my own doing, and three knee surgeries. Some women have three abortions.

WHEN GOD WAS PRO-CHOICE: A GLIMPSE INTO HISTORY

In 1975, the evangelical press Zondervan published an ethics book by Norman Geisler, a leading Christian apologist both then and in the intervening decades. In it, Geisler said, 'Abortion is not murder, because the embryo is not fully human – it is an undeveloped person.'[4] Not all Christians of the time agreed with him, but his perspective was well within the mainstream of Christian opinion at the time.

A few years ago, I was helping to clean out old files for the Washington Association of Churches when I ran across an old mimeographed six-page pamphlet from 1978 titled 'Abortion: An Ecumenical Study Document'.[5] The pamphlet did not contain a position statement. Quite the opposite, in fact. From the beginning, the authors explain that such an agreement is impossible:

> Clearly there is no Christian position on abortion, for here real values conflict with each other, and Christian persons who seek honestly to be open to God's call still find themselves disagreeing profoundly.

At the time, five years had passed since the US Supreme Court's *Roe v Wade* decision legalising abortion, and the Church, broadly, was wrestling with ethical and spiritual complexities that the decision brought to the surface. In the absence of an agreement, the study group articulated a set of shared values and then assembled statements from member denominations.

Some of the contents would come as little surprise to anyone aware of today's struggles over abortion ethics and rights. For example, the Catholic representative pronounced that even when pregnancy threatens a mother's life abortion 'increases the overall tragedy'. Catholicism has wavered over the centuries about when a foetus becomes a person with a soul, but the hierarchy has been consistent in its opposition to abortion after ensoulment, which is now proclaimed to happen at conception.

What might be surprising is how little the other denominations agreed. Consider the following statements:[6]

- 'Because Christ calls us to affirm the freedom of persons and the sanctity of life, we recognize that abortion should be a matter of personal decision.'
  – American Baptist Churches
- 'The ALC recognizes the freedom and responsibility of individuals to make their own choices in light of the best information available to them and their understanding of God's will for their lives, whether those choices be in regard to family planning or any other life situations.'
  – American Lutheran Church
- 'The Christian Church (Disciples of Christ) believes that the mother has an overwhelming stake in her own pregnancy, and to be forced to give birth to a child against her will is a peculiarly personal violation of her freedom ....

The fetus is seen as a potential person, but not fully a person in the same developed sense in which the mother is a person with an ability to think, to feel, to make decisions, and choices concerning her own life. ... That prior right however, carries with it a tremendous responsibility, for human life, even potential human life is valued.'

    – Christian Church (Disciples of Christ)

- 'Abortion should be accepted as an option only where all other possible alternatives will lead to greater destruction of human life and spirit. ... We support persons who, after prayer and counseling, believe abortion is the least destructive alternative available to them, that they may make their decision openly, honestly, without the suffering imposed by an uncompromising community.'

    – Church of the Brethren

- 'Christians have a responsibility to limit the size of their families and to practice responsible birth control. ... Where there is substantial reason to believe that the child would be deformed in mind or body, or where the pregnancy has resulted from rape or incest ... termination of pregnancy is permissible.'

    – Episcopal Church

- 'The status of the fetus is the key issue. That status is affected by consideration of the fact that it is the organic beginning of human life. Further, its status is defined by its stage of development, its state of well-being, and its prospects for a meaningful life after its birth.'

    – Lutheran Church in America

- 'Human life develops on a continuum from conception to birth. At some point it may be regarded as more "personal" and higher in "quality." At some undesignated time, the value of this life may actually outweigh competing factors; e.g., the vocational and social objectives of the family, etc.'

    – United Church of Christ

- 'Our belief in the sanctity of unborn human life makes us reluctant to approve abortion. But we are equally bound to respect the sacredness of the life and well-being of the mother, for whom devastating damage may result from an unacceptable pregnancy. In continuity with past Christian teaching, we recognize tragic conflicts of life with life that may justify abortion.'

    – United Methodist Church

- 'The artificial or induced termination of pregnancy is a matter of the careful ethical decision of the patient, her physician, and her pastor or other counselor and therefore should not be restricted by law ....'

    – United Presbyterian Church

As a psychologist, what I find most interesting about these statements is how they vary in terms of black-and-white thinking versus shades of complexity. For Washington's Catholic bishop, life became precious when an egg was fertilised, and aborting a foetus, even to save someone like Savita Halappanavar who desperately wanted to live, was evil – a violation of natural law. Other theologians took the view that a human being emerges gradually and gains moral standing over time or that many different kinds of good must be weighed: the well-being of the mother, for example, or her right to self-determination, or the goals of the family. The Episcopal assertion that limiting family size is not merely a right but a responsibility took readers into different moral territory. And, of course, there were shades of variation in terms of who should make the decision.

I, myself, disagree to a greater or lesser extent with many of these statements. For me, morality is about the lived experience of sentient beings – beings who can feel pleasure and pain, preference and intention, who at their most complex can live in relation to other beings, love and be loved and value their own existence. These – not simply human DNA – are the traditional elements of personhood, and they are present to some degree in species other than humans, which means we have moral obligations toward them in proportion to what they are able to experience. *What are they capable of wanting? What are they capable of feeling?* These are the questions my husband and I explored with our kids when they were figuring out their responsibility to their pet chickens and guinea pigs. It was a lesson that turned expensive, when the girls stopped drinking milk from cows that didn't get to see the light of day or eat grass, but it's not one I regret.

By contrast, the attributes of personhood are wholly absent in the human embryo, with some emerging gradually over the course of gestation. The cranium is empty even after rudimentary reflexes emerge because the nervous system develops late in the game. *Do unto others as they want you to do unto them says* the Platinum Rule, but an embryo or early foetus is incapable of experiencing or wanting anything. It is a potential person, and in my moral universe real people count more than potential people.

Who Decides?

In my moral universe, like that of the Episcopal in the abortion study document, family planning is not only a right but a responsibility. My husband and I felt a responsibility to make parenthood decisions with a mind to not only our well-being but that of our children, our family and our community. For me, parenting begins before conception, and carrying forward that first infected pregnancy would have violated my sense of what it means for me to parent well, even when it is painful.

I have said, in this context, that abortion is a positive social good and that I experience our abortion as a blessing – and a gift of the two beloved daughters I now cherish. But should I have the right to impose my values – and own sense of obligations – on you? How about your parent or spouse? How about your doctor or legislator? How about a priest or judge?

When our deep values come into conflict or when the unexpected threatens to harm our family or derail our dreams, each of us wrestles alone or in the company of loved ones and chosen advisors. Sometimes we do prefer to hand off hard decisions to another person, or to an authority figure. And sometimes an authority figure claims that right.

The Catholic hierarchy claims officially to represent the will of God, and in that role asserts that any legal option for women or couples to end unwanted or unhealthy pregnancy degrades life for us all. But believers don't all agree. Some say, rather, that their sense of the sacred is precisely what makes them believe that childbearing should be a matter of intention and choice.

So, who decides? That is the question. In voting to repeal or retain the Eighth Amendment, you are choosing who will make future decisions. In fact, you are really facing two questions:

- Who, if anyone, do I want to make this kind of parenthood decision for me?
- In this situation, am I willing to impose my values legally on my fellow citizens or do I prefer to let them choose whether or not to carry forward a budding life based on their own values?

You are being asked to decide who decides.

References

Bongaarts, John, John Cleland, John W. Townsend, Jane T. Bertrand and Monica Das Gupta (2012) *Family Planning Programs for the 21st Century: Rationale and Design*, New York, NY: Population Council, www.popcouncil.org/uploads/pdfs/2012_FPfor21stCentury.pdf

Geisler, Norman (1975) *Ethics: Alternatives and Issues*, Grand Rapids, MI: Zondervan, cited in www.patheos.com/blogs/slacktivist/2017/06/08/groovy-relic-forbidden-evangelical-past/#7XWbDd5vaZO0YOpX.99.

Hatcher, Robert, James Trussell, A.L. Nelson, W. Cates, D. Kowal and M. Policar (2011) *Contraceptive Techology*, twentieth revised edition, New York, NY: Ardent

Media, Contraceptive Technology, www.contraceptivetechnology.org/wp-content/uploads/2013/09/CTFailureTable.pdf.

Tarico, Valerie (2015) 'I Am Pro-Abortion, Not just Pro-Choice: 10 Reasons Why We Must Support the Procedure and the Choice', *Salon*, 24 April, www.salon.com/2015/04/24/i_am_pro_abortion_not_just_pro_choice_10_reasons_why_we_must_support_the_procedure_and_the_choice/.

Washington Association of Churches (1978) *Abortion: An Ecumenical Study Document*, Washington Association of Churches, Washington State Catholic Conference, https://valerietarico.com/2012/11/11/abortion-an-ecumenical-study-document-autumn-1978/.

ENDNOTES

[1] Tarico (2015).

[2] Bongaarts, Cleland, Townsend, Bertrand and Das Gupta (2012).

[3] Hatcher, Trussell, Nelson, Cates, Kowal, and Policar (2011).

[4] Geisler (1975).

[5] Washington Association of Churches (1978).

[6] These quotes are all taken from Washington Association of Churches (1978).

ALL LIVES MATTER

Karen Gaffney

In a recent issue of *Down Syndrome World* magazine,[1] Michelle Sie Whitten, the President and CEO of the Global Down Syndrome Foundation[2] made reference to a beautiful painting that was done about 500 years ago, in the year 1515. This painting, *The Adoration of the Christ Child*, hangs in the Metropolitan Museum of Art in New York City. I was surprised to learn of this painting, and it caused me to do some research to learn more about it, because the painting had special meaning for me. I always like to do research on things that interest me, and this certainly did.

According to the Metropolitan Museum of Art, the actual painter is unknown but believed to be a 'follower of Jan Joest of Kalkar (Netherlandish, active ca. 1515).' The Museum offers this description:

> The fourteenth-century mystic Saint Bridget of Sweden recounted Christ's birth after experiencing a vision. The 'great and ineffable light' she described as emanating from the Child is the most compelling feature of this picture… [www.metmuseum.org/art/collection/search/436781][3]

Please take a moment and look at the painting with me. I hope you see what I see in this painting. Do you happen to notice the young person who is next to Mary amongst the angels knelt in prayer around the Baby Jesus? That young person has Down syndrome. The 'great and ineffable light' that Saint Bridget describes was captured by the painter and surrounds those kneeling around the child. If you look closely, you will see the young man looking in from the window. I believe that he has Down syndrome as well. And then take a minute to look at the faces of the cherubs above. Do you see the face of Down syndrome in some of them as I do?

Well, with all due respect to the Metropolitan Museum of Art, I have a different view of the 'most compelling feature' of this painting. For me, the 'most compelling feature' of this painting is the 'great and *ineffable* light' shining on

The Adoration of the Christ Child by a follower of Jan Joest of Kalkar; from the Jack and Belle Linsky Collection, 1982. Reproduced with permission from The Met, New York.

the faces of Down syndrome! 'Ineffable'; I had to look that up because I had not heard that word before. It means:

- Too overwhelming to be expressed or described in words; inexpressible: ineffable beauty
- Too awesome or sacred to be spoken: God's ineffable name

A painter, in 1515, capturing the birth of Jesus, also captured the face of Down syndrome. A painter in 1515 felt it was important to show the 'great and *ineffable* light' from the baby Jesus shining on the face of Down syndrome. Yes, the baby Jesus, just hours old, shining a light on the face of Down syndrome, for the entire world to see. Those of us who look like the young girl, the boy looking in from the window, and the cherubs above, didn't even have a label yet, but a painter in the year 1515 thought it was important to show a light 'too awesome or sacred' for words coming from the baby Jesus to light our way. And this is where I will start my story.

I am Karen Gaffney and although I am from the States, I am very proud of a family tree whose strong roots are anchored here in your country, in Ireland. I come from a large family of Gaffneys and Lynchs, O'Connells, Garitys, Hedigans, McGees and Durnins, just to name a few. And we are very proud of our Irish heritage.

Oh, and by the way, I have Down syndrome, so now you know why I am so interested in that beautiful painting. Now, it is important to me to explain to anyone who will listen, Down syndrome is not a disease, you can't catch it from someone, it's not contagious, and I don't 'suffer' from it; I just have it, that's all.

I would like to use the space I have here to make a case for Down syndrome. I would like to help you see that Down syndrome is a life worth choosing, it is a life worth living, and it is a life worth saving. I guess you could say, it is a life worth shining a light on.

Now, you might want to know, 'What's different about someone with Down syndrome anyway?' So, let me explain something that many of you reading this probably learned a while back but may have forgotten by now. And that is that all of us have a set of chromosomes in every cell in our bodies, 23 pairs actually, 46 in total. Well, I have one more chromosome than most of you reading this. I have 47 chromosomes in every cell in my body. The scientists took time to map out all our chromosomes and to give a number to each pair. And, as it turns out on what should be the 21st pair of chromosomes for me, and for everyone else like me, there is an extra piece, so instead of two '21's', I have three. Sometimes they call this 'Trisomy 21'.

It is just a tiny piece of material that is so small you can only see it with a special microscope, but that's where the trouble starts, and so do the differences. Those of us with Down syndrome look differently than others; in fact we look a lot like the children and the angels in the painting I told you about. Sometimes we don't hear as well as others, we don't see as well either, and sometimes we don't learn as fast as others. But we can learn, and I will talk more about that in a bit.

Now, you might be wondering why we call it 'Down syndrome'; why not something like 'Up syndrome' or at least something more positive than Down? Well, it turns out about 150 years ago, long after the painting was made, there was a Doctor John Langdon Down in England who first determined that all of us who look like the children and some of the cherubs in the painting have similar characteristics. He didn't know about the extra chromosome; that came much later. But unfortunately, we inherited his name anyway. Leave it to the British to give us a name like that!

We didn't even know about the 21st chromosome we all share until about 60 years ago, much later than the work by Dr Down. I learned about Dr Jerome Lejeune when I was working on my Associate of Science degree at Portland Community College. He was a genetic researcher in France and it was his research team that led to the discovery that all of us with Down syndrome 'ROCK' an extra chromosome. Now, I am sure those weren't his *exact* words upon the discovery. But from what I have learned about him, I bet they are pretty close.

I learned that Dr Lejeune had devoted his life to finding ways to improve the lives of those of us who were born with the extra chromosome. It was *never* his intention to have his discovery lead to tests that would prevent our lives. In fact, the Jerome Lejeune Foundation[4] was started by Dr Lejeune and his family to carry out his work on the behalf of all of us who have the extra chromosome. The Jerome Lejeune Foundation is hard at work both in the States and in Paris, France, where he lived and raised his family, doing medical research to make our lives better. I have often thought that we should change the name of 'Trisomy 21' to Lejeune syndrome. That sounds better than 'Down' to me!

I wonder how many of you reading this have met someone with Down syndrome. I will bet that many of you have. Maybe you have a sister or brother, a cousin, an aunt or an uncle with Down syndrome. Maybe we were in your classes in school. You've seen us in church, or at the grocery store. Maybe there is a swimmer with Down syndrome on your son's swim team. I certainly hope so. And now, you all know one more person with Down syndrome: me, and I am very happy to meet you.

Another thing you should know about me, besides the fact that I have Down syndrome, is that I am an athlete. If you could see a picture of me, you would probably say 'She doesn't look much like an athlete to me! She is only 4 feet, 10 inches tall and she weighs 90 pounds AND she walks with a cane!'

Well, looks can be deceiving sometimes. You see, I am a long-distance open water swimmer. I mean, a really L-O-N-G long-distance swimmer. A few years back six of us from my home town in Portland, Oregon boarded a plane for England to go for a little swim over there. We took on the English Channel. After landing in London, we made our way to Shakespeare Beach in Dover. We had trained together for over a year to get used to the cold water and the long distance of the English Channel. You see, no wetsuits are allowed for a recognised Channel swim. It seems the first person to swim the Channel did it that way, and he got to make all the rules for the rest of us. So, getting used to both the cold water and the long distance took a great deal of time and practice for all of us.

We swam the relay from Dover all the way across the Channel to Cap Blanc-Nez on the coast of France. It is about 21 miles straight across the Channel from Dover to Cape Blanc. But our team swam about 35 miles because of the currents and tides that day. We each swam for an hour at a time, then the next swimmer took over. We alternated like that all the way across the Channel. With my team's help, I became the first person with Down syndrome to swim a relay across the English Channel!

I didn't stop with the English Channel. I kept on swimming into the record books. My longest open water swim was a nine-mile solo swim straight across the width of Lake Tahoe in the US. I swam from the Nevada shore of the Lake to the California shore and it took me a little over six hours to complete.

I also like to tell people that I am the first person with Down syndrome to 'Escape from Alcatraz'. I am sure many of you are familiar with the famous prison that sits in the middle of the San Francisco Bay. Now it is no longer in operation, but they used to put all the most dangerous prisoners there, because they thought no one could escape from that island. Well, I am happy to report that I have! I have done that swim from Alcatraz Island, where the prison used to be, all the way across the San Francisco Bay sixteen times now. And unlike some famous prisoners who have attempted that swim, I have lived to tell about it.

I have done many other open water swims in Donner Lake, the Boston Harbor, a five-mile swim from Molokini to Wailea Beach in Maui and an eight-and-a-half mile swim from Vermont to New York on Lake Champlain.

And thanks to my friend Dr John Redmond, who lives near Dublin, and his wife Anne Marie, I have even completed an open water swim in Ireland. I was invited to swim Dun Laoghaire Harbour in an open sea swim a few years ago.

Swimming nine miles nonstop in 60-degree water is pretty hard for anyone to do, with or without Down syndrome. Dodging jelly fish in the English Channel is pretty tough too. And dealing with the 'washing machine waves' of the San Francisco Bay can take anyone down. But working to stay included in a regular classroom setting and getting my regular high school degree and a two-year college degree was a lot harder than *any* of the long-distance swims I have tackled. However, with a great deal of support from my family and teachers along the way, I made it.

Today, I have a part-time job working about twenty hours a week doing clerical work at Oregon Health Sciences University in Portland, Oregon. I also work part-time in my non-profit organisation to advocate for Down syndrome. And I swim two miles a day six days a week so that I can be ready for the next big open water swim.

Over the last fifteen years I have talked with audiences all around the world about the importance of inclusive education for people like me with Down syndrome and other disabilities. I have shared my experiences and have helped to influence change and raise expectations of others about what people like me can accomplish. I also talk about the importance of regular exercise for everyone, but especially for people like me.

We have made a great deal of progress in the last 60 years for people with Down syndrome and their families all over the world. It is hard to believe that 60 years ago students like me didn't even have a place in school classrooms in the States. While many families were turning their backs on institutions, and keeping children with Down syndrome in a home environment with their brothers and sisters, the neighbourhood school was off-limits.

But with hard work and perseverance that all changed. In the early 1960s and 1970s we had parents, along with all the friends and supporters they could enlist, knocking down doors, pulling out all stops, standing up for our rights and getting legislation passed that allowed people like me into the classrooms of the 1980s and 1990s. For many of those parents, it was too late for their own children, but they made it happen for my generation.

Many young people with Down syndrome who are around my age are part of the first generation of early intervention programmes, inclusion in schools, speech therapy, physical therapy, regular exercise, and RISING EXPECTATIONS.

We owe a great deal to the generations before us. They all had the courage to see things differently, to ignore old data. They helped families say no to institutions and they spent more than a generation paving the way for us, imagining all sorts of new possibilities; education, inclusion and independence. All things the generation before me did not have for their children, but that generation worked hard to make it right for my generation. They opened the doors for us, and we walked right in. Their hard work was not in vain. We showed them the possibilities.

As we turned the corner into the twenty-first century, we have young people with Down syndrome all over the country, all over the world actually, graduating from their high schools, learning employable skills, living and working and contributing in the communities around them. All doing ordinary and extraordinary things that would not have been thought possible even 60 years ago.

Take the time to search for the Down syndrome support organisations all around the world and read about people just like me, who battled their way through school, got regular diplomas, and are working hard to live and grow in their communities. Read about accomplished actors and musicians, dancers, golfers, public speakers, black belts in taekwondo and a few long-distance swimmers! Read about the jobs they hold in their communities. They are all showing that people with Down syndrome certainly do have a place in this world. With advancements in education, medical care and inclusion in the lives around us, we can overcome the obstacles of an extra chromosome. We can learn and grow and contribute to the lives around us. Isn't that what humanity is all about?

Now, at this point, some of you might be asking yourselves, 'Why is this so important for us to understand all this progress? What's the major point here?'

Well, I'll tell you why this is important. Just as we were making so much progress, as I like to say 'rewriting the story on Down syndrome', something else was happening too. As we turned the corner into the twenty-first century, Down syndrome had become a target of a whole new industry. You see, a whole industry had grown up to develop 'prenatal screening' that identifies Down syndrome in the womb. The test is easy to do and can count chromosomes. So, before we can even take our first breath, our life can be cut short. Abortion of the unborn child is taking its toll on Down syndrome.

But that cannot happen in Ireland, because your country has chosen to stand up for the voice of the unborn child. Today, in your country, you have chosen to honour all life, including the life of the unborn child.

In many countries around the world, medical professionals, even today, do not provide timely and accurate information about what Down syndrome is like today. They still use old and outdated information that reflects the past, not the present. Many times a parent may hear that this extra chromosome the baby is carrying is 'not compatible with life'. Not compatible with life? So, think about that for just a minute, think about your cousin, your brother or sister, the person you see in the grocery store, the child in your son's class, the little girl you see at Mass. Are WE not compatible with **LIFE?**

Thankfully, in my country, and in several countries around the world, we have many parents who will say, 'I know a different Down syndrome' or 'Wait a minute … let me learn more about this.' But sadly, those parents have to push back on a medical community that is quick to advise termination in the countries that allow that, instead of education and learning about Down syndrome in the twenty-first century.

Many parents who are raising children with Down syndrome will tell you they were scared, very scared, when they first heard that their child will be born with an extra chromosome. Who wouldn't be scared? *Choosing Naia*, by Mitchell Zuckoff,[5] is a real-life account of one family's experience of learning that their baby would be born with Down syndrome and all they went through. Many families all around the world would tell similar stories that Naia's mom and dad tell. But they put the life of their unborn child ahead of their fears and Naia is today is off to college! You can read about her progress in a 2016 Boston Globe article written by her mother.[6] I think you would agree that our world is better with Naia in it. Our world is better with Down syndrome in it.

I always have a hard time when someone says, 'But it is my body, I should have the right to choose what I do with my body.' And to that I would say, 'Yes, you can make choices for yourself, but you cannot take another person's life from them. It is the unborn baby's body too, is it not? The unborn baby cannot yet speak up for himself or herself. So, someone somewhere has to stand up for those who can't yet speak for themselves. Today, that's Ireland.'

Ireland today protects those of us with Down syndrome from being terminated at will. Ireland today protects the life of any unborn child with or without Down syndrome. Ireland today is a leader for humanity. We have come so far in the quality of life for those of us with Down syndrome, just in the last 60 years, can't you just imagine how far we will go in the next sixty years if we can be saved from prenatal death in countries all around the world?

It is a wave of humanity that lifted us out of institutions, and brought us home, got us into schools, fixed our broken hearts, our faulty hearing, our bad respiratory systems. There is a tremendous push for medical research all around the world, led by phenomenal organizations like the Global Down Syndrome Foundation, the Linda Crnic Institute,[7] the Jerome Lejeune Foundation, the LuMind Foundation[8] and many others, to find ways to fight the bad effects of that extra chromosome. These organisations don't want to screen us out; they want to fix what is hurting us. It will require a wave of humanity to stop the targeting of Down syndrome around the world, and Ireland can lead that wave!

This brings me back to the beautiful painting, *The Adoration of the Christ Child*, and the message I believe it holds for all of us around the world. It is my prayer that the 'great and ineffable light', a light 'too awesome and sacred for words' that shines on the faces of Down syndrome in this painting, will shine in the hearts and minds of the wonderful people of Ireland as you choose once again to protect the life of the unborn child.

References

Global Down Syndrome Foundation, www.globaldownsyndrome.org.

Jerome Lejeune Foundation, www.fondationlejeune.org and www.lejeunefoundation.org.

Linda Crnic Institute, www.globaldownsyndrome.org/our-story/linda-crnic-institute/about-the-linda-crnic-institute-for-down-syndrome/.

LuMind RDS Foundation, www.lumindrds.org.

Met, The (n.d.) *The Adoration of the Christ Child*, www.metmuseum.org/art/collection/search/436781, last accessed 21 December 2017.

Sie Whitten, Michelle (2017) 'Letter from the Editor', *Down Syndrome World*, No. 3, https://downsyndromeworld.org/.

Temple Fairchild, Tierney (2016) 'A Homecoming for Naia', *Boston Globe*, 23 November.

Zuckoff, Mitchell (2003) *Choosing Naia: A Family's Journey*, Boston, MA: Beacon Press.

Endnotes

1   Sie Whitten (2017).
2   www.globaldownsyndrome.org.
3   The Met (n.d.).
4   French site: www.fondationlejeune.org; US site: www.lejeunefoundation.org.
5   Zuckoff (2003).
6   Temple Fairchild (2016).
7   www.globaldownsyndrome.org/our-story/linda-crnic-institute/about-the-linda-crnic-institute-for-down-syndrome.
8   www.lumindrds.org.

The Broad and Varied Middle Ground

Kate O'Connell

People talk about giving the gift of life, or being blessed with life – as if some otherworldly force benevolently dictates the beginning of a new being. Some people – and they are many – believe there is an otherworldly force and he decides not just your ability to have a healthy child, but indeed whether you could have an unhealthy one. He decides what happens to you in your life, and what happens to you when that life ends. He is the moral judge, jury and executioner to your immortal soul and he is watching you.

I was reared with this ideology, along with my five siblings – and it's an ideology that I am raising my three children with now. I don't consider it too much harm for them to take part in the established rites of passage that almost all Irish children participate in. We listen with interest as they excitedly tell us garbled stories involving superhero-style Judeans and Transformer-like ascensions. I smile with my husband when they argue about where bunnies and eggs come into the equation, rationalising the lifecycle of an egg versus a furry mammal and wondering if maybe the eaten chocolate eggs will miraculously reappear, uneaten, three days after the event.

Because it doesn't do them any harm, we figure, and it didn't do us any harm – and we managed to grow up relatively unscathed by dogma. We managed to get our education and develop critical thought as well as principled ideals. We are neither overly virtuous and righteous nor immoral and unjust. Like many other ordinary Irish people, we just get on with our lives, work hard and strive to be happy. We try not to dwell on the miserable stories, the negativity and the sad things we encounter throughout our lives in work, and in our families.

Experience has taught me over the years not to judge, to leap to conclusions or to assume. When a prescription from a maternity hospital gets thrust at me, I don't ask if there's a baby. When a woman who looks visibly pregnant, her eyes red from tiredness and tears, hands you a script for medicine to help her deliver her beloved, but now lost, baby – you learn pretty fast.

There are pharmacies that would turn patients like that woman away today – in Ireland, right now, in 2018. Because they can conscientiously object to even having the medicine in stock. They are perfectly within their rights to do so. They can coldly tell that woman that she and her miscarriage can take themselves somewhere else if they want that sort of thing.

As if the woman chose to lose her baby. As if she deserved it and it happened for an otherworldly reason.

Those places are littered around Ireland and are more numerous than you might think. I'd hazard a guess that all of them are in receipt of state payments for dispensing medicines under the medical card scheme, the long-term illness scheme, or any of the schemes that require them to have a contract with the state for the safe storage, sale and supply of medicines. Your taxes, whether you like it or not, are providing an income and a wage for people who may hold ideologically polar-opposite opinions to you.

If you believe in giving women the care they want, or need, at the desperate times in their lives then you're probably unhappy and uncomfortable with your taxes being spent in a way that supports a view contrary to that.

Your idea of what is morally right or wrong is irrelevant to them – they are private enterprises, who can rightfully decide what they sell and what price they charge for it too. They have the law on their side and, callous as it may seem, they are protected and shielded by their right to conscientiously object to your prescribed treatment.

But then, more than €1.3 million of your taxes were distributed between Anew and Cura in 2015 – two crisis pregnancy agencies that operate under the auspices of unbiased counselling, but have an avowedly prolife ethos. Cura, which is supported by the Irish Catholic Bishops' Conference, received €50,000 from the Irish Episcopal Conference that year too.

Those who would retain the control over women as it is enshrined in the Constitution seem to have a serious problem with the idea that their taxes might fund anything they consider morally wrong. They are outraged, angry, upset.

INDIGNITY

I sat down with a young woman recently who was outraged, angry and upset. Last year she had to travel for a termination. She told me about discovering that she was pregnant, alone in the toilet at her workplace. She rang numerous GP surgeries to see if they offered scanning, because she had been having periods up to a month before the test, but she wanted to know how far along she was.

All the surgeries either said they didn't have the capacity to see her or that she would be better off trying to get an appointment at a maternity hospital. She had limited means and considered ordering tablets online to self-medicate. She was frightened that the tablets would damage her, that they wouldn't have the right ingredients, that she could have a reaction to them and she wouldn't know where to go if that happened. In the end she flew to the UK with her partner three weeks after finding out she was pregnant.

She described to me the redbrick house on the tree-lined avenue in Liverpool, the pale and anxious faces in the waiting room, the variety of women who sat patiently waiting for their name to be called.

She talked about the indignity of being sent to the public toilet of the clinic and pushing tablets high up into her cervix.

She said she saw three other Irish women there, two of whom took calls from their children at home as the school day ended in Ireland.

She was scanned and told that in spite of earlier predictions that she was only a few weeks pregnant, she was further along than expected. She had a surgical termination later that evening, once the nurses were satisfied and certain that she was staying overnight in Liverpool. Because she had been disguising her trip as a holiday, she had booked two nights in a hotel in the city.

She told me how she bled heavily for days, how she took painkillers for the cramping and how she recalls vomiting with pain off the edge of her bed into a Penneys bag.

What she remembered most was the overarching indignity and shame of it all.

FEAR

Another woman confided in me about her termination a few years ago. We weren't friends but I had dealings with her through work. She was poor, had limited education and was quite a vulnerable person, both physically and mentally. She found herself pregnant by a man who should never have taken advantage of her, but did so anyway.

She had no family support, received minimal benefits and had no source of income. She went to a moneylender and borrowed what she could, flew to the UK and booked into a hostel, where she stayed in a shared room of bunk beds.

She talked about the fear, the pain and not knowing what to do. She didn't understand some of the things that medical staff were saying and she was too frightened and embarrassed to ask them to explain things in simpler terms. She didn't reveal the psychiatric illnesses she was living with, for fear that somehow this might mean being refused treatment. She felt it was her fault, that what she was doing made her a bad person and that maybe she deserved the pain and the suffering as a sort of penance.

She came back home to Ireland the next day to try to recover, and to attempt to make some money to pay off the moneylender.

She only told me about it after everything had happened; I hadn't seen her for a while and I had wondered where she had been. She seemed frightened even to talk about it, afraid of legal and moral repercussions.

What she remembered most was the fear, how she was terrified she wouldn't be able to pay the money back and how afraid she was of people finding out.

THE MIDDLE GROUND

There wasn't a stage in my life that I can clearly identify as the moment that I became pro-choice. I honestly don't think there is for anyone. Most people I meet don't feel aligned to the fervently pro-choice or the fervently no-choice groupings, seeing themselves instead as somewhere in the middle. The broad and varied middle ground. If you ask them some direct questions and challenge them to try to relate to a woman seeking an abortion, they invariably feel uncomfortable and awkwardly say things like 'Look I don't want to know, I don't want to be involved – it should be between a woman and her doctor, that conversation ...', or 'Sure there's no right answer is there, I think I'm pro-life, but when you hear of poor women having strokes or dying then I don't know what I am' or, 'I'm pro-life but I wouldn't object to a woman who was raped being able to get an abortion, sure she didn't set out to have sex.'

If you ask people, 'Why do you think a woman would want an abortion?', the same awkwardness ensues. 'Well I suppose because she doesn't want to be pregnant', or 'I don't think any woman would ever want an abortion would they?' (And truly, no woman ever *wants* an abortion – but sometimes *they need one*.)

Keeping the Eighth Amendment in place as it is does not solve any of the problems that the middle ground have with abortion. By virtue of the fact that there are circumstances in which they feel abortion should be provided, they are effectively in favour of repeal without subscribing to the strong pro-choice ethos associated with most 'repealers'.

The other side of the debate know this. They recognise that the middle ground is where most people are, and that this grouping will ultimately decide the result of the referendum. Their tactics seem to be based largely around instilling fear, distrust and confusion so that the majority of people err on the side of caution and leave the amendment untouched – as a sort of 'lesser of two evils' approach to an issue they're not quite sure how to handle.

You will see and hear these tactics all around you during a campaign, as myths and untruths are spread like fake news – tactics that are so commonplace nowadays, it shouldn't be hard to spot them.

One of the most frequently thrown about of these myths is that the Eighth Amendment has saved 100,000 lives. It's plastered all over pamphlets handed out in front of the Dáil, on the tip of every pro-life pundit's tongue during interviews, and, controversially, sprawls across a billboard in Northern Ireland that was recently challenged and upheld. This is heralded as a victory by the Both Lives Matter campaign, but the language used by the Advertising Standards Authority tells a different story.

Their official line read, 'Because we considered that readers would understand the figure to represent an estimate, we concluded that the claim was unlikely to materially mislead readers.' But you could say that roughly translates to, 'The public will know better than to take this "research" seriously.'[1]

The public should know better and, frankly, they can. It doesn't take more than ten minutes to read through the gilded report[2] that the '100,000 lives' line comes from to see its many gaping holes. For a start, the report clearly states that the research was commissioned by the Pro-Life Campaign.

The premise behind the entire report is also deeply flawed, framed by taking the known number of abortions had by Irish women who travelled, over the span of two decades, and then subtracting that figure from a series of assumed abortions that would have happened (but didn't) if the Eighth Amendment were not in place. It uses other countries' abortion rates as a stand-in for these non-existent Irish abortions. Confused? You should be; the assertion of these grounds as anything more than madmen musing is preposterous.

When searching for sources in this infamous report, a single website can be found, squished between two back to back typos. On this site, which is made up of a strange collection of statistics on geysers, physics and *Star Trek*, alongside abortion, the author uses the following disclaimer, 'The reader should be aware that abortion statistics are often hard to obtain, and those statistics that are available are frequently inaccurate', before offering up data from the Global Life Campaign, yet another example of agenda-driven research collection.[3]

As opposed to the guessing game this report made of what Ireland's abortion rate could have been over the last twenty years, the reality of the last four decades – under the anvil of the Eighth Amendment – is a devastating laundry list of cases that resulted in untimely deaths. Moreover, *the evidence is clear*: women who do not want to be pregnant will find a way to end their pregnancies. We are lucky, in Ireland, to be so near to the UK and its safe, legal abortion access. A minimum of ten to twelve women leave Ireland every day to seek termination services abroad.[4] These services are most often sought out by women who find themselves in unplanned pregnancies, and the choice to end these pregnancies is often based on any number of reasons. I've already offered up the stories of two women, from two wildly different places in life, who chose to end their pregnancies. The circumstances of their relationships and their financial capacities are just two of the factors that led to the decision they made.

To some people, no matter how much anecdotal evidence you share or personal encounters they have for themselves, these everyday, relatable women will sound like outsiders in the abortion-seeking crowd. The shame shrouding female sexuality has let a pervasive untruth about people in need of an abortion be perpetuated – that exclusively young, promiscuous and irresponsible women are the only ones who desire access to services – and this takes over our dialogue on the matter.

In fact, the majority of women who seek abortions are already mothers.[5] Some of the reasons they give are:

- Their families are complete; they have five or six children already.
- They cannot financially support a child.
- They have a disability themselves.
- They suffered life-changing effects to their bodies in previous pregnancies.
- They don't feel it is the right time in their lives, due to their careers or schooling.
- They are single and barely able to support themselves.
- Many used contraception that failed, or they used contraception improperly.

These women know what will and won't work for themselves and their loved ones. To be clear, they don't owe us these explanations, but here they are, for you all to see – someone's deeply personal and complicated decision, each one just some of the dozens of reasons women will seek an abortion.

Another from the myriad of myths surrounding abortion is the claim that a baby's heart beats just 21 days after conception. Sitting in a session of the Joint Committee on the Eighth Amendment of the Constitution, this was put forth to the masters of the Rotunda Maternity Hospital and the simultaneous grace and force with which they asserted the facts of foetal development at this stage was applaudable. There is no heart, in the way one might picture it, at 21 days. There is a small tube that pulsates, and this is what will become a heart. But this is no powerful, blood-pumping, four-chambered organ; it's conjured up to try to pluck at people's heartstrings. And why use a heart as the example? Why not lungs, or kidneys? Are they not cute enough?[6]

Having a discussion about abortion is difficult enough without misconstrued facts at the centre. These conversations deserve nuance and reason, not radical overstatements designed to dominate someone's emotions.

There are other attempts to muddy the waters on foetal development too, like the claim that a foetus will feel excruciating pain if, at any gestation, an abortion is obtained. Research is frequently evolving in this area, but can confirm that the earliest the nervous system is developed enough to experience pain would be 24 weeks, and could be as late as 30.[7] The only situation in which a doctor would induce delivery at this stage of a pregnancy would be for someone whose health, or the health of their foetus, is at risk.

No doubt you know people who had their pregnancies ended earlier than expected – because their health was deteriorating, or the foetal growth had tapered off – so doctors moved quickly to deliver the baby and protect both mother and child. Technically, that is a termination of pregnancy – because pregnancy is a state of being that comes to a conclusion. All of us were born when a pregnancy was terminated. All of us are here because a woman protected and nurtured us with her body.

The notion that a woman would wake up one day 22 weeks pregnant and decide to get an abortion is absurd, but more than that, it is deeply offensive. We need to be challenging this notion every time its ugly head is reared. Women have suffered unimaginably in this stage of a very much wanted pregnancy, waiting for test results, or by putting their own lives and health at risk to save their pregnancies.

Organisations that cite statistics on botched abortions pull their data from cases where women die for lack of abortion aftercare, which is largely due to the travel Irish women are condemned to, or from the painful cases of fatal foetal abnormalities, where a woman has labour induced in order to give birth to her baby and be with the child for however many minutes or hours she gets. They are babies who would otherwise die in utero and be stillborn. The accusation that these infants are being left in cold hospital corridors is a malicious mischaracterisation of a terrible decision some women are presented with.

Similarly, the idea that every woman must be mentally and emotionally equipped to give birth to a baby who will only be with them for a matter of hours, or be wealthy enough to go somewhere else to handle their personal tragedy, is cruel. I am so comforted to hear that there are women who can find solace from the pain by sharing fleeting time with their child in their arms.

But for every woman who finds closure in those moments, another woman may find profound and lasting trauma.

Instead of facing this trauma, they are forced to endure a different one. Boarding a plane or a boat to find their way to another country, where a different doctor will have to hear their story. They have to carry their own medical records, concealed for privacy in coats or handbags instead of filing cabinets. They have to rattle off their medical histories, hoping not to forget any essential information in their nervousness and haste. They will take the hand of whoever accompanied them instead of going to work that day, assuming their partner or loved one is financially capable of purchasing airfare as well.

After the procedure, they return to hotel rooms instead of homes. The bodies of their babies may be cremated, and their ashes mailed to them in a parcel a few weeks later. A burial would require smuggling the babe's body home, stopping every few hours to change the disposable ice packs that line the coffin, placed there to preserve the precious little body of a much wanted and much loved family member.

How dare we ask these women to act like criminals in order to mourn and honour the child they lost?

The other kind of abortions we see at 22 weeks are the product of the mother's failing health as opposed to that of the foetus. And again, women who get to this point in pregnancy know they are pregnant and want to be pregnant – this cannot be emphasised enough. As a woman's health comes into question, doctors prepare to do everything they can to protect mother and child. But the dilemma the Eighth Amendment causes is that it forces doctors to ask the question, 'Is she dying yet?' before they can act.

As a doctor in Ireland, if you intervene too soon you could be pulled up on criminal charges and imprisoned for fourteen years. Intervene too late, and your patient and the baby could die. In no other area of healthcare do we ask doctors to wait until a patient is on the edge to act.

Here again, we do ourselves a disservice by pretending maternal health is a simple matter. There are an endless number of circumstances in which a simple medical concern could be compounded by other circumstances and health could rapidly deteriorate. These situations are complex and time-sensitive, and I believe we can all agree that in that moment, a woman and her doctor should be able to efficiently consult and act without the hindrance of fear or legal repercussions.

The meaning of the word 'risk' is another idea that deserves our time and attention. Not every woman has the same things at stake in a pregnancy. If a woman is 42 years old and desperate for her first child, she may be willing to put everything on the line to continue with this pregnancy. But a mother of three has children she needs to return home to, and may justifiably not be willing to push the limits of her health to go through with another pregnancy. Likewise, a younger woman who can try again may choose to end a pregnancy that poses a substantial risk to her life.

These realities of life shouldn't be dismissed because they make an abortion narrative easier to digest. Abortion decisions are complex because life is complex. That's the only simple statement we should really be able to make on the matter.

Moving further into the sea of misinformation that swarms around in the public sphere is the claim that Ireland is one of the safest places to be pregnant and give birth. It is true that Ireland is higher in the ranking of low maternal mortality,[8] but an essential element of this is our proximity to the United Kingdom. Dr Sabaratnam Arulkumaran, author of the report on Savita Halappanavar, was a witness before the Oireachtas Committee on the Eighth Amendment and he was straightforward in his testimony on the nature of this relationship. If Irish women did not have the ability to travel to the UK and seek abortion services there, or use more recent services of safe abortion pill delivery, the maternal mortality rate would skyrocket as these same women turn to dangerous at-home methods, or face risks to their lives, in order to conduct an abortion in their home country. Women who are part of migrant or asylum-seeking communities here in Ireland are limited even further due to their financial or immigration status. Liberal neighbouring abortion laws are what preserve Ireland's status as a safe place to be pregnant, not the Eighth Amendment.

There are many people who would, along these lines of maternal safety, rebuke the facts of Savita Halappanavar's death. It is disgraceful that conversations surrounding her case sometimes happen with callous disregard while her loved ones look on, trying to find both peace of mind and justice for her untimely death. The matter deserves more tact and dignity than it is given by some who refute the cause her name has become associated with, and I wish to handle it with brevity and sensitivity here.

The report on Savita's death states that she died due to mismanagement of sepsis. The argument put forth is that this is where the matter stops. That because the Eighth Amendment is not scribed in black and white as the cause of death, it cannot be culpable. This wilfully overlooks the reality that the doctors managed her condition in the way they felt they had to with the looming Eighth Amendment in place. Had there been no Eighth Amendment, Savita's request for an abortion would have been granted, before it was too late.

Her case was a culmination of doctors feeling their hands are tied until the clock is ticking, and of the complexities of maternal health that are glossed over in debate after debate. Regardless of its original intent, and the intent behind the *Protection of Life During Pregnancy Act* that followed, her tragic loss was the clear product of the Eighth Amendment in action.

We owe Savita and every other woman living in Ireland more than good intentions. We owe them sound policy. We owe them bodily autonomy. We owe them dignity. We owe them change.

Further tumbling down the rabbit hole of insensitive inventions leads me to address another subject more deserving of nuanced and tasteful discussion than is usually offered, and that is the data surrounding Down-syndrome-related abortions. The easy part of this conversation is to immediately quash any suggestion that a nation, be it Iceland or Denmark, has a goal of eliminating Down syndrome. This is not true. It is, in fact, outrageous.

Doctors from the Rotunda Maternity Hospital have spoken of their experiences with diagnoses of Down syndrome while testifying before the Eighth Amendment Committee, and the data from Ireland is as follows: 57 per cent of people who receive a prenatal diagnosis of Down syndrome travel, leaving 43 per cent of people who choose to proceed with the pregnancy.[9] This is a reflection of balanced advising that happens between doctors and patients when this diagnosis is delivered.

An element of this discussion that often goes missing is the spectrum on which conditions like Down syndrome exist. Some people receiving the news that their child has Down syndrome are also learning that their child is unlikely to survive until birth. Others know they will have a child, but do not know the extent to which their condition will dictate their participation or level of ability to engage with others and live a full, happy and independent life. Questions of your own capacity to care for another human with additional needs are deeply personal and require an honest assessment of your finances, emotional support networks, flexibility of time and lifestyle. The law should have no place in these considerations.

We should be doing more to address the concerns of people living with or caring for someone with a disability. Problems with under-resourcing and access should not suddenly matter when they make for an argument against abortion rights, and go ignored at all other hours. It is advances in the disbursement of services paired with calm, compassionate conversations that will help temper concerns surrounding disability and abortion.

Another celebrated and frequently echoed slogan of the pro-life movement is that 'adoption is an option', and yes this is true. Someone should really pat them on the back for this marvellous observation, as they rarely talk about options or choice in respect to medical care during pregnancy and afterwards.

What adoption is *not* is a comparable solution to ending an unwanted pregnancy. Aside from the emotional aspect of adoption that involves carrying a child to term and then giving it away, there is so much more to a pregnancy than its end result.

To be pregnant is to sacrifice your body to the whims of morning sickness, swollen joints, back pain, exhaustion, overwhelming cravings, cracked and bleeding nipples, haemorrhoids, varicose veins and more serious but also quite common conditions like gestational diabetes, organ damage or organ failure, pre-eclampsia, risk of stroke, paralysis, incontinence, double incontinence, prolapsed uterus, vaginal tears and fissures, and mastitis.

It requires time off work to attend additional doctor visits. It demands money for new clothes to drape over a growing belly and a more conscious diet including supplemental vitamins. Pregnancy sends your hormones into a spin, setting your mental health down an unknown path. People you bump into will ask all sorts of invasive questions – 'Oh, who's the father? When are you due? Boy or a girl?' – that you may not want to focus on when the baby is meant to be given away. Then, of course, is the actual act of giving birth, which is not exactly a walk through the park. And once you've checked out of the maternity ward, once again, the people who knew you as pregnant only the week before will ask, 'How are you and the baby? Can I see pictures? What name did you choose?'

There is a significant emotional and financial cost to pregnancy. You cannot erase nine months of pregnancy when you put a child up for adoption. It is not so simple as to do it and forget about it. Once a birth mother, always a birth mother. Children are not born in a vacuum and do not grow up without wondering where they came from. Adoptive parents are excellent, wonderful, nurturing people who give many children a chance in life they might otherwise not receive.

What person would be happy to learn that they are only here because their mother was detained and forced to carry her pregnancy to term, risking her health and life, resenting every moment of it? Every mother should be a willing mother, every child a wanted child. We heard harrowing evidence at the Committee from psychiatrists, who say their clinics are full of adults who were unwanted children, neglected and abused, left in dirty nappies and ignored, starved of love throughout their lives. One psychiatrist talked of the long-term psychological damage this has on people, how they have depression and mental illness as adults and fear becoming parents themselves because their harrowing start in life has left them feeling they don't know how to correctly love or parent a child.[10]

Finally, I'll turn to the notion that keeping a pregnancy that resulted from rape is a matter of hope. Not entirely different than the cases of parents finding peace in giving birth to a child with a fatal foetal condition, some women have testified to finding comfort in the gift of a child who has come out of their horrific experience. I am moved to know that these women have found such peace. But this is not everyone's reaction. For many women, the pregnancy would stand as a constant reminder of their pain – an additional, inescapable trauma. It is unreasonable and unjust to ask everyone to carry out their pregnancies on the grounds that some people have found joy in them.

Some proponents of forcing a rape survivor to remain pregnant against her will, will argue that it is for her own mental health, referring to the damage of abortion regret on the mind. There is no evidence of this.[11] There are as many reactions to having abortions as there are people who get them, and they are dependent on the unique set of circumstances each woman has in her life. There is evidence, however, of the harm forcing someone to remain pregnant does to mental health. Anyone with sincere concern for the victim would act on these facts and not their own delusions.

So, I'd like to return you to that fated and vast middle ground, the sprawl of people who have been so lucky as to never need a fully formed opinion on the matter of abortion. These are the people who will decide whether or not we see a repeal. They will decide because they are many. But before they decide, they will listen.

I may not remember the moment I became pro-choice, but in the next year there is potential for thousands of people to have their moment. To connect the dots, follow personal beliefs to their logical conclusions. But these epiphanies do not simply fall out of the ether. They are the products of education, experience and time. They are born out of conversations we have in our granny's kitchen and sitting in a pub with passers-by.

We have to talk about abortion, albeit awkward or enraging or sad or confusing. If we don't engage people in the middle ground, they will not be there when history stands ready to change.

'Why do you believe in abortion only in the cases of rape, incest and fatal foetal abnormality? To spare them suffering?'

Here is what I mean when I say that these middle grounders, when well informed, are more pro-choice than they know. The average of all the undecided or moderate opinions on abortion looks something like the above. And it is true that people don't believe a woman should be punished for things out of her control. You can't limit abortion to the parameters of rape and fatal foetal or set gestational limits without still inflicting pain upon these women.

Talk to these middle grounders about the reality of a 'moderate' law. Push them. Ask them everything. How would you prove you were raped? Would you need a rape kit? Do you have to have filed criminal charges? What if your rapist is not convicted and you have already been given an abortion? Is that now a crime? Putting a burden of proof on survivors will traumatise her again.

Gestational limits are the exact kind of thing that fail women dealing with the tragedy of a fatal foetal diagnosis. What if she is 23 weeks pregnant and the limit is 22? There will always be someone who is beyond the limit in need of an abortion, and we have to ask what she will do then. If you believe in sparing these women their suffering, you have to trust them with a liberal abortion policy.

The middle ground believe in dignity, therefore the middle ground believe in repeal. We must pursue these conversations, so that the middle ground can have their moment.

Experience has taught me over the years not to judge, to leap to conclusions or to assume.

I hope as a country we all can learn not to judge others for the decisions they make. Let we who are without sin cast the first stone.

REFERENCES

Aiken, Abigail R.A., Kathleen Broussard, Dana M. Johnson and Elisa Padron (2017) *Qualitative Findings to Accompany Written Statement to the Joint Oireachtas Committee on the Eighth Amendment, October,* www.oireachtas.ie/parliament/media/committees/eighthamendmentoftheconstitution/Professor-Abigail-Aiken,-Briefing-Document-2-of-2---Qualitative-Findings-Brief.pdf.

British Pregnancy Advisory Service (2016) 'Abortion Statistics Show Increase in Abortions to Older Women, Mothers, and Those in Relationships', *BPAS*, 17 May, www.bpas.org/about-our-charity/press-office/press-releases/abortion-statistics-show-increase-in-abortions-to-older-women-mothers-and-those-in-relationships/.

Department of Health (UK) (2016) *Abortion Statistics, England and Wales: 2016,* www.gov.uk/government/uploads/system/uploads/attachment_data/file/652083/Abortion_stats_England_Wales_2016.pdf.

Irish Times (2017) 'Ad Claiming 100,000 Lives Saved by NI Abortion Laws "accurate"', *Irish Times*, 2 August, www.irishtimes.com/news/ireland/irish-news/ad-claiming-100-000-lives-saved-by-ni-abortion-laws-accurate-1.3174415.

Jacobson, Thomas W. and Wm. Robert Johnston (2016) 'Abortion Worldwide Report Released', *Johnston's Archive*, http://johnstonsarchive.net/policy/abortion/awr.html.

Lee, Susan J., Henry J. Peter Ralston, Eleanor A. Drey et al. (2005) 'Fetal Pain: A Systematic Multidisciplinary Review of the Evidence', *Journal of the American Medical Association*, Vol. 294, No. 8, pp. 947–954.

Mahony, Rhona and Fergal Malone (2017) 'Health Care Issues Arising from the Citizens' Assembly Recommendations: Masters of the National Maternity Hospital, Holles Street and the Rotunda Hospital', Submission to the Joint Oireachtas Committee on the Eighth Amendment, 11 October, http://oireachtasdebates.oireachtas.ie/debates%20authoring/DebatesWebPack.nsf/committeetakes/EAJ2017101100002?opendocument#W00050.

O'Kane, Veronica (2017) 'Risks to Mental Health of Pregnant Women', Submission to the Joint Oireachtas Committee on the Eighth Amendment, 25 October, http://oireachtasdebates.oireachtas.ie/Debates%20Authoring/DebatesWebPack.nsf/committeetakes/EAJ2017102500002?opendocument#F00200.

Pro-Life Campaign (2016) *The 8th Amendment: Ireland's Life-Saving Provision*, 7 September, https://prolifecampaign.ie/main/wp-content/uploads/2016/09/ProLife Campaign_Actuarial_Report_and_Commentary_7September2016.pdf

Save the Children (2015) *The Urban Disadvantage: State of the World's Mothers 2015 – The Complete Mothers' Index 2015*, www.savethechildren.org/atf/cf/%7B9def2ebe-10ae-432c-9bd0-df91d2eba74a%7D/SOWM_MOTHERS_INDEX.PDF.

ENDNOTES

1 *Irish Times* (2017).
2 Pro-Life Campaign (2016).
3 Jacobson and Johnston (2016).
4 Department of Health (UK) (2016).
5 British Pregnancy Advisory Service (2016).
6 Mahony and Malone (2017).
7 Lee, Ralston, Drey et al. (2005).
8 Save the Children (2015).
9 Mahony and Malone (2017).
10 O'Kane (2017).
11 Mahony and Malone (2017); see also Aiken, Broussard, Johnson and Padron (2017).

When Life Triumphs in Ireland, the World Will Pay Attention

Declan Ganley

The debate that Ireland will have in 2018 is one where the fundamental values of what we stand for as a society will be at stake. It will say much about us as a people and, whatever the result, a powerful message will be sent to the rest of the world about what we value, or what we do not.

The world in 2018 is a small place. Oceans that once divided us even from knowledge of each other's existence are now traversable by plane in a matter of hours. Something that happens in Ireland can be read about, or watched, within mere seconds in New Zealand. Where once the people of the world were divided by language, an article written in Arabic can be passed through Google Translate and broadly understood in seconds by a person who has never spoken the author's tongue.

In this shrinking world, where the differences and distances between us grow smaller every day, the impact of a single nation's decision will reverberate around the world. What we do in the ballot box will be debated and discussed across the globe, and the people of Earth will take note of the message that we send them.

The Eighth Amendment to our Constitution, adopted in 1983, recognises the right to life of the unborn child, and, with 'due regard to the equal life of the mother, guarantees in its laws to respect, and, as far as practicable, by its laws to defend and vindicate that right'.

We are, so far as I know, the only country on Earth to recognise in our Constitution the equal value of the unborn child and the woman who will become that child's mother. Other countries have rendered abortion illegal, but none have so eloquently affirmed in their constitution the idea that an unborn child is just as much a part of our society as any of the rest of us.

This idea that an unborn child is equal to the rest of us is the matter at the very heart of this debate. Those who would delete those words from our

Constitution contend that it places women in danger – a charge for which there has never been any evidence – and further, that even if it does not place women in danger, that it is wrong for the state and society to equate the life of an adult woman with that of the child she is carrying.

It is important to note at this point that it is not the position of the Irish Constitution, Irish case law, or this author, that a woman's rights do not take precedence, when a conflict arises, over the rights of her unborn child. No institution, country or medical ethics book in the world advances the idea that a woman should ever be permitted to lose her life in order to save that of the child within her. Irish law already recognises that in the tragic situations where a pregnancy threatens the life of a woman, the life of the child within her cannot be protected at the cost of her own.

What those who advocate for legal abortion would do is to go further than this position, and grant to a pregnant woman the right to proactively seek the termination of the life of the unique human individual within her on a discretionary basis. They would remove any and all constitutional or legal protection for the unborn, and declare that the unborn have no rights at all. For after all, if one has no right to remain alive, then all other rights become somewhat useless.

In any honest debate, it is important to recognise those parts of your opponent's argument that have merit. Pregnancy, they rightly note, is a phenomenon unique to those who are in possession of a womb. Pregnancy is a condition that for some women carries increased medical risks. Not all pregnancies, tragically, are consensual. Nor, equally sadly, are all pregnancies successful. Women will sometimes experience the horrors of bearing a child with a medical condition that means their child will not long survive the world outside the womb. My own family had a taste of that worry, two decades ago, when my wife and I were told by a New York doctor that our daughter would be condemned to suffer a life-limiting condition and that he advised an abortion of our baby, something we immediately ruled out. As it turned out, the diagnosis was, to say the least, too pessimistic, and we are the proud parents of a bright and healthy young woman today. But the worry of that moment will live with me forever.

For other women, pregnancy is just a burden that comes upon them at the wrong point in their lives, complicating and undoing the path they had seen lying before them until that point. Women with an unwanted pregnancy are no less worthy of our compassion than those with a pregnancy forced on them by a rapist, or a pregnancy blighted by an illness that strikes at the child in the womb.

It is important that any argument against abortion recognises that there always have been, and always will be, for whatever reason, those women who do not wish to be pregnant who find themselves pregnant nonetheless. And it must be recognised openly that it is our position that they should not be permitted to ask the state or their doctors to end a healthy pregnancy if in so doing they take the life of an unborn child. The pro-life position does place a limit on the rights of a pregnant woman, and there is little to be gained from denying that.

In order to justify the restriction we place on the mother, it is necessary therefore to make a positive argument for the humanity of her unborn child. We must establish that the unborn child is human, and has a right to life, and that the baby deserves protection by our laws and our Constitution.

The most common position adopted against this proposition is that an unborn child is not a person, but a potential person. Much like a seed is not a tree, but a potential tree. The argument made by those who would legalise abortion is that to compare a seed to a tree is absurd, and that therefore the two should not be treated equally. Of course, a sapling is not a tree, either, and it is equally absurd to compare a ten-year-old tree to one that has seen a hundred summers and towers over it. At what point does the seed become a tree? Is it after it sprouts its first roots? Is it when it is a foot tall? Ten feet? This isn't a question that gets answered, because it is indefinable.

What we do know is that if a seed is destroyed, it will never become a tree. Since for the most part there is not much legal protection for the lives of trees and seeds, this is a not a matter that concerns the laws of the land to any great degree.

Of course, people are not seeds, and fully grown adults are not trees. We can say with certainty that very regularly, without external interference, a foetus will become a baby, who will become a toddler, who will grow into a child, and then a teenager, and then a young person, and then an old person. A toddler is not a teenager. A toddler is merely a potential teenager. A teenager is merely a potential old person.

At any other point along the journey of potential that we call life killing is unlawful. It is unlawful precisely because the act of killing is, in essence, the theft of potential. By killing a toddler we have stolen his or her future. When somebody dies young, we often mourn them with more sorrow than when somebody dies in their ninetieth year. We mourn more for the lost potential of their life than we do when a life has exhausted the known limits of that human potential.

In every other part of our life, the loss of potential life is considered the greatest of human tragedies. It is odd then, that 'it's only potential life!' should be thrown around with such argumentative glee by our opponents in this debate.

We know that the unborn child is human because we can scientifically prove it. Before we address the science, though, we should remember that we also know that unborn life is human life because of the way women who are pregnant talk about it. I have never met a woman who tells me that she's happily pregnant with a foetus, or a clump of cells, or a blastocyst. Women who are pregnant speak of the love they bear their babies. When they tragically miscarry, they speak of losing their child.

In the referendum we are about to have, women who, facing the horror of a seriously and terminally ill child, chose to have an abortion, will speak of their pain at not being able to have a funeral. That pain is understandable and tragic. But it should make us ponder why it is exactly that a child terminated in these circumstances is worthy of a funeral, and a child terminated at the same gestational age in an unwanted pregnancy is not worthy of the same care, or even referred to as human at all. In these cases, it appears, the pro-choice position is that the humanity of the unborn child is decided by the love borne for it, or not borne for it, by its parents.

Pro-choice advocates often say that an unborn child is not human because of the stage of development it has reached. The ideas that it does not have consciousness, cannot feel pain or is incapable of independent survival are arguments put forward regularly for the proposition that its life is not worthy of protection. But these arguments are exposed by the argument around pregnancies blighted by terminal illness, which are often referred to as 'deeply wanted pregnancies'. In these situations, the real line that is drawn between life and death is not a biological one at all, but an emotional one. The humanity of the unborn child is determined entirely by how we feel about it. This is deeply troubling, and should make us think.

Science leaves us in little doubt as to the truth of whether an unborn child is a human individual. It is a simple point, but often worth repeating, that each of us has a unique genetic code, replicated in no other human, and no other living organism ever to have been found on Earth. Each of us is the only creature ever to have borne the DNA that makes us who we are. That DNA, that signature that makes us who we are, is generated at our conception. It determines mundane things like our hair colour (a moot point in my own case), our eye colour and how tall we will grow. It also endows us with unique talents, ranging from the international soccer player, to the scientist, to the person without any notable gifts beyond the ability to listen and make others feel better.

Every person born into our world has the unique ability to do good, and to make the world a better place. Even if in their lives they make it a better place only for one or two other people they have accomplished and delivered something valuable for all of us. Every abortion deletes, and removes from all of us, a little bit of our future. We lose people of all imaginable talents and variations.

Whatever is coded in their veins is taken from us, and what we are left with is a void where that person should have been.

In this campaign, I hope we will hear from those people who were almost taken from us, but were not. Gianna Jessen turns 40 years old on the day I write this. In April 1977 she had a birthday unlike that of most of us, when she was brought into the world prematurely as the result of an abortion gone wrong. Gianna was born weighing only 2 pounds, and condemned by her premature delivery to live the rest of her days with cerebral palsy. Despite this tragic start to her life, she walks amongst us today, as human as you or I. What makes her different is that to the doctor who delivered her, Gianna was not human at all. She was just a clump of cells.

Abortion can only be permitted if the person who is being aborted can be stripped of all humanity. We see this in action in the arguments for abortion every day, and in the terminology used, as we have just discussed. In this respect, abortion differs in no way from every other great and unjust persecution throughout human history. No monster from our past has ever successfully pursued mass murder without first convincing those who supported the murders that it was not people who were being killed, but something lesser. 'Subhuman' is an epithet that has been applied to the Slavs, to gypsies, to Jews, to homosexuals, to Catholics, to Protestants, and to non-believers. In each case, it has been used to justify their persecution and their slaughter.

In the United States, to justify slavery, black people were explicitly valued as being worth three-fifths of a white person. Because slaves were deemed to be property, and not people, their rights were forfeited. In this, one of the most grievous stains on the history of the Western world, we see clearly that to justify persecution on a massive scale we have to pretend that the people we are persecuting are not our equals.

Some advocates of abortion openly admit that the unborn child is, in fact, human. In a piece in *Salon* magazine in 2013, the pro-choice writer Mary Elizabeth Williams posited the question 'So what if abortion ends life?'[1] It is worth quoting her in part (I encourage readers to read the whole thing):

> When we on the pro-choice side get cagey around the life question, it makes us illogically contradictory. I have friends who have referred to their abortions in terms of 'scraping out a bunch of cells' and then a few years later were exultant over the pregnancies that they unhesitatingly described in terms of 'the baby' and 'this kid'. I know women who have been relieved at their abortions and grieved over their miscarriages. Why can't we agree that how they felt about their pregnancies was vastly

different, but that it's pretty silly to pretend that what was growing inside of them wasn't the same? Fetuses aren't selective like that. They don't qualify as human life only if they're intended to be born ....

But we make choices about life all the time in our country. We make them about men and women in other nations. We make them about prisoners in our penal system. We make them about patients with terminal illnesses and accident victims. We still have passionate debates about the justifications of our actions as a society, but we don't have to do it while being bullied around by the vague idea that if you say we're talking about human life, then the jig is up, rights-wise ....

And I would put the life of a mother over the life of a fetus every single time – even if I still need to acknowledge my conviction that the fetus is indeed a life. A life worth sacrificing.

Williams' case is summed up almost entirely in her final four words, 'a life worth sacrificing'. It is important to address this argument head on, because it is a view that is increasing in popularity as science and reason continue to demolish the argument that the unborn human individual is not human at all. The debate is moving more and more in the direction of whether it is permissible to kill, or sacrifice, an unborn child for being an impediment to the mother.

The analogies that Williams draws here – to patients with terminal illnesses, criminals on death row, accident victims, and men and women in other nations whose lives are lost in wars – are worth exploring. In none of those examples is a life 'sacrificed'. We do not sacrifice a patient with a terminal illness, even as we allow them to die. Their deaths are not in the service of our own advancement, but are seen universally for the tragedies they are.

For those who support the death penalty (I am not amongst their number, and believe it should be abolished) execution is not a sacrifice, but a punishment. Nobody, I believe, argues for abortion on the basis that the unborn deserve to be punished. Indeed, the only category of killing in which the 'sacrifice' analogy could possibly be drawn is the loss of innocent lives in a military or security operation where people other than the primary target of the strike lose their lives.

Of course, in those situations, we are outraged and horrified. Thousands march against war every year, globally, precisely because such 'sacrifices' are so repugnant to them. We refer to the 'horrors of war' because of incidents like those Williams is referring to. If the best argument for abortion is that it is no worse than accidentally dropping a missile onto a wedding party, I would submit that the argument being made is not particularly strong, since opposition to such killing is almost universal.

As to the argument that Williams makes that she 'would put the life of a mother over the life of the fetus every single time, even if I still need to acknowledge my conviction that the fetus is indeed a life'[2], I can think of no more succinct expression of the core pro-life position.

What Williams is arguing is not for valuing the life of the mother greater than the life of the unborn child, but instead for not valuing the life of the unborn child at all. Because how can you value a life if your intent is its destruction? That is not possible.

To justify abortion therefore, the most serious pro-choice advocates have developed a final argument, which states that even as we recognise the unborn child is human, and even as we recognise that it has rights, abortion does not really kill the child actively, but instead simply denies it the right to inhabit a female body to which it has no right.

As with Ms Williams above, it is important, if we are to refute this argument, to quote it fairly. The argument I refer to was developed by the pro-choice philosopher Judith Jarvis Thompson:[3]

> I propose, then, that we grant that the fetus is a person from the moment of conception. How does the argument go from here? Something like this, I take it. Every person has a right to life. So the fetus has a right to life. No doubt the mother has a right to decide what shall happen in and to her body; everyone would grant that. But surely a person's right to life is stronger and more stringent than the mother's right to decide what happens in and to her body, and so outweighs it. So the fetus may not be killed; an abortion may not be performed.
>
> It sounds plausible. But now let me ask you to imagine this. You wake up in the morning and find yourself back to back in bed with an unconscious violinist. A famous unconscious violinist. He has been found to have a fatal kidney ailment, and the Society of Music Lovers has canvassed all the available medical records and found that you alone have the right blood type to help. They have therefore kidnapped you, and last night the violinist's circulatory system was plugged into yours, so that your kidneys can be used to extract poisons from his blood as well as your own. The director of the hospital now tells you, 'Look, we're sorry the Society of Music Lovers did this to you – we would never have permitted it if we had known. But still, they did it, and the violinist is now plugged into you. To unplug you would be to kill him. But never mind, it's only for nine months. By then he will have recovered from his ailment, and can safely be unplugged from you.' Is it morally incumbent

on you to accede to this situation? No doubt it would be very nice of you if you did, a great kindness. But do you have to accede to it? What if it were not nine months, but nine years? Or longer still? What if the director of the hospital says 'Tough luck. I agree. But now you've got to stay in bed, with the violinist plugged into you, for the rest of your life. Because remember this. All persons have a right to life, and violinists are persons. Granted you have a right to decide what happens in and to your body, but a person's right to life outweighs your right to decide what happens in and to your body. So you cannot ever be unplugged from him.' I imagine you would regard this as outrageous, which suggests that something really is wrong with that plausible-sounding argument I mentioned a moment ago.

This is perhaps the most powerful argument for abortion, and the one that most people who are pro-life feel challenged to respond to. It concedes what we know to be true – that the unborn child is a human individual with rights – and counters with a powerful example of what is at the core of the pro-choice case – the idea that a woman should not be deprived of bodily autonomy. It deserves a serious response.

We should begin of course by noting that being tied to a bed with an unconscious person for nine months would be a terrible sentence for anybody. It is not, however, analogous to pregnancy. The overwhelming majority of pregnant women do not lose their mobility. They do not lose their freedom to come and go as they wish, and, in general, live their lives exactly as they would were they not pregnant at all.

As in all of life, however, there are exceptions to this. A small percentage of women suffer pre-eclampsia, or an incompetent cervix, and find that they are limited in their mobility like the person tied to the violinist. Of course, the difference between these pregnant women (indeed all pregnant women), and the person tied to the violinist is that a pregnant woman has a relationship with her unborn child that the unwitting supporter of our unconscious violinist simply does not. The argument for abortion here rests on the notion that despite the differing relationships, a mother has no more responsibility to her own child than she does to an unconscious violinist. This is clearly false. You or I would not be judged by society to be bad people if we did not feed the homeless on a daily basis. If, on the other hand, we chose not to feed our own children, society and the legal system would judge us to be failing in our responsibilities. This pro-choice argument relies strongly on the idea that the unborn is a child to whom we have no responsibility as parents – a notion at variance with our understanding of parental responsibility in every other area of life.

Another flaw in this argument for abortion is the difference between unplugging from the violinist on the one hand, and abortion on the other. In one case, support is simply being withdrawn. Abortion is not merely the withdrawal of support, but the active act of killing. Trying to compare a saline injection to stop a heart to 'withdrawing support' is a bit like if we tried to justify murdering somebody with a pillow by saying that we were merely withdrawing oxygen and allowing nature to take its course.

Finally, we must consider the troublesome question of responsibility. In the example cited by Dr Jarvis Thompson, the person attached to the violinist is entirely innocent of any act that put the violinist into his condition. In pregnancy this is not the case, since in the vast majority of pregnancies the child is created by a consensual act involving two people. I think most people would consider themselves obligated to aid the violinist had they been responsible for his condition, via a car accident or some other horrible incident. Equally, when we cause somebody to be dependent upon us, we do bear some responsibility for their condition.

This last point is obviously not relevant when somebody is raped. In these criminal cases, the woman is in no way responsible for the creation of the child. It is understandable then that there are those who, feeling human sympathy for a woman whose life has been changed utterly against her will, believe that in such circumstances abortion should be permissible.

There are several things to consider when discussing abortion in such a difficult case. The first is whether the circumstances of a person's conception changes what they are. Earlier in this chapter, we discussed the phenomenon whereby people who are pro-choice in Ireland will advocate for abortion in some circumstances on the basis that parents should be allowed to have a funeral and a coffin for their terminally ill baby. In other circumstances, these same pro-choice campaigners would deny a healthy baby aborted at the same gestational age any right to a funeral, a coffin, or even the name 'baby'. In these cases, pro-choice campaigners decide whether a person is human based on whether they are loved. In the case of rape, the distinction relates to the circumstances of conception.

We can say, without fear of contradiction, the following: a child aborted because of a fatal foetal illness and given a coffin and a funeral is exactly the same thing as a child aborted on the same day because he or she was conceived in rape. The only thing that separates them is how we think of them. Both children are equally innocent.

In cases of rape, there are two arguments commonly used to justify the exception. The first is the fact of the rape, which amounts to punishing the unborn child for the crimes of its genetic male parent (I will not use the term 'father' here, since no rapist deserves the title). The second is that a woman should not be burdened with a child she did not choose to conceive. The best way to balance this conflict is not to eliminate the child, but to seek to place it with those many adoptive parents who so badly want to love children of their own.

It is on this final point that I wish to conclude. Almost every single abortion of a healthy pregnancy has one thing in common – that the child being carried is not believed to be wanted. Because these children are not wanted, we indulge in the fantasy that they are not children at all. We consign ourselves to the kind of doublethink where a woman sixteen weeks pregnant, on a bus on the way to an abortion clinic, is said to be carrying a foetus, whereas the woman twelve weeks pregnant on the same bus is expecting a baby. This is dehumanisation, a mental trick we play on ourselves as a species. Every time throughout history that we have deployed this mental trick, thousands and millions have suffered. Abortion is no different.

What separates those two growing children on that bus? Why is one deserving of life, and the other not? The answer comes down to the fact that one child is loved for its potential, and the other is feared for its potential.

There are some cases, tragically, where a life cannot be saved. A case where a child is very ill and unlikely to survive means that there is little we can do. But where a child is simply not loved, or feared for what it might do to a young female life? In those cases, we can do so much better than abortion. In a world where so many couples struggle from infertility, and lose sleep, hope and relationships for the desire for a child, we can do so much better than abortion.

For 24 years, Ireland has been a beacon of hope for the world, showing the rest of the world that it is possible to be a modern country without killing your unborn children on an industrial scale. Our Constitution has demonstrated that we can value the lives of women and their children equally, with due regard for each partner in that foundational relationship. We are being asked to change that now, and we should think very carefully before we do. Following the herd to a place that has left countries like Iceland 'free' of people with Down syndrome is a darker path than Ireland's Constitution.

It is often said by pro-choice advocates that no woman wants to have an abortion, but that some women need abortions. I think they are half-right. It is true that no woman wants to have an abortion, because abortions are traumatic, physically and emotionally. It should never be true that a woman needs an abortion, because when she feels that way it is because the rest of us have not been as supportive as we are called to be.

In 1916, those who declared Irish independence called on us to cherish all the children of the nation equally. Tragically, we have not always lived up to that mandate. What we have never done before, and should not do now, is to consciously abandon it. Children, and their mothers, deserve much better. Let Ireland's Constitution and our Eighth Amendment serve as a light to light the world and guide it to a future where all of humanity can be loved and no individual is cast aside by society as 'unwanted'. In Ireland we are better than that, as a nation; it's our calling and we are up to the challenge.

REFERENCES

Jarvis Thomson, Judith (1971) 'A Defense of Abortion', *Philosophy & Public Affairs*, Vol. 1, No. 1, Fall, http://spot.colorado.edu/~heathwoo/Phil160,Fall02/thomson. htm.

Williams, Mary Elizabeth (2013) 'So What if Abortion Ends Life?', *Salon*, 23 January, www.salon.com/2013/01/23/so_what_if_abortion_ends_life/.

ENDNOTES

[1] Williams (2013).
[2] *Ibid.*
[3] Jarvis Thomson (1971).

Journey to Change:
Why the Eighth Amendment Has to Go

Catherine Connolly

Sheila Hodgers, a young, married Dundalk mother of two, died on 19 March 1983 at Our Lady of Lourdes Hospital in Drogheda, after giving birth to a premature baby girl who died almost immediately after birth. Sheila had become pregnant while receiving treatment for a recurrent cancer. The hospital had refused to allow her to stay on the treatment because it would harm her unborn child. She was also denied an x-ray and pain relief. Her husband had asked at various stages for an abortion, early delivery of the baby or a Caesarean section. All were refused. Mrs Hodgers died two days after her daughter and by then she had tumours everywhere: on her neck, her legs, her spine.[1]

The inhuman medical treatment, or more accurately the lack of treatment, afforded to Sheila Hodgers occurred less than six months before the people of Ireland voted to ratify an amendment to the Constitution which provides that:

> The State acknowledges the right to life of the unborn and, with due regard to the equal right to life of the mother, guarantees in its laws to respect and as far as practicable, by its laws to defend and vindicate that right.

By inserting this article into the Constitution, which became law on 7 October 1983, it was clear that the pain, anguish and death of Sheila Hodgers had not led to any period of meaningful reflection or learning on the part of Irish society. Rather, the cold ambition of preventing abortion was to be at any cost to the life and health of women. It was also in complete denial of the reality of thousands of pregnant women who travel out of the country each year to obtain an abortion, including, of course, the year that the amendment was passed in 1983.

That this was the position was evident from the number of pregnant women who found themselves before one legal forum or another in this country or abroad, including the District, High and Supreme Courts together with the Court of Justice, the European Court of Human Rights and two UN committees.

The unique and varied circumstances arising in each of these cases highlight in a most acute way the challenges and obstacles faced by these pregnant women. To the fore of course in all the situations depicted is the Eighth Amendment and the detrimental effects of decisions made thereunder on women's lives and health.

Given that abortion was already prohibited in Ireland by virtue of section 58 of the *Offences against the Person Act* 1861 and given that the *Health (Family Planning) Act* 1979 also sets out the statutory prohibition of abortion, why did the people of Ireland vote to amend the Constitution in the manner they did?

It is clear that two Court judgments, one by the Supreme Court in Ireland and an earlier case by the Supreme Court in the United States, caused alarm bells to ring for those who wanted abortion prohibited in Ireland with absolute certainty.

Of particular relevance in this regard is the Supreme Court judgment in *McGee v The Attorney General* in 1974.[2] The court recognised a right to marital privacy and that right included the right to access and use contraceptives. Following this decision, the most serious concerns were expressed by pro-life groups that a subsequent case might extend the right to privacy to include a right to abortion, notwithstanding that in the course of its judgment the Court also recognised the right to life of the 'unborn'. Moreover, just the previous year the US Supreme Court in *Roe v Wade*[3] in 1973 found that the fundamental right to privacy allowed a right to abortion. Both decisions served to galvanise and intensify the campaign to insert a 'pro-life' article into the Constitution, culminating in the 1983 referendum.

The debate therefore in the run-up to the referendum on Eighth Amendment in September of that year was formulated in stark black-and-white terms, with the full intent of giving certainty to an area where certainty could and should not apply. Moreover, that determined attempt to guarantee certainty and to control women's decisions and their bodies continued after the insertion of the Eighth Amendment into the Constitution. In the ensuing years, applications came before the courts, seeking to restrict the nature of the information and advice pregnant women were entitled to receive in relation to the procurement of an abortion outside of Ireland.

In 1988 for example, the Supreme Court gave judgment in a case brought by the Society for the Protection of the Unborn Child (SPUC) and known as *AG (SPUC) v Open Door Counselling Ltd and Dublin Well Woman Centre*.[4] The Supreme Court granted a perpetual injunction preventing the organisations in question from assisting pregnant women within the state to travel abroad to obtain abortions, whether by referring them to relevant clinics or by informing them of the identity, location of and method of communications with the clinics. The Supreme Court also declared that the acts which the defendant organisations were restrained from doing were 'unlawful having regard to the provisions of Article 40.3.3 of the Constitution'.[5]

Open Door Counselling Ltd and Dublin Well Woman Centre then took a case to the European Court of Human Rights, which gave judgment on 29 October 1992.[6] The Court found that Ireland had violated Article 10 of the European Convention on Human Rights guaranteeing freedom of expression. It also held that the Irish Courts' injunction against Open Door and Well Woman from receiving or imparting information on abortion services legally available in other countries was disproportionate and created a risk to the health of women seeking abortions outside the state.

The following year, in 1989 in *SPUC v Grogan*,[7] SPUC brought another application to the High Court seeking an injunction restraining certain student groups from distributing information on abortion services in the United Kingdom. Again, the matter ended up in the European Courts. This time the legal forum was the Court of Justice by way of referred questions from the High Court seeking clarification on the correct meaning of certain provisions of European law on which the student groups sought to rely.

Sensibly, the High Court made no order in relation to the application for an injunction, pending the decision of the Court of Justice. SPUC, however, appealed to the Supreme Court, which granted the injunction but did not overturn the decision of the High Court to refer the questions to the Court of Justice.

Finally in 1991, the Court of Justice ruled that abortion could constitute a service under the founding treaty of the EU and therefore a member state could not prohibit the distribution of information by agencies having a commercial relationship with abortion clinics. The Court went on to find however that since the student groups had no direct links with abortion services outside of Ireland, they could not claim protection of European Community law.

Following this decision, SPUC went back to the High Court in 1994 and sought, and was granted, a permanent injunction by the High Court restraining the activities complained of. That order remained in place for four long years until, on appeal, the Supreme Court finally lifted the injunction in 1998.[8]

In addition to the applications as set out above, the chilling effect of the Eighth Amendment was clearly exposed in 1992 in the X Case. The circumstances of this case are worth noting and the following facts are as set out at page 11 of a 48-page Supreme Court judgment:

The first-named defendant is a fourteen-and-a-half-year-old girl and the second- and third-named defendants are her parents. Upon the facts proved in the High Court, the first-named defendant was, in the month of December 1991, raped, and as a result of such rape became pregnant of which fact she and her parents became aware at the very end of January 1992. The rape was then reported to the Garda Síochána and a statement given by the first-named defendant to them of the facts surrounding the alleged rape.

All of the defendants were distraught as a result of the revelation of the fact of rape and as a result of the fact that the first-named defendant was pregnant and after careful consideration all of them reached a decision that she should travel to the United Kingdom and undergo an operation for abortion. The family informed the Garda Síochána of that fact and inquired from them whether any particular process was available for testing the foetus so aborted in order to provide proof in any subsequent charge of the paternity of the accused. The Garda Síochána apparently submitted that inquiry to the Director of Public Prosecutions and he in turn communicated the information thus arising to the Attorney General.

The Attorney General on 7 February 1992 having applied ex parte to Costello J in the High Court, obtained an order of interim injunction restraining the first-named defendant and the other defendants from leaving the country or from arranging or carrying out a termination of the pregnancy of the first-named defendant. At the time that order was ready to be served on the defendants they apparently had left this country and were in England arranging for the carrying out of the termination of the pregnancy. Upon being informed whilst there of the order which had been made by the court, they returned to this country.[9]

Such are the stark facts of how a traumatised fourteen-year-old girl, pregnant as a result of rape, was subjected to repeated trauma, directly consequent on the interpretation of the Eighth Amendment by state agencies and an experienced judge of the High Court, along with the appalling failure of successive governments to enact the necessary legislation.

On appeal to the Supreme Court, the injunction preventing the fourteen-year-old from travelling abroad was overturned and in the course of his judgment, Chief Justice Finlay set out the very limited circumstances in which a woman can access an abortion in this country as follows:

I, therefore, conclude that the proper test to be applied is that if it is estab-lished as a matter of probability that there is a real and substantial risk to the life, as distinct from the health, of the mother, which can only be avoided by the termination of her pregnancy, such termination is permissible, having regard to the true interpretation of Article 40.3.3 of the Constitution.[10]

The judgment given by Justice Niall McCarthy in this case is worthy of particular note in that it highlights both the complexity of the issues facing pregnant women and their families pursuant to the Eighth Amendment and the appalling absence of appropriate legislation. More particularly, he says:

In the context of the eight years that have passed since the amendment was adopted and the two years since *Grogan*'s case, the failure by the legis-lature to enact the appropriate legislation is no longer just unfortunate; it is inexcusable. What are pregnant women to do? What are the parents of a pregnant girl under age to do? What are the medical profession to do? They have no guidelines save what may be gleaned from the judgments in this case. What additional considerations are there? Is the victim of rape, statutory or otherwise, or the victim of incest, finding herself pregnant, to be assessed in a manner different from others? The amendment, born of public disquiet, historically divisive of our people, guaranteeing in its laws to respect and by its laws to defend the right to life of the unborn, remains bare of legislative direction. Does the right to bodily integrity, identified in *Ryan v Attorney General* (1965) IR 294 and adverted to by Walsh J in *SPUC v Grogan*, involve the right to control one's own body?[11]

Given the clear articulation by the Supreme Court justice of the complex issues pertaining in this area, and given that he had excoriated the Oireachtas for failing to legislate, what was the response of the then government to this judgment? Regrettably, before the year was out, it had gone down the road of yet another divisive referendum, which took place on 25 November 1992.

In this second referendum on abortion, less than ten years since the first, voters were asked to decide on three separate proposed amendments to the Constitution. The first sought to remove the risk of suicide as grounds for a termination. The second proposed amendment sought to establish the right to travel abroad, including travel for the purpose of procuring an abortion. The third sought to establish the right to disseminate and obtain information within Ireland in relation to procuring an abortion abroad.

The people of Ireland by a majority rejected the first amendment and thereby refused to remove the risk of suicide as a ground for abortion from the Constitution but passed the second and third amendments resulting in the Thirteenth and Fourteenth Amendments to the Constitution setting out an express right to travel and to access the necessary information to obtain an abortion abroad.

It took another three years before the *Regulation of Information (Services outside the State for Termination of Pregnancies) Act* 1995 was enacted, the effect of which is to restrict free communication between women with unintended/ crisis pregnancies and their doctors and prohibits doctors from directly referring women to abortion services or making appointments for them in abortion clinics. Moreover, along with these restrictions, the campaign to remove suicide as a ground for obtaining an abortion in Ireland continued and resulted ten years later in a third referendum in 2002. Fortunately the proposed amendment was rejected, albeit by a small majority of the electorate, with 50.42 per cent voting against the removal of the suicide ground and 49.58 per cent for its removal, with a voter turnout of just 42.89 per cent.[12]

In tandem with, or subsequent to, the above referenda and court applications seeking to restrict the grounds for an abortion and/or to restrict a pregnant woman's right to information and/or to travel abroad for an abortion, another series of cases highlighted the detrimental consequences of the Eighth Amendment on women's lives and health.

In 1998 in *A & B v Eastern Health Board, District Judge Mary Fahy and C*[13] the Court was once again faced with a child, pregnant as a result of rape, six years after the X Case. In accordance with the wishes of the thirteen-year-old child, the Eastern Health Board, under whose care that child had been placed by the Court, obtained an order to take C abroad for an abortion. Her parents, however, appealed the order to the High Court in order to prevent their daughter travelling to the United Kingdom for an abortion. Pursuant to the test set down in the X Case, the High Court accepted that the child in question might commit suicide unless allowed an abortion, and therefore there was a real and substantial risk to her life. This judgment is significant in confirming once again that a termination was legally permissible in Ireland but only in the very limited circumstances set down in the X Case.

That a traumatised thirteen-year-old girl, pregnant through rape should have to endure District and High Court proceedings to access what the courts accepted was the required medical treatment was unconscionable. Yet the proceedings, which directly arose from the Eighth Amendment and the failure of successive governments to enact the necessary legislation, did not serve as a catalyst for change.

Rather, the judgment galvanised another campaign for a further restrictive referendum in 2002 as set out above. All the while of course more and more pregnant women found themselves before the courts.

In all of these cases, where the circumstances of each pregnant woman varied enormously and included a diagnosis of fatal foetal abnormality, access to cancer treatment, and a medical clinical determination that a pregnant woman had suffered brain stem death, the brutality and inhumanity of the legal regime in operation is clearly exposed.

In 2006 for example, the *D v Ireland* case[14] concerned the applicant known as D, who was pregnant and where a fatal foetal abnormality had been diagnosed. The applicant had been forced to go to England to terminate the pregnancy and argued that this was a breach of her rights under the European Convention of Human Rights. In the event, the European Court of Human Rights ruled the case inadmissible because all domestic remedies available in Ireland had not been exhausted by the applicant. The government's case, which was accepted by the Court, relied on the argument that in the applicant's particular circumstances she could have been legally entitled to an abortion in Ireland should she have gone through the Irish courts system.

It is particularly difficult, however, to accept the *bona fides* of the government's argument given that Ireland was once again heading for its second divisive referendum, fixed for 6 March 2002, at the same time as D had been given the diagnosis and also given its utter failure to enact the required legislation ten years after the X Case. To coldly set out that D should go to every court in the country in the first instance, and then, if necessary, to the European Court of Human Rights is particularly disingenuous given D's circumstances as set out in the judgment:

> The applicant was devastated by the loss of her twins and dismayed by the prospect of carrying the pregnancy to term. She felt unable to tolerate the physical and mental toll of a further five months of pregnancy with one foetus dead and with the other dying. She did not consider any legal proceedings in Ireland at that point, but rather made arrangements to travel to the UK for an abortion. She felt unable to inform her family doctor and submitted that her health insurance did not cover the abortion costs. While she explained her wish to terminate the pregnancy to Doctors X and Y, they were 'very guarded' in their responses indicating that they 'appreciated that she was not eligible for an abortion in Ireland'. Hospital B 'thought she could not take her notes with her if she travelled abroad'. She did not clarify whether she brought a copy of her

file and medical records to the UK or who made the appointment for her but confirmed that she had been 'unable to obtain a referral'.[15]

The following year, in 2007, the Miss D Case[16] revealed the extent of the actions a state body was prepared to take to control a woman's life pursuant to its interpretation of the Eighth Amendment. This time, a seventeen-year-old with an anencephalic pregnancy and under the care of the HSE found herself before the courts having failed to obtain the HSE's permission to travel abroad to obtain an abortion. Not satisfied with the young woman's refusal to say she was suicidal in order to obtain that abortion in Ireland, the HSE wrote to the Garda Síochána to request that they arrest Miss D if she attempted to leave the jurisdiction. They also requested the Passport Office to refuse to issue her with a passport. Miss D was obliged to bring High Court proceedings against the HSE to allow her to travel. Although severely traumatised by the fact that her baby would not survive, Miss D said that she was not suicidal. The High Court found that there was nothing to prevent Miss D from travelling and she was entitled to do so.

The judgment of the European Court of Human Rights in the next case was given as the country entered the second decade of the twenty-first century, almost 27 years after the insertion of the Eighth Amendment into the Constitution and in the context of the continued failure of successive governments to enact the appropriate legislation. *A, B and C v Ireland*[17] concerned applications by three pregnant women who by virtue of the provisions of the Irish Constitution were obliged to travel outside the jurisdiction to avail of abortion services. There was no legislation governing the process to be followed. The Grand Chamber of the European Court of Human Rights unanimously ruled that Ireland's failure to implement the existing constitutional right to lawful abortion when a woman's life is at risk violated Applicant C's rights under Article 8 of the European Convention of Human Rights. The court also ruled that the three women challenging Ireland's ban on abortion did not have an effective remedy available to them under the Irish legal system either in theory or in practice.

Following the publication of this judgment and resulting media attention, Michelle Harte came forward to tell us her story. In 2010 she had become unintentionally pregnant while suffering from a malignant melanoma. Doctors at Cork University Hospital advised termination because of a risk to her health. The decision however was referred to an ad hoc ethics committee. After an appalling delay, the hospital refused to authorise an abortion on the basis that her life was not under 'immediate threat'. Michelle Harte was obliged to travel to the United Kingdom for an abortion while severely ill and had to be assisted onto the plane. Her case was subsequently settled in July 2011 on the basis of the previous ruling of the European Court of Human Rights in the *A, B and C v Ireland* case. Michelle Harte died from cancer in 2011.[18]

It took the death of another unfortunate woman, however, for the government to begin the process of introducing the legislation required since 1983. On 28 October 2012, Savita Halappanavar, a 31-year-old woman, who was 17 weeks pregnant, died in Galway University Hospital in circumstances where she was refused a termination during an inevitable miscarriage because a foetal heartbeat was detectable. The subsequent report into her death, amongst other findings, found an over-emphasis on the need not to intervene until the foetal heart stopped, together with under-emphasis on managing the risk of infection and sepsis.[19]

The following year, in July 2013, the *Protection of Life During Pregnancy Act 2013* was finally enacted. The primary purpose of the Act was to implement the 1992 judgment of the Supreme Court in the X Case and the subsequent 2010 European Court of Human Rights judgment in *A, B and C v Ireland*, and to provide for lawful access to abortion where a pregnant woman's life is at risk, including the risk of suicide. Of course, by the time it became operational on 1 January 2014 it had become abundantly clear that both the Eighth Amendment and the 2013 Act were not fit for purpose and were actually detrimental to women's lives and health.

In the meantime, women continue to make decisions as best they can in the shadow of a legal system that both criminalises and disempowers them while removing their voices completely from the process. It also completely denies their reality. In 2016, at least 3,265 Irish women had abortions in the UK clinics with an unknown number elsewhere.[20] In addition, courtesy of the research carried out by Dr Sally Sheldon at the University of Kent, it is now known that also in 2016 there were approximately 3,000 requests for abortion pills from Northern Ireland and the Republic combined to the two biggest providers of online abortion medication in the United Kingdom.[21] All of these women are currently excluded from the Irish healthcare system. They have to make their own care arrangements and their medical management and outcomes are not monitored by the Irish healthcare system. Moreover, they experience an unacceptably low standard of healthcare. Furthermore, pregnant women continue to come before one legal forum or another because either the existing legal mechanisms allow for the most intrusive interventions into women's lives and/or Ireland's restrictive abortion laws are not compliant with human rights legislation.

The stark facts as set out in the judgment delivered on 26 December 2014 in *PP and the Health Service Executive*[22] highlight just how far the tentacles of the Eighth Amendment extend into a woman's life and death. A medical determination had been made on 3 December 2014 that the woman who was the subject of these proceedings had suffered brain stem death and both her father and the father of the unborn child were so advised on the same day. The woman was 26 years old, pregnant with her third child and the pregnancy was at the gestational age of 15 weeks at the time of her death. The doctor and hospital in question, however, made a decision to maintain the woman on life support for the duration of the pregnancy. In the circumstances as set out to him, and wanting his daughter to have a dignified death, PP was obliged to bring High Court proceedings seeking to have the medical measures discontinued. The Court acceded to her father's request on 26 December, 23 days after the woman suffered 'brain stem death'. Significantly, evidence given during the case confirmed that medical staff had informed the father that, for legal reasons, they felt constrained to put his daughter on life support because her unborn child still had a heartbeat. Further evidence given to the court indicated that 'a study of the notes brought home that the doctors in the Dublin hospital were clearly concerned, having regard to the mother's pregnancy, not to do anything that would "get them into trouble from a legal point of view and were awaiting legal advice".[23] Indeed in its judgment granting the father's application, the High Court said 'To maintain and continue the present somatic support for the mother would deprive her of dignity in death and subject her father, her partner and her young children to unimaginable distress in a futile exercise which commenced *only* [emphasis added] because of fears held by treating medical specialists of potential legal consequences.'[24]

9 June 2016 saw the United Nations Human Rights Committee give its judgment in *Amanda Jane Mellet v Ireland*.[25] It held that Ireland's abortion law violated Amanda Mellet's human rights under the International Covenant on Civil and Political Rights. The foetus she was carrying was diagnosed with a fatal foetal abnormality. Irish law, as we know, criminalises abortion except in the very restricted circumstances outlined in the X Case and the subsequent 2013 Act, thus compelling her to travel to the United Kingdom for an abortion. As highlighted by Máiréad Enright, this is the first time that any international court or human rights body has found that the criminalisation of abortion is in itself a violation of women's human rights.[26] The Committee held that the Irish law violated her right to freedom from inhuman and degrading treatment, violated her rights to privacy and bodily integrity, violated her right to freedom from discrimination and violated her right to seek and receive information.

One year later, in June 2017, in *Siobhán Whelan v Ireland*,[27] the UN Human Rights Committee ruled for the second time that Ireland's abortion laws subjected a woman to cruel, inhuman and degrading treatment. Again Ms Whelan was denied access to abortion services in Ireland following a diagnosis of fatal foetal impairment.

There is absolutely no doubt in my mind that more and more cases will continue to come before the Courts as long as the Eighth Amendment remains part of the Constitution. Seventy years after this country passed the *Republic of Ireland Act* 1948, by which it would declare itself a republic the following year, it is time to remove the Eighth Amendment from the Constitution and place the pregnant woman at the centre of a rights-based process. A process that will enable and empower her to meet the challenges posed in any given pregnancy and to make her own informed decisions as to the best way forward.

REFERENCES

A and B v Eastern Health Board, Judge Mary Fahy and C and the Attorney General (notice party) [1998] 1 IR 464.

A, B and C v Ireland [2011] 53 EHRR 13.

Amanda Jane Mellet v Ireland, CCPR/C/116/D/2324/2013, www.reproductiverights. org/sites/crr.civicactions.net/files/documents/CCPR-C-116-D-2324-2013-English-cln-auv.pdf.

Attorney General v X [1992] 1 IR 1.

Attorney General (SPUC) v Open Door Counselling Ltd and Dublin Well Woman Centre [1988] IR 593.

Cullen, Paul (2012) 'State Settled with Cancer Patient', *Irish Times,* 22 November, www. irishtimes.com/news/state-settled-with-cancer-patient-1.555035.

D v Ireland, Application No 26499/02 ECtHR (28 June 2006).

Department of Health (UK) (2016) *Abortion Statistics, England and Wales: 2016,* www.gov.uk/government/uploads/system/uploads/attachment_data/file/652083/ Abortion_stats_England_Wales_2016.pdf.

Elections Ireland (n.d.) '25th Amendment: Protection of Human Life in Pregnancy', *Elections Ireland,* https://electionsireland.org/results/referendum/refresult. cfm?ref=200225R.

Enright, Máiréad (2016) 'Amanda Jane Mellet v Ireland – The Key Points', *Human Rights in Ireland,* 9 June, http://humanrights.ie/uncategorized/amanda-jane-mellet-v-ireland-the-key-points/.

Health Service Executive (2013) *Final Report: Investigation of Incident 50278 from Time of Patient's Self-Referral to Hospital on the 21st of October 2012 to the Patient's Death on the 28th of October, 2012,* June, www.hse.ie/eng/services/news/nimtreport50278.pdf.

McDonald, Dearbhail (2007) 'Miss D: My Story', *Irish Independent,* 12 May, www. independent.ie/irish-news/miss-d-my-story-26288744.html.

McGee v Attorney General [1974] IR 284.

Open Door and Dublin Well Woman v Ireland (14234/88) [1992] ECHR 68 (29 October 1992).

O'Toole, Fintan (2003) 'The Ugly Politics of the Womb', *Irish Times*, 5 August, www.irishtimes.com/opinion/the-ugly-politics-of-the-womb-1.368580.

PP v Health Service Executive [2014] IEHC 622.

Roe v Wade [1973] 410 US 113.

Sheldon (2016) '"How Can a State Control Swallowing?" Medical Abortion and the Law', *University of Kent*, www.kent.ac.uk/law/mabal/Medical%20Abortion%20and%20the%20Law_web.pdf.

Siobhán Whelan v Ireland, CCPR/C/119/D/2425/2014 [2017], http://tbinternet.ohchr.org/Treaties/CCPR/Shared%20Documents/IRL/CCPR_C_119_D_2425_2014_25970_E.pdf.

Society for the Protection of Unborn Children Ireland Ltd v Grogan, [1989] 1 IR 753.

SPUC Ltd v Grogan and Ors (No. 5) [1998] 4 IR 343.

ENDNOTES

1   O'Toole (2003).
2   *McGee v Attorney General* [1974].
3   *Roe v Wade* [1973].
4   *Attorney General (SPUC) v Open Door Counselling Ltd and Dublin Well Woman Centre* [1988].
5   *Ibid*, p. 617.
6   *Open Door and Dublin Well Woman v Ireland* [1992].
7   *Society for the Protection of Unborn Children Ireland Ltd v Grogan* [1989].
8   *SPUC Ltd v Grogan and Ors* (No. 5) [1998].
9   *Attorney General v X* [1992], p. 11.
10   *Ibid*, p. 20.
11   *Ibid*, p. 40.
12   Elections Ireland (n.d.).
13   *A and B v Eastern Health Board, Judge Mary Fahy and C and the Attorney General (notice party)* [1998].
14   *D v Ireland* (2006).
15   *Ibid*, para. 4.
16   McDonald (2007).
17   *A,B and C v Ireland* [2011].
18   Cullen (2012).
19   Health Service Executive (2013).
20   Department of Health (UK) (2016).
21   Sheldon (2016).
22   *PP v Health Service Executive* [2014].
23   *Ibid*, p. 8.
24   *Ibid*, p. 28.
25   *Amanda Jane Mellet v Ireland* (2013).
26   Enright (2016).
27   *Siobhán Whelan v Ireland* (2017).

Debating the Eighth — The Future of the Right to Life: The Irish Legal Context and the United Nations Perspective

Róisín Bradley

Debate, discourse and engagement with contrasting opinions help shape and develop our thoughts and principles. These, in turn, inform our national conversations. As democrats, we should value an open marketplace of ideas within which both policies and the theories that underpin them are examined. In Ireland today, among the most hotly debated topics is abortion and the future of the Eighth Amendment of the Irish Constitution (Article 40.3.3°). The Eighth Amendment states that:

> The State acknowledges the right to life of the unborn and, with due regard to the equal right to life of the mother, guarantees in its laws to respect, and, as far as practicable, by its laws to defend and vindicate that right.

Part I of this chapter shall examine three possible approaches and their most likely respective outcomes: repeal, replace and retain. An analysis of the legal implications of each shall be discussed in turn. In Part II, the question of abortion within the covenants and conventions of the United Nations shall be examined. Issues such as the legal status of the unborn, the protection of mothers, and the effects of current Irish and British legislation shall be touched on throughout this paper.

Before the adoption of the Eighth Amendment in 1983, there was a possibility that the liberalisation of the availability of abortion could have been achieved through the judicial system. The Supreme Court had already, in the case of McGee v Attorney General,[1] recognised within the right to marital privacy the right to obtain contraceptives. This mirrored an earlier development in the US where, in the case of Griswold v Connecticut,[2] the US Supreme Court applied the principle of privacy in the context of contraception. The precedents established in Griswold were further developed to introduce a broad 'right' to abortion in the famous case of Roe v Wade.[3] There is argument to support the claim that McGee had similar potential in the Irish context.[4] This was precluded when a majority of the electorate, on 7 September 1983, voted to insert Article 40.3.3° into the Constitution, ostensibly preventing future members of the judiciary from determining abortion policy. Discontentment in certain quarters with Article 40.3.3° persisted over the years, even after the enactment of the Protection of Life During Pregnancy Act 2013.

This has brought about our current position, the creation of the Citizens' Assembly and, subsequently, the formation of the Joint Oireachtas Committee on the Eighth Amendment. The Citizens' Assembly recommended that abortion should be made lawful, up to twelve weeks' gestation, 'without restriction as to reason'. This was accepted by the Oireachtas Committee 'provided that it is availed of through a GP-led service'.[5] Currently, under the Eighth Amendment, legislation must be enacted in compliance with the principle that the right to life of the mother and the unborn child are equal. The legal implication of this is that a woman cannot seek to use any of her other constitutional rights, such as privacy or autonomy, in order to have her pregnancy terminated. To legislate for abortion (beyond the X Case parameters)[6] the Constitution must first be changed by both Houses of the Oireachtas and by referendum.[7] The Oireachtas Committee have favoured 'replacing Article 40.3.3 with a constitutional provision giving exclusive authority to the Oireachtas to legislate on the issue of termination of pregnancy, free from the legal uncertainty of constitutional challenge and judicial intervention'.[8] This will mean that any subsequent legislation cannot be constitutionally challenged. The government have approved a 'repeal and enable' clause which will give explicit power to the Oireachtas to legislate on the matter at its discretion. In the words of Taoiseach Leo Varadkar, 'It is the case that once that article [the Eighth Amendment] is removed from the Constitution and the Oireachtas is enabled to make new laws, that we cannot tie the hands of a future Oireachtas.'[9] Essentially, the repeal and enable provision will ensure that the Oireachtas is not restricted by either implied or unenumerated rights existing elsewhere in the Constitution which afford protection of the right to life to the unborn. According to the Taoiseach, 'we can never give total certainty ... we cannot set in stone what the new law will be forever.'[10] This is a clear indication that over time the legislation will broaden.

PART I

Repeal

In the ongoing discussion about Article 40.3.3° there are those who advocate that it should be repealed in its totality. If a referendum results in a majority of voters choosing to repeal, the landscape of Irish human rights will be significantly shifted. Although certain aspects of the law post-repeal are unclear, one thing is not: the Oireachtas would have total freedom, authority and discretion to legislate on this issue as it sees fit. There would no longer be an obligation to refer to Article 40.3.3° and the Oireachtas could, therefore, introduce abortion as liberally or restrictively as it wished as time goes by. Some of those advocating for the repeal of the Eighth Amendment want unrestricted abortion on request to be introduced by law. The Coalition to Repeal the Eighth Amendment has stated that:

> Denial of a woman's right to decide if or when to have children is a grave denial of her human right to freedom and wellbeing. ... Only a tiny proportion of women have abortions for what most people see as 'exceptional circumstances'. ... A legislative model for abortion based on restrictions rather than on what women actually need is entirely ineffective, as it takes no account of the complexity of women's lives and of the wide range of reasons why they decide to have an abortion. ... It is not enough to provide treatment only in medical emergencies and only then where there's a 'real and substantial risk' to a woman's life as opposed to her health.[11]

To legislate in accordance with these demands would mean that the protection of life currently afforded to the unborn would be completely stripped away. Unborn children would have no status or explicit protection under the Constitution. The extreme view is that abortion should be permitted even as a form of contraception on the basis that the right to autonomy and the right to 'choose' trump all other human rights. On this view, the right to life of the unborn baby matters little and whatever intrinsic value it may have certainly does not come close to that of the mother. This is essentially a statement that some lives matter more than others.

Opinion also exists that a repeal of Article 40.3.3° would not necessarily lead to abortion on request.[12] The Oireachtas could choose to give significant legislative rights to the unborn and seek to exclude extremely broad access to abortion. There is already and will continue to be inconsistency about what repeal actually means and what it could lead to. Professors Enright and de Londras express the same concern. 'Excising the constitutional provision would rid Article 40.3.3° of any further effect, ostensibly leaving the contours of abortion law for political settlement in the Oireachtas. However, it is not necessarily clear that the effect of repeal would be quite as straightforward as this suggests.'[13] They express concern that the Constitution may contain some 'loose threads' that could influence the judiciary in future cases 'so that the Constitution may be said to contain a meaning not anticipated by the repeal campaign.'[14] Should Article 40.3.3° be removed, dicta from previous cases remain,[15] which suggest that the unborn actually had a right to life within the Constitution even before the insertion of the Eighth Amendment.[16] However, the suggestion that these cases would be used to assert a constitutional right to life for the unborn post-repeal is 'unlikely—given that the express purpose of a repealing amendment would be to de-constitutionalise abortion.'[17]

Professor Whyte's analysis of the law on abortion in a post-repeal situation clarifies this. Article 40.3.3° 'provides the sole constitutional protection for the right to life of the unborn' therefore, 'it is not possible to argue, post deletion of the Eighth Amendment, that the right to life of the unborn still enjoyed some residual constitutional protection by virtue of other provisions of the Constitution.'[18] If it were argued that the unborn retained some rights then it would effectively render a vote to repeal the amendment futile. Imposing limits on access to abortion post repeal of the Eighth Amendment 'would be to read the decision of the People to remove constitutional protection for the unborn as somehow still subject to the implicit right to life of the unborn.'[19] The idea of repealing Article 40.3.3° but retaining some constitutional protection for the unborn implies that a right to life is implicit not only in Article 40.3.3° but, also, in other constitutional provisions. Therefore, if it is assumed that a vote to repeal would mean that the majority are voting to 'de-constitutionalise abortion' in order to allow for the introduction of abortion legislation, then it appears that an outright repeal of the Eighth Amendment would mean abortion on request as the unborn would no longer have constitutional protection.

Replace

There are those who argue that some degree of consensus could be reached by introducing abortion in limited, rare circumstances. This could be done by amending Article 40.3.3° rather than repealing it in full. It shall be argued that replacing the Eighth Amendment with a provision permitting abortion up to twelve weeks' gestation 'without restriction as to reason' is, in fact, not a centre-ground approach in practice. It must be remembered that 'restrictive abortion' is a difficult standard to maintain. One needs only to look across the water at our nearest neighbour. The British Abortion Act 1967 was intended by most of those who voted in favour of it to make abortion available only in extreme situations – the 'hard cases'. Even Lord Steel, who introduced the legislation as a Private Member's Bill, has acknowledged that the Act has become something it was never intended to be. The following extract from a newspaper article quoting him highlights his concern: 'Lord Steel, architect of the 1967 Abortion Act, says today that abortion is being used as a form of contraception in Britain and admits he never anticipated "anything like" the current number of terminations when leading the campaign for reform.'[20] The language of the 1967 Act was formed with the intention that the availability of abortion be restrictive in nature. However, application of the legislation quickly broadened to evolve into the situation that Britain currently has, which is effectively abortion on request, with almost 200,000 abortions taking place each year. The supposedly restrictive provisions of the Act were utterly ineffectual in prohibiting this.

One circumstance that is often discussed as a possibility for allowing the introduction of limited or restrictive abortion is in cases of babies with terminal illnesses or life-limiting conditions. Under the Abortion Act 1967, Ground E provides for abortion, without time limits, in cases where 'there is a substantial risk that if the child were born it would suffer from such physical or mental abnormalities as to be seriously handicapped'.[21] A 2013 Parliamentary Inquiry into Abortion on the Grounds of Disability confirmed that it is legal to terminate a pregnancy up to full-term, which is 40 weeks, on the grounds that the child has such a disability.[22] Table 9(a) of the 2016 abortion statistics published by the UK Department of Health shows the medical conditions for which abortions under Ground E were performed in England and Wales.[23] In 2016, 3,208 abortions in total were performed under Ground E. Of those, 177 were for spina bifida and 791 were for 'other congenital malformations' including of the ear, eye, face and neck, and also minor conditions like cleft lip and cleft palate which could be rectified by simple surgical procedures. Of the chromosomal disorders, 220 abortions were performed for the condition of Edwards syndrome and 83 abortions performed for Patau syndrome, while 706 abortions took place where the pre-born baby was diagnosed with Down syndrome. In 2016, there were 219 abortions for babies diagnosed with anencephaly.

As these records show, abortion in cases of 'severe disabilities' are more frequently performed on unborn babies with non-fatal conditions such as Down Syndrome because in reality, the number of pre-born foetuses diagnosed with more life-limiting conditions like Edwards syndrome or anencephaly are extremely small.[24] Babies with Down syndrome could and would be aborted under similar terms in Ireland without Article 40.3.3° because that condition is a chromosomal disorder and is therefore a 'disability'. It is not possible to introduce abortion on strictly limited and exceptional circumstances. It is inevitable that these circumstances will broaden. For instance, Table 2 of the abortion statistics published by the UK Department of the Health record that 38 per cent of legal abortions carried out in 2016 were obtained by women who have previously had an abortion under the 1967 Act. In numerical form, that 38 per cent translates to 71,126 repeat abortions.[25]

There is concrete evidence to show that over time a greater number of abortions take place following the legalisation of abortion. This is clearly demonstrated by the 2016 abortion statistics. In 1968, records show that 23,641 abortions took place. In 2016, that number has increased to 190,406.[26]. These facts, among numerous other elements, indicate that, far from being restricted to exceptional cases, abortion in Britain is widely available. Clearly, the 1967 Act is failing to do what Parliament had intended, given the high percentage of pregnancies ending in abortion. There is no reason to expect that whatever little restrictions are implemented in Irish law would be more effective than those in Britain or any other European country with abortion. Subject to whatever restrictions might be contained in a replacement Article 40.3.3°, it is likely that the Oireachtas, in legislating for abortion, would look to British abortion legislation for inspiration and guidance in publishing the Heads of the Bill prior to the referendum.[27] It is arguable that the twelve-week proposal is even more liberal than the British regime. Abortion is legal in England up to 24 weeks under the 1967 Act. Whenever there is a substantial risk to a woman's life, whether physical or mental, or if the baby has a foetal abnormality, then abortion is permitted up to birth. There is no age limit for accessing abortion.[28] That is the reality of the type of 'restrictive' abortion regime implemented in England and Wales.

Retain

In the event that the people vote to retain the Eighth Amendment, the status quo will remain unchanged. Since there are various common misconceptions about the current effects of the Amendment, it may be useful at this point to clarify some of these. According to Professor Fergal Malone, Master of the Rotunda Hospital, the Eighth Amendment is having a deleterious effect on the medical care given to pregnant women in Ireland. He told the Oireachtas Committee on the Eighth Amendment that 'Obstetricians and maternity hospitals in Ireland should be able to provide complete and appropriate healthcare services to their patients without the threat of a criminal conviction'.[29] He also stated that Section 22 of the Protection of Life During Pregnancy Act 2013 specifies that 'no prosecution would occur without the consent of the Director of Public Prosecutions, and presumably this would unlikely be given in a situation where a doctor or hospital was acting in good faith to care for a patient in a difficult circumstance'.[30] It seems that there is not medical consensus that the Amendment restricts medical practice. Professor John Bonnar, in his submission to the All-Party Oireachtas Committee on the Constitution,[31] as Chairman of the Institute of Obstetricians and Gynaecologists, in May 2000 stated that an obstetrician would not view intervening in a case of pre-eclampsia, cervical cancer or ectopic pregnancy as abortion. That is because medical procedures such as these are the necessary treatments needed to care for the health and save the life of the mother. The Eighth Amendment allows for these procedures. No doctor has ever been imprisoned for performing any such operations. Abortion is directly interfering in a pregnancy to intentionally end the life of a baby. Lifesaving medical treatments are certainly not the same.

Section 7 of the Protection of Life During Pregnancy Act 2013 affirms Professor Bonnar's interpretation. Section 7 is titled 'Risk of Loss of Life From Physical Illness' and provides that:

It shall be lawful to carry out a medical procedure in respect of a pregnant woman, in the course of which, or as a result of which, an unborn human life is ended where—

a. she has been examined by two medical practitioners who jointly certify in good faith that
   i. there is a real and substantial risk of loss of the woman's life from a physical illness and,
   ii. that risk can only be avoided by performing the medical procedure.

It should be noted that Section 7 merely placed on statutory footing what had hitherto been standard best medical practice.

One aspect of this debate which everyone can agree on is surely this: the mother's life and well-being are imperative. The mother is not secondary to her baby; her right to life is not and should not be lesser than her unborn child's. Their lives are equal: 'The State acknowledges the right to life of the unborn and, with due regard to the equal right to life of the mother ...'.[32] Any treatment or legislation, regulation or practice that subjects the mother to a lesser standard of healthcare is directly opposed to the meaning of the Eighth Amendment. Moreover, this is an issue of equality. This debate concerns equality between the lives of the mother and the baby, but also equality of opportunity. An argument often disseminated in this debate is that a woman should be allowed to access abortion where a pregnancy may jeopardise her career potential. Women should not be forced to choose between their careers and the lives of their children. The system should be and can be changed to suit working mothers. A man would never be told that he cannot excel in his career once he becomes a father. Pregnancy and motherhood should never be used as an obstacle to prevent a woman from excelling in her career. In any case, the experience of other countries shows that introducing abortion will not mean the end of such workplace bias and gender discrimination.

PART II

The United Nations

The preamble of the 1959 United Nations Declaration of the Rights of the Child (henceforth UNDRC) states that '... the child by reason of his physical and mental immaturity, needs special safeguards and care, including appropriate legal protection, *before as well as after birth*' (emphasis added). The United Nations Convention on the Rights of the Child (hereafter UNCRC), which is based upon the UNDRC, quotes this in its preamble. Article 6, paragraph 1 of the UNCRC declares that: 'States Parties recognise that every child has the inherent right to life.' Furthermore, Article 6, paragraph 2 calls upon States Parties to 'ensure to the maximum extent possible the survival and development of the child.' In light of paragraph 1, reference to the development of the child in paragraph 2 could be argued to include development in the womb. Article 24 provides that States Parties 'recognise the right of the child to the enjoyment of the highest attainable standard of health ...'. In addition, paragraph 2(d) calls upon States Parties to implement this right and take suitable measures to 'ensure appropriate pre-natal and post-natal health care for mothers'.[33] In conjunction, these articles indicate that the right to life extends both to the born and the unborn.

Principle 5 of the UNDRC states: 'The child who is physically, mentally or socially handicapped shall be given the special treatment, education and care required by his particular condition.' We, as a society, should not opt to view those who are not 'able bodied' as less deserving of the right to life. Every human being is valued simply by virtue of his or her humanity, regardless of condition or illness. They are equally part of the human family to which we all belong. Our laws should reflect that principle, but should also make it a practical reality for babies diagnosed with disabilities and their families. Rather than advocating the premature ending of the life of a disabled child, we should implement these standards wherever we fall short in doing so.

Recently, the UN Committee on the Rights of Persons with Disabilities (CRPD) addressed the question of laws providing for abortion on grounds of disability (including so-called 'fatal foetal abnormalities') in a submission on the draft General Comment No. 36 of the UN Human Rights Committee on Article 6 of the International Covenant on Civil and Political Rights (ICCPR).[34] Paragraph 9 of the draft General Comment No. 36 calls for States to introduce abortion '... where the pregnancy is the result of rape or incest or when the foetus suffers from fatal impairment'. In response, the CRPD proposed that the aforementioned be deleted, stating that 'Laws which explicitly allow for abortion on grounds of impairment violate the Convention on the Rights of Persons with Disabilities (Art., 4, 5, 8). Even if the condition is considered fatal, there is still a decision made on the basis of impairment. Often it cannot be said if an impairment is fatal. Experience shows that assessments on impairment conditions are often false. Even if it is not false, the assessment perpetrates notions of stereotyping disability as incompatible with a good life.'[35]

The status of the Committee Against Torture, Inhumane and Degrading Treatment in relation to Ireland's abortion laws must be highlighted in order for our obligations, if any, be made clear. On 27 and 28 July 2017, the body responsible for monitoring states' adherence to the United Nations Convention against Torture and Other Cruel, Inhuman or Degrading Treatment or Punishment (CAT) reviewed Ireland. In its Concluding Observations, the Committee expressed concern at the 'severe physical and mental anguish and distress experienced by women and girls regarding termination of pregnancy due to the State policies'.[36] It called for Ireland to make abortion available. However, the opinion of the Committee is simply just that: an opinion. Moreover, while Ireland signed the Optional Protocol to the CAT in 2007, Ireland has not ratified it.[37] Ireland is, therefore, under no obligation to comply with the opinion of the Committee, contrary to what we are led to believe. Nor are there any sanctions for non-compliance.

The UN Human Rights Committee (HRC) comprises eighteen independent experts who monitor the implementation of the ICCPR by States Parties. The HRC is not a court, nor is it any kind of legislature. In 2002, the Irish Supreme Court stated that 'the notion that the "views" of the committee could prevail against ... a properly constituted [Irish] court is patently unacceptable' and would violate our Constitution. The Court also found that the Covenant itself did not give 'any binding effect to the views expressed by the committee' and that the HRC cannot give 'any form of judgment or declare any entitlement to relief'.[38] Use of the word 'views' in Article 5, Paragraph 4 of the Optional Protocol [to the ICCPR] demonstrates that the Committee's concluding observations are advisory in nature rather than obligatory and, furthermore, there is no enforcement mechanism.[39] The view of the Committee should not and does not compel us to make any rash changes to our law.

Article 6 of the ICCPR states that 'Every human being has the inherent right to life. This right shall be protected by law. No one shall be arbitrarily deprived of his life.' There is divergence between this clause of the ICCPR and the opinion of the HRC and CAT that some human beings, i.e. those who are unborn, do not have the right to life. There is inconsistency between, on the one hand, the view of abortion and the right to life of the unborn taken by the HRC and CAT and, on the other hand, the view of the CRPD and of the above articles and covenants which afford some protections and value to foetal life. In fact, the HRC itself contradicts this principle in its own General Comment No. 36 when it declares that the right to life is 'the supreme right', not 'a core right' or 'one of the most important rights': it is the supreme right. The only time the HRC seems to deviate from this principle is in its views on abortion. The HRC, by disregarding and isolating the rights of an entire sector of society, risks destroying its own credibility as a defender of human rights. It could even be argued that by making such commentary on an issue this controversial, in an attempt to put international pressure on States Parties to introduce abortion, the Committee is acting ultra vires (beyond its powers).

The Human Rights Committee cannot claim to be a universal human rights body if it goes beyond the remit of other regional bodies such as the European Court of Human Rights (ECtHR). The CAT and HRC both undermine the right to life, and are much more extreme in what they recommend regarding abortion in comparison to actual supranational courts like the ECtHR. From the case of ABC v Ireland, states have a legitimate interest in protecting the right to life of the unborn.[40] The HRC is directly putting itself in contention with this finding. In ABC, the first two applicants contested that their rights under Article 8 of the European Convention on Human Rights (ECHR) had been breached due to the prohibition of abortion in Ireland.[41] The third applicant, C, claimed that she had no means of establishing her right to a lawful abortion in Ireland on the grounds of a risk to her life due to the absence of legislation interpreting Article 40.3.3°. This, she claimed, was a breach of Article 8. The first applicant, A, was unmarried with four children and was an alcoholic. All of her children were in foster care and she was living in poverty. B was seeking an abortion as she felt she was unable to care for a child on her own at that particular time in her life. C was in remission from cancer and had been advised that it was not possible to predict the effect that her pregnancy would have on the development of the cancer.

In respect of A and B, the Court held that restrictions on the availability of abortion in Ireland did not amount to a disproportionate interference with their rights under Article 8. However, given the ethical issues surrounding abortion and the importance of the public interest in the matter, the Court held that the state had a broad margin of appreciation in determining whether a fair balance was struck between the right to life of the unborn and the applicants' conflicting Article 8 rights. The interference with Article 8 was proportionate in these two instances. However, in respect of applicant C, a different approach was taken. The Court held that the state had violated the ECHR by failing to provide an accessible procedure that allowed a woman to establish whether she qualified for a legal abortion under Irish law. The ECtHR did not, however, accept the argument that Article 8 conferred a right to abortion.[42] Following this decision, the Protection of Life During Pregnancy Act 2013 was introduced. The Act now sets out the procedures for obtaining a lawful abortion.[43]

In conclusion, the ECtHR has not allowed for the liberalisation of abortion. The HRC, then, should certainly not go beyond the jurisprudence of the ECtHR in the manner which they have. Comparing a UN treaty monitoring body, like the HRC, with the European Court of Human Rights is like comparing the Oireachtas Joint Committee on the Eighth Amendment with the Supreme Court. The views of the HRC carry political weight, certainly. But in the instant case, it is troubling that they call for the extreme modification of abortion laws without any argument presented by the HRC to justify it having done so. There are three major differences that must be highlighted:

1. Many members of the HRC are not lawyers, have never served as members of the judiciary and are not democratically elected. They are volunteers. Whereas the ECtHR is comprised of qualified lawyers, appointed by the Parliamentary Assembly,[44] whose job it is to interpret the European Convention on Human Rights.[45]
2. What the HRC is proposing is so extreme. The language used by the ECtHR in ABC respects the sovereignty of member states to regulate on contentious social issues as they see fit. Member states enjoy a 'wide margin of appreciation'.[46] This is in contrast to the language used by the HRC in their draft General Comment No. 36 that 'States parties *must* [emphasis added] provide safe access to abortion to protect the life and health of pregnant women …'.[47]
3. This is highlighted further by the fact that no other body has taken such a wide interpretation. The HRC does not have a right to create new human

rights law; its function is to interpret the ICCPR. Its claim has no legal standing.

CONCLUSION

Liberal societies have always protected the weak and the vulnerable. As a Western, democratic nation we should maintain this protection. Article 40.3.3°, the Eighth Amendment to the Irish Constitution, should be retained in full without alteration. In addition to its lethal consequences for unborn babies, abortion is a traumatic, upsetting, frightening and unpleasant experience for most women.[48] The introduction of abortion in restrictive circumstances by way of legislation is unachievable, as can be seen from the examination of British legislation and its effects. The prime effect of retaining the Eighth Amendment is the protection of the lives of mothers and babies. Their lives are not in competition; both are equally invaluable. Our present laws reflect this. I have every faith our society will continue to do so too.

BIBLIOGRAPHY

Table of Cases

Irish Cases

Attorney General v X [1992] 1 IR 1
Finn v Attorney General [1983] IR 154
G v An Bord Uchtála [1980] IR 32
Kavanagh v The Governor of Mountjoy Prison [2002] 3 JIC 0103
McGee v Attorney General [1974] IR 284
Norris v Attorney General [1984] IR 36

UK Cases

Gillick v West Norfolk and Wisbech Area Health Authority [1985] 3 All ER 402 (HL)
R (on the application of Sue Axon) v The Secretary of State for Health & Anor [2006] EWHC 37 (Admin), [2006] 1FCR 17

US Cases

Griswold v Connecticut [1965] 381 US 79
Roe v Wade [1973] 410 US 113

ECHR Cases

ABC v Ireland [2011] 53 EHRR 13

Table of Legislation

Irish

Protection of Life During Pregnancy Act 2013, s7, s8, s9, s22

UK

Abortion Act 1967
Human Fertilisation and Embryology Act 1990, s1(1)(d)

References

All-Party Oireachtas Committee on the Constitution (2000) *Fifth Progress Report: Abortion*, http://archive.constitution.ie/reports/5th-Report-Abortion.pdf.
Article 40.3.3° Irish Constitution.
Article 15.2.1° Irish Constitution.
Article 15.4.1° Irish Constitution.
Article 8 European Convention on Human Rights.
Department of Health (UK) (2016) *Abortion Statistics, England and Wales: 2016*, www.gov.uk/government/uploads/system/uploads/attachment_data/file/652083/Abortion_stats_England_Wales_2016.pdf
Enright, Máiréad and Fiona de Londras (2014) 'Empty Without and Empty Within: The Unworkability of the Eighth Amendment after Savita Halappanavar and Miss Y', *Medico-Legal Journal of Ireland*, Vol. 20, No. 2, pp. 85–90.
Glynn, Brendan (2016) 'How Unenumerated Rights Have Created a More Tolerant and Liberal Ireland', *Irish Law Times*, Vol. 34, No. 14, pp. 202–204.
Irish Human Rights and Equality Commission (2017) *Ireland and the Convention against Torture: Submission to the United Nations Committee against Torture on Ireland's Second Periodic Report*, July, www.ihrec.ie/app/uploads/2017/07/Ireland-and-the-Convention-against-Torture.pdf.
Joint Committee on the Eighth Amendment of the Constitution (2017) *Majority Report on the Eighth Amendment of the Constitution*, www.oireachtas.ie/parliament/media/committees/eighthamendmentoftheconstitution/Report-of-the-Joint-Committee-on-the-Eighth-Amendment-web-version.pdf.
Kenny, David (2017) *The Constitution and Legislation: The Making and Changing of Laws*, submission to the Citizens' Assembly, www.citizensassembly.ie/en/The-Eighth-Amendment-of-the-Constitution/Final-Report-on-the-Eighth-Amendment-of-the-Constitution/Appendix-E-Volume-1.pdf, pp. 221– pp.

Malone, Fergal (2017) *Testimony to the Joint Oireachtas Committee on the Eighth Amendment*, 11 October, www.oireachtas.ie/parliament/media/committees/eighthamendmentoftheconstitution/Opening-Statement-by-Professor-Fergal-Malone,-Master-of-the-Rotunda-Hospital-Dublin.pdf.

MerrionStreetNews (2018) 'Post Cabinet Press Conference 29ᵗʰ January 2018', *YouTube*, www.youtube.com/watch?v=4VJvaWTU_gM.

Ó Cionnaith, Fiachra (2017a) 'Vote to Repeal 8th Amendment Will Not Lead to Abortion on Demand, Committee Hears', *Irish Examiner*, 27 September.

Ó Cionnaith, Fiachra (2017b) 'Rotunda Master before Eighth Committee', *Irish Examiner*, 11 October.

O'Connell, Hugh (2016) 'Labour Wants to Replace the Eighth Amendment with a UK-Style Abortion Law', *TheJournal.ie*, 18 February, www.thejournal.ie/labour-abortion-law-2611642-Feb2016/.

Parliamentary Inquiry into Abortion on the Grounds of Disability (July 2013), http://dontscreenusout.org/wp-content/uploads/2016/02/Abortion-and-Disability-Report-17-7-13.pdf.

Royal College of Obstetricians and Gynaecologists (2011) 'The Care of Women Requesting Induced Abortion: Evidence-Based Clinical Guideline Number 7', November, www.rcog.org.uk/globalassets/documents/guidelines/abortion-guideline_web_1.pdf.

Smith, Ailbhe (2017), *Paper of the Coalition to Repeal the Eighth Amendment Delivered to the Citizens' Assembly*, 5 March, www.citizensassembly.ie/en/Meetings/Coalition-to-Repeal-the-Eighth-s-Paper.pdf.

United Nations Committee Against Torture, Inhumane and Degrading Treatment (2017) *Concluding Observations on the Second Periodic Report of Ireland*, July, http://tbinternet.ohchr.org/Treaties/CAT/Shared%20Documents/IRL/INT_CAT_COC_IRL_28491_E.pdf.

United Nations Committee on the Rights of Persons with Disabilities (2017) *Comments on the Draft General Comment No 36 of the Human Rights Committee on Article 6 of the International Covenant on Civil and Political Rights*, November, www.everylifecounts.ie/am-site/media/uncommitteeondisabilities.pdf.

United Nations Convention on the Rights of the Child.

United Nations Declaration of the Rights of the Child (1959).

Ward, Lucy and Riazat Butt (2007) 'Too Many Abortions: Lord Steel', *The Guardian*, 24 October.

Whyte, Gerry (2017) 'Repeal or Replace? The Legal Implications of Amending Article 40.3.3', Paper presented at the Abortion, Disability and the Law Conference, Dublin, 20 October.

Women Hurt (2017) *Submission of Women Hurt to the Citizens' Assembly*, www.citizensassembly.ie/en/The-Eighth-Amendment-of-the-Constitution/Final-Report-on-the-Eighth-Amendment-of-the-Constitution/Appendix-E-Volume-2.pdf.

Wu, J., A. Springett and J.K. Morris (2013) 'Survival of Trisomy 18 (Edwards Syndrome) and Trisomy 13 (Patau Syndrome) in England and Wales: 2004–2011', *American Journal of Medical Genetics Part A*, Vol. 161A, pp. 2512–2518.

ENDNOTES

1   [1974] IR 284.
2   [1965] 381 US 79.
3   [1973] 410 US 113.
4   Glynn (2016).
5   Joint Committee on the Eighth Amendment of the Constitution (2017), p. 11.
6   *Attorney General v X* [1992] 1 IR 1.
7   For information on this see Kenny (2017).
8   Joint Committee on the Eighth Amendment of the Constitution (2017), p. 4.
9   MerrionStreetNews (2018), at 18:55.
10   *Ibid* at 19:15.
11   See Smith (2017), p. 5.
12   Ó Cionnaith (2017a).
13   Enright and de Londras (2014), p. 89.
14   *Ibid*, pp. 89–90.
15   See *G v An Bord Uchtála* [1980] IR 32, the judgments of Walsh J. in *McGee v Attorney General* [1974] 1 IR 284, McCarthy J. in *Norris v Attorney General* [1984] IR 36, and Barrington J. in *Finn v Attorney General* [1983] IR 154.
16   Enright and de Londras (2014), p. 90.
17   *Ibid.*
18   Whyte (2017).
19   *Ibid.*
20   Ward and Butt (2007).
21   As amended by the *Human Fertilisation and Embryology Act* 1990, see section 1(1)(d).
22   *Parliamentary Inquiry into Abortion on the Grounds of Disability* (2013).
23   Department of Health (UK) (2016).
24   See, for example, Wu, Springett and Morris (2013)
25   See Table 2 in Department of Health (UK) (2016), p. 26.
26   In 2007, the highest recorded number of abortions in Britain (205,598) took place.
27   The Irish Labour Party have already done so. See O'Connell (2016).
28   See Royal College of Obstetricians and Gynaecologists (2011), p. 24. See also *Gillick v West Norfolk and Wisbech Area Health Authority* [1985] 3 All ER 402 (HL) and *R (on the application of Sue Axon) v The Secretary of State for Health & Anor* [2006] EWHC 37 (Admin), [2006] 1FCR 17.
    In *Gillick*, Lord Frazer set out the criteria for any young person under sixteen years of age who refuses to involve their parents. A doctor or clinician is justified in proceeding without the parents' consent or knowledge if:
    a) the young person will understand the advice; b) she cannot be persuaded to inform her parents or to allow the doctor/clinician to inform her parents that she is seeking an abortion; c) she cannot be persuaded to inform her parents or to allow the doctor/clinician to inform

her parents that she is seeking contraceptive advice; d) she is likely to begin or to continue having sexual intercourse with or without contraceptive advice; e) unless she receives contraceptive advice or treatment, her physical or mental health, or both, is likely to suffer; f) her best interests require the clinician/doctor to give her contraceptive advice, treatment or both without parental consent. The case of *Axon vs The Secretary of State for Health* confirmed that the *Gillick* judgement also extends to cover abortion.

29   Malone (2017), p.7. See also Ó Cionnaith (2017b).

30   Malone (2017), p. 7. Section 22, *Protection of Life During Pregnancy Act* 2013: '(1) It shall be an offence to intentionally destroy unborn human life.

(2) A person who is guilty of an offence under this section shall be liable on indictment to a fine or imprisonment for a term not exceeding 14 years, or both.

(3) A prosecution for an offence under this section may be brought only by or with the consent of the Director of Public Prosecutions.'

31   All-Party Oireachtas Committee on the Constitution (2000), pp. 44–45.

32   Article 40.3.3° of the Irish Constitution.

33   Article 24, para 2(d) of the UNCRC.

34   Article 6 of the ICCPR: 'Every human being has the inherent right to life. This right shall be protected by law. No one shall be arbitrarily deprived of his life.'

35   United Nations Committee on the Rights of Persons with Disabilities (2017).

36   United Nations Committee Against Torture (2017), para 31.

37   See Irish Human Rights and Equality Commission (2017), p. 4.

38   *Kavanagh v The Governor of Mountjoy Prison* [2002] 3 JIC 0103.

39   Article 5.4 of the Optional Protocol to the ICCPR: 'The Committee shall forward its views to the State Party concerned and to the individual.'

40   [2011] 53 EHRR 13.

41   Article 8.1, ECHR: 'Everyone has the right to respect for his private and family life, his home and his correspondence.

2. There shall be no interference by a public authority with the exercise of this right except such as is in accordance with the law and is necessary in a democratic society in the interests of national security, public safety or the economic well-being of the country, for the prevention of disorder or crime, for the protection of health or morals, or for the protection of the rights and freedoms of others.'

42   *ABC v Ireland* [2011] 53 EHRR 13 para 214.

43   The provisions governing lawful abortions are as follows: Section 7 where there is a risk of loss of life from physical illness; Section 8 where there is risk of loss of life from a physical illness in an emergency situation; and Section 9 where there is a risk of loss of life from suicide.

44   Article 22, ECHR: 'The judges shall be elected by the Parliamentary Assembly with respect to each High Contracting Party by a majority of votes cast from a list of three candidates nominated by the High Contracting Party.'

45   Article 21, ECHR: 'The judges shall be of high moral character and must either possess the qualifications required for appointment to high judicial office or be jurisconsults of recognised competence.'

46   [2011] 53 EHRR 13.

47   See General Comment No. 36, para 9.

48   See Women Hurt (2017), p. 655. You can also view their website at www.womenhurt.ie.

FROM *SPUC v GROGAN* TO STUDENTS4CHOICE: THE HISTORY OF ABORTION LAW IN IRELAND, AND THE CASE FOR STUDENT ACTIVISM

Kevin Keane

The student movement has been one of the great forces for social advancement in Ireland and across the world over the last half-century. From the Civil Rights Movement in the US, to the nationwide labour strikes in Paris in 1968, to the Tiananmen Square Massacre in Beijing in 1989, students have been integral to social change in every corner of the globe. Here in Ireland, students have unquestionably been at the forefront of change. Higher education policy has been shaped by student activism, as has the advent of marriage equality. Students led the campaign to boycott apartheid South Africa, and students have been instrumental in the fight for reproductive rights in Ireland for over 30 years.

Over the course of the coming pages, I will outline the shameful history of Ireland's treatment of women who need access to abortion, in order to demonstrate the atmosphere in which the student movement has been actively campaigning for over 30 years. Students have led the charge in every aspect of the struggle for reproductive rights in Ireland, from the provision of condoms in the 1970s, to the seminal case of *SPUC v Grogan*, through to Strike4Repeal and Students4Choice. Using the example of the student movement's successful campaigning for marriage equality, I will highlight the power the student movement has to effect fundamental social change in Ireland. Finally, I will argue that not only should students' unions have a voice in this campaign, we should be doing everything in our power to contribute to the national campaign to Repeal the Eighth Amendment. I will argue that students are disproportionately affected by the Eighth Amendment, and that now is the time for students to stand up and shape the Ireland of the future.

Ireland has some of the most restrictive abortion law regimes on Earth. In Europe, only Poland and Malta make it more difficult to access abortion than Ireland. The restrictive nature of the law in Ireland has very real impacts – in 2015,

3,451 people travelled to the UK for abortions. 63 women per week, or 9 every single day. In the 34 years since the implementation of the Eighth Amendment, over 160,000 women have travelled overseas to access abortions. As a direct result of the Eighth Amendment, we have witnessed some of the most gruesome, harrowing case law with which the Irish courts have ever had to deal.

Our troubled history of abortion access dates as far back as 1861, and the *Offences Against the Person Act*. This Act criminalised abortion in all its forms, and threatened women who chose to access abortion with 'penal servitude for life'. Punishment was just as severe for those who were found to have assisted in the procurement of an abortion. Indeed, Mamie Cadden was sentenced to death by hanging under the Act in 1956, for carrying out backstreet abortions. Although her sentence was ultimately commuted to a lifetime of penal servitude, the law of the land was comprehensive and extreme in its pursuit of those who engaged with abortion in any way.

When the United Kingdom extensively liberalised its abortion legislation in 1967, Ireland was forced to look inward for the first time, and examine its position. Rather than acknowledge the reality – that thousands of women were travelling every year from Ireland to the UK – the most powerful forces in Irish society at the time deemed it necessary to copper-fasten the oppression already enshrined in our domestic law. Towards the end of the 1970s and into the early 1980s, Ireland's Catholic, conservative, male-led special interest groups began to gather their forces. In January 1981 they convened and created the Pro-Life Amendment Campaign (PLAC). The sole aim of PLAC was to turn Ireland into the only democratic country in the world with a Constitutional ban on abortion. The success of this stunningly sectarian organisation is perhaps the clearest possible sign of the stranglehold of the Catholic Church on Irish life and politics at the time. Of the thirteen bodies explicitly listed as members of the campaign, ten were exclusively Catholic. The remaining three were, for all intents and purposes, exclusively Catholic organisations.[1] All of PLAC's membership were clear on one thing – that they wanted a Constitutional amendment that would guarantee 'the absolute right to life of every unborn child from conception'.[2]

Against this incredibly well-resourced and organised bloc, there stood only a small coalition of pro-choice activists. Ireland simply wasn't ready to defy the Church's rhetoric on such a fundamental social issue, and the Amendment passed with a significant majority on 8 September 1983. Article 40.3.3 of the Irish Constitution then read, and still reads to this day:

The state acknowledges the right to life of the unborn and, with due regard to the equal right to life of the mother, guarantees in its laws to respect, and as far as practicable, by its laws to defend and vindicate that right.

It did not take long for the dire consequence of Ireland's repressed and oppressive relationship with pregnancy and women's rights to rear its ugly head. Just four months after nearly two-thirds of the Irish electorate voted in favour of the Eighth Amendment, Ann Lovett tragically died. Ann was a fifteen-year-old schoolgirl who, on 31 January 1984, left school and walked to the local grotto, where she gave birth to a baby boy under the watch of a statue of the Virgin Mary. She stayed there for several hours, in the cold and rain. Her stillborn infant was wrapped in her coat when she was found. Ann Lovett died shortly after being rushed to hospital. Her story instantly became international news, and shone the harshest possible light on the oppressive nature of conservative Ireland, which allowed a fifteen-year-old child to suffer alone, in the dark and cold, because of our backward attitudes to sex and pregnancy.[3]

Possibly the most famous case in Irish judicial history is that of *Attorney General v X*,[4] heard in 1992, in which a fourteen-year-old girl (named only as X in the courts and media in order to protect her identity) fell pregnant as a result of a rape perpetrated by her neighbour. It later transpired that she had been the victim of ongoing abuse over a period of years. Her family supported the decision to travel to the UK in order to access an abortion, but in the interests of the pending case against her abuser, X's parents asked the Gardaí, prior to travelling to the UK, if DNA evidence obtained from the foetus after the abortion was completed would be admissible in court. The Gardaí reported the family's intention to travel to the UK to the Attorney General, who immediately went to the High Court to seek an injunction to stop the child leaving the country. Although they were already in London by the time the injunction was granted, X's family decided to return to Ireland without following through with the abortion.

Unsurprisingly, the abused child at the centre of this legal debacle was deeply traumatised by the events as they had unfolded, and became suicidal. She told her mother of her intention to jump in front of a train in London, and was in a deeply disturbed state when she returned to Ireland. Despite the fact that a clinical psychologist very clearly deemed X to be at risk of suicide, Judge Costello in the High Court was adamant. Eleven days after X and her parents returned to Ireland from the UK, he granted another order, which said that the right to life of the unborn could not be interfered with, and that X was to be restrained from leaving the jurisdiction for a period of nine months. The judge openly acknowledged X's suicidal ideations, and explicitly gave greater protection to the life of the foetus than that of the fourteen-year-old girl who had been raped and subjected to the torture of travelling to London for an abortion, only to be brought home at the eleventh hour. He justified his decision by saying that X had a supportive family, and that they would 'help her through the difficult months ahead'.[5] The result of the High Court ruling, had it gone unchallenged, would have been to effectively imprison the teenage survivor of abuse in Ireland, regardless of the mental trauma that such imprisonment would inflict upon her, in the interests of a foetus conceived as a result of rape.

Thankfully, the Supreme Court saw sense and overturned the judgment delivered in the High Court. The majority of the Supreme Court said that a woman had a right to an abortion under Article 40.3.3 if there was 'a real and substantial risk' to her life. This right did not exist if there was a risk to her health but not her life; however it did exist if the risk to her life existed due to the possibility of suicide. The ruling permitted X to access abortion, but she miscarried before the procedure could be carried out.

The response to the X Case was instant and momentous in Irish society. Thousands of people took to the streets on both the pro- and anti-choice sides of the argument, and the newspapers spoke of little else for months.

Shortly after the Supreme Court concluded its deliberations, the government brought forward three referenda to the Irish people:

- The Twelfth Amendment: if passed, would have banned any access to abortion, regardless of whether the woman were suicidal
- The Thirteenth Amendment: specified that the ban on abortion would not stop women travelling abroad in order to access abortion
- The Fourteenth Amendment: specified that it would not be illegal to spread information about abortion services abroad

The Twelfth Amendment was defeated, but the Thirteenth and Fourteenth both passed into law. There was a further attempt in 2002 to ban abortion on the grounds of risk to life of the mother by suicide, which also failed. In fact, every single time the Irish people have had the chance to liberalise abortion access in Ireland since 1983, they have done so.

This may in large part be due to the harrowing and traumatic succession of cases that have followed the X Case. The C Case, where a young child was raped by a friend of her family, and was forced to go through High Court proceedings in order to be allowed travel to the UK, is a clear example.[6] Another is the case of Miss D, when in 2007 a teenage girl wished to travel to the UK to abort her pregnancy, due to a diagnosis of anencephaly (the absence of a major portion of the brain, skull and scalp) in the womb. Despite the fact that it is legal to travel for access to abortion, the HSE lied to her, telling her that they had an order banning her from travelling. They went as far as to threaten to physically restrain her if she sought to leave the country. The Y Case saw an asylum seeker, who has no right of travel outside the jurisdiction, attempt to access abortion services here in Ireland. She became deeply suicidal upon learning of her pregnancy, which was the result of rape in her country of origin. She was unsuccessful in her application, and after she began a hunger strike the High Court granted an order to hydrate her against her will. The X Case should have allowed her access to abortion, and yet her baby was delivered, after sustained forced hydration, by Caesarean section.[7]

One of the most well known cases resulting from the Eighth Amendment in recent years is that of Savita Halappanavar. Savita died in 2012 as a result of the Eighth Amendment, and the murkiness of the law surrounding it. The timeline of her final days is horrific, and is itself a damning indictment of the Eighth Amendment. Savita presented to University Hospital Galway seventeen weeks into a much wanted pregnancy, complaining of back pain. She was sent home, but the pain continued to get worse and she returned that night. The following day, she was told that she would suffer an 'inevitable miscarriage'. Despite this, as her conditions worsened, the following day she was told a termination would not be possible, because Ireland is a 'Catholic country'. Her doctor later told the inquest that if they had been in a country where abortion was legal, Savita would have been offered one. Her condition continued to deteriorate, and she was in excruciating pain. Her blood pressure was unrecordably high, and she was diagnosed with sepsis and an infection in the foetal membrane. Five days after checking in to hospital with back pain, she was moved to the High Dependency Unit, where finally the doctors deemed it possible to order a termination. In the operating theatre, Savita spontaneously delivered a dead baby girl. Over the next two days, Savita's condition continued to worsen, and she died in agony, just over a week after checking in to hospital. While it is true that Savita died of septicaemia, a timely abortion would have saved her life. However, the doctors treating her were shackled in their treatment of her by the law. They could not even countenance a life-saving termination until Savita was in such dire health that it was too late.[8]

The Eighth Amendment has been the direct cause of some of the most heinous, inhumane and abhorrent decisions our courts have ever made. It has been the cause of tragedy, anguish and incalculable suffering, and it will continue to be so, every day, until it is entirely repealed.

Students' unions have been campaigning for choice for as long as the Eighth Amendment has been in place. Union members were active in the campaign against the Amendment in the first instance, and opposed it wholeheartedly once it was enacted. The unions were not alone in seeking to influence abortion access after 1983. The Society for the Protection of the Unborn Child (SPUC) took centre stage in litigation following the Eighth Amendment. SPUC was an avowedly anti-choice organisation which arose out of the Pro-Life Action Committee. It was essentially a group of lawyers who, according to one High Court judge, had 'assumed the self-appointed role of policing' the effects of the Eighth Amendment.[9]

SPUC sought to frustrate the student movement and its allies at every turn. SPUC is at the centre of the vast majority of the early litigation in the aftermath of the Eighth Amendment, and students' unions were their foil in arguably the most pivotal of those cases, *SPUC v Grogan*. Interestingly, that early litigation was not focused on the substantive right which the Eighth Amendment restricts – access to abortion in Ireland. Those cases came later, and are outlined above. Instead, the courts dealt with the right to travel for abortions, or, more specifically, the right to provide information about abortion clinics to women travelling to the UK or elsewhere. While I do not intend to forensically examine the so-called 'information cases', it is useful to give a brief overview of the facts, to contextualise the work of the students' unions at the time.

The first of these cases was *Attorney General (SPUC) v Open Door Counselling*. SPUC sought to shut down counselling services to women experiencing crisis pregnancies on the basis that they provided non-directive information about abortion clinics in the UK if their patients asked for it. They would also help to book flights and facilitate the journey, if necessary. SPUC argued that Article 40.3.3 restricted this activity, and that the counselling services were in breach of the Constitution. The Supreme Court agreed, and they were no longer permitted to refer patients to clinics, help with travel arrangements, or even provide the contact details of the clinics.

The *Open Door* case in the Supreme Court was a significant victory for SPUC, and very much framed the debate between SPUC and the student movement. At the time, the provision of contact details of clinics was the symbolic battleground, and the students' unions were ready to do battle. The first skirmish between SPUC and students arose in 1988, in *SPUC v Coogan*. At the time, UCDSU published a welfare guide with helpful information and tips on student welfare for the coming year. Included in that guide were the telephone numbers of abortion clinics in the UK. SPUC brought the students' union to the High Court, requesting that they not publish the information in the coming year. The High Court rejected their application, because SPUC had no standing to require UCDSU to do anything. In the Supreme Court, the students' union was less successful. The court rejected the idea that SPUC had no standing to take the case, on the basis that the courts should respond to any request that the right to life of the unborn be protected, if brought forward by a party with a legitimate interest. The Court looked at SPUC's track record and deemed them sufficiently legitimate as to have standing.[10]

Coogan did little more than set the stage for *SPUC v Grogan*, which is likely the most high-profile legal case a students' union has ever been a part of in Ireland. It ultimately progressed all the way to the European Court of Human Rights. Three students' unions were parties to the case: the Union of Students in Ireland (USI), UCDSU and TCDSU. In the aftermath of *Coogan*, SPUC sought an undertaking from the students that no pro-abortion information, or particularly the contact information of abortion clinics, be published in future welfare guides. When they failed to get that undertaking, SPUC went to the High Court to force the matter, and sought an injunction against the unions.[11]

SPUC v Grogan was drama of the highest order, played out on the national stage. At the centre of the case was Ivana Bacik, who later went on to serve in Seanad Éireann as a member of the Trinity panel of Senators, and as Leader of the Labour Party in the Seanad. She also became the Reid Professor of Criminal Law in Trinity – a position she holds to this day. At the time, she was a young, newly elected students' union president in Trinity College, and was taking a sabbatical year from her law degree to work for the students' union.

Shortly after SPUC's interim injunction was granted, newspaper reports began to surface accusing the student leaders, specifically Ivana, of continuing to circulate abortion clinic contact details. SPUC immediately demanded in the High Court that she and the other TCD students' union officers be jailed for contempt of a court injunction. Although officers of both USI and UCDSU were also parties to the proceedings, and subject to the injunction, it was only the four TCDSU officers threatened with jail. This was due to the fact that Trinity's Freshers' Week began a week earlier than UCD's, and so Bacik and her team began to distribute Freshers' packs, including the abortion information in question, before any of the other parties to the injunction.

The team of four sabbatical officers in Trinity knew that they were in grave danger of being committed to prison before they began to distribute the information. In fact, Mary Robinson, a Trinity Senator at the time, advised Bacik to pack a bag in readiness for her committal to Mountjoy Prison. The sabbatical team had agreed ahead of time that should they be deemed to be in breach of the court order, that they would risk a find of contempt of court and the consequent jail time – they had committed to standing over their principles, and spending as much time as was necessary behind bars. They knew by taking that stand, that they would expose themselves to personal financial liability, and risk bankruptcy. Four young students, on the cusps of their careers, were willing to stand against the might of SPUC and their allies, regardless of the personal toll it may have taken.

Such was the team's certainty that jail would be the outcome of any injunction hearing, that when word came to them that summons were on their way to the union offices in Trinity, they ran through the building in order to avoid being served the summons. Ultimately, the court servers were successful in their pursuit of the officers, and a hearing was set. Naturally, the mood in Trinity's students' union offices would have been extremely tense: the four officers were all in their early twenties, none had any previous experience of the penal system, and all four were facing jail for an indefinite period of time. At the time, Mountjoy was the prison for which they seemed destined. The potential jailing of four students' union sabbatical officers was in every newspaper, and a prison officer from the women's wing in Mountjoy took it upon herself to visit the sabbatical officers prior to their court date. The warning she gave Bacik was stark – prison conditions for young, vocal Trinity activists in Mountjoy would be uncomfortable, to say the very least.

Ultimately, Bacik and her team avoided jail. The High Court refused to hold the officers in contempt, on the basis that the submitted newspaper reports constituted hearsay, and hearsay is not sufficient grounds for imprisonment.

The case continued to the Supreme Court, which ruled in favour of SPUC. The position of the Court was that any assistance provided to women seeking abortions was in violation of Article 40.3.3, and repugnant to the Constitution. The Court granted an interlocutory injunction against the unions, banning the publication and distribution of any of the abortion clinic contact details that the unions had fought to protect.

SPUC v Grogan progressed to the European Courts, where two questions were essentially at play: was the provision of abortion a service under European Community law, and if so, could the ban on providing information about that service be considered a breach of Community law? The Court found that although abortion, when provided legally in a member state, did in fact constitute a service, the information ban at hand was too tenuous to be considered a restriction under European Community law. The result of this was a permanent injunction placed on the unions, banning all provision of abortion clinic details indefinitely. While *SPUC v Grogan* may be considered a loss for the student movement, it had huge impact. It inspired a new wave of students to engage with pro-choice campaigning, and very much set the stage for students' unions to lead the charge in the run-up to a Repeal referendum.

It is in this climate that student activists, and students' unions around the country, are now organising to fight the oppressive power of the Eighth Amendment, and to demand its complete repeal. The first step for any students' union before it can take any stance at all on an issue like Repeal is to secure a mandate from the students they represent. The last three years have seen students' unions around the country adopt overwhelmingly pro-Repeal positions. The majority of students' unions in universities and institutes of technology the length and breadth of Ireland have passed mandates, by referendum of all students, to support Repeal of the Eighth Amendment. There is not a single students' union across the country that has failed to pass a pro-choice referendum, or that are mandated to campaign against choice. In UCC, 84.4 per cent of students voted for the students' union to adopt a pro-choice position. In DCU, an incredible 88 per cent of students wanted the students' union to campaign for Repeal. The student movement, clearly, is united – the vast majority of students are ardently in favour of Repeal. Trinity is no different – in 2014, a referendum of all students saw a landslide 73 per cent mandate to campaign for pro-choice legislation returned.[12]

This unity is driven in no small part by the Union of Students in Ireland (USI). USI is Ireland's national students' union, and boasts a membership of well over 370,000 students from almost every higher education institution in Ireland. Trinity is a proud member, and we have learned a huge amount about pro-choice campaigning from the example of USI. The only notable institutions that are non-members of USI are UCD and the University of Limerick. The power of such a vast network of activists and student leaders shouldn't be underestimated, particularly when it comes to campaigning for social justice issues.

The power of such a well-organised national campaigning machine was never clearer than during the marriage equality campaign. USI did an excellent job of mobilising the student bodies in every college and university to campaign actively for a Yes vote. It is well documented that the youth vote played a pivotal part in the victory of the Yes Equality campaign, and without USI and the work of its dozens of member organisations, that campaign would have looked very different. USI placed significant emphasis on registering students to vote with the upcoming referendum in mind. It saw tremendous success – in Trinity alone we registered over 3,500 students that year, and over 27,000 students registered nationally. USI's enormous focus on voter registration during the marriage equality campaign has continued since: voter registration has become an annual feature of students' union work. The result of that voter registration drive is an engaged network of young people, still in college or recently graduated, who are registered and ready to vote. Over the past four years, we estimate that over 50,000 students have been registered. They are the same students who have overwhelmingly voted in support of Repeal in union referenda, and they will have their voices heard when the time comes to go to the national ballot box.

The campaign for marriage equality was hugely important for the student movement in Ireland, and USI particularly. Quite apart from voter registration, student voices were at the forefront of shaping the campaign itself. Laura Harmon, President of USI at the time, is widely seen as having been an instrumental force in the campaign, and the national student movement gained great credit for the success of the referendum. Ruairí McKiernan, writing in the *Huffington Post*, summed up the campaign by saying: 'Young people have been heroes in this.'[13] Politicians from across the spectrum were also quick to heap praise on the young people of Ireland in the aftermath of the referendum. The then Tánaiste Joan Burton said that 'the student movement can just be incredibly proud of what you have helped to achieve,'[14] while the then Minister of State for Equality, Aodhán Ó Ríordáin, said: 'I fundamentally believe that if it wasn't for what USI did from the beginning with the registration campaign, I don't think we would have had a public consciousness of the importance of getting registered to vote, the realisation that this referendum was coming, and the importance of it.'[15]

USI is doing all it can to prepare the national student body for a Repeal referendum: Students4Choice is USI's banner for all its Repeal activism. In 2012, USI joined Action on X, a campaign group at the time led by Ailbhe Smyth and Sinéad Kennedy, two figures who then established the Coalition to Repeal the Eighth Amendment.

Students4Choice has seen huge success. At the annual March for Choice in September 2017, organised by the Abortion Rights Campaign, over 1,000 students from all over the country gathered in Trinity's Front Square before joining the march. Speaking to the crowd, Síona Cahill, then USI Deputy President, said 'this isn't political theory … this isn't philosophical debate or an argument to be won or lost – this is about real people, with real, hard choices, and we respect and trust them to make those decisions', and that 'choice is the middle ground' when it came to the growing activism by students around reproductive rights over the preceding two decades.[16]

In autumn 2016, USI, along with numerous students' unions and college societies, submitted a detailed document to the work of the Citizens' Assembly, which was created to look at the Eighth Amendment of the Irish Constitution, and to make recommendations on whether a referendum should be put to the public on the issue. Following on from this submission, USI was selected to present to the Citizens' Assembly in March 2017. Annie Hoey, then President of USI, highlighted why access to abortion services and adequate reproductive health care services are a student issue, while also highlighting the long, and often illegal, history of the student movement campaign in fighting for reproductive rights. In her speech, Hoey declared:

> 'There are many students who are members of students for choice for whom never personally want to access abortion services, But they vehemently believe that the choice should still remain for Irish women .... They do not believe that a person's womb should be governed by the constitution.'[17]

She then called on the Citizens' Assembly to recommend a referendum to repeal the Eighth Amendment.

Individual students' unions have also committed significant resources and energy to the upcoming campaign. In Trinity, Repeal is the union's number one priority this year. If you were to walk through any part of Trinity, you would inevitably see someone wearing a Repeal jumper. We are placing a huge emphasis on training our students so that they can contribute meaningfully and powerfully to the national campaign, just as we did during marriage equality. We are also working to educate and activate sections of the student community who wouldn't automatically engage with pro-choice activism, by bringing the conversation to them, and ensuring that Repeal is a central part of the college psyche. Trinity played a central role in the Strike4Repeal, which took place on International Women's Day (8 March) in 2017. Thousands of people, both students and others, took to the streets to voice their fundamental abhorrence of our laws as they stand. Trinity students covered windows and statues in black bags and the iconic Strike logo was to be seen everywhere. The atmosphere throughout the university was electric, and there was a palpable sense of fury throughout the corridors and across the cobblestones, which has not abated.

In many ways, the Ireland of 2018 is a fundamentally different one to the Ireland that allowed Ann Lovett to die alone all those years ago. We have cast aside our slavish devotion to the arbitrary diktats of the Catholic Church. We have never been more open and healthy in our attitudes to sex and feminism, and we are, in many respects, able to measure up to our European and democratic neighbours in social justice and equality. Many of those hard-fought gains can be traced back to the influence of the student movement, and it is progress of which we are extremely proud. There is, however, a black mark on our progress. We can never truly take our place as an open, progressive and equal European country as long as the Eighth Amendment persists. We can never be proud to call ourselves Irish, as long as we exile half our population overseas to abortion clinics in the

UK. The student movement has had enough. We are preparing for a referendum. We are training, and educating ourselves. We are ready to once more usher in a new era of social equality into Ireland, and we will not be stopped.

We must Repeal the Eighth.

References

A. and B. v EHB and C. [1997] IEHC 176.

Attorney General v X [1992], IESC 1.

Baker, Sinéad (2015) 'Students Played a Decisive Role in Achieving Marriage Equality, USI Hears', *University Times*, 28 May.

Baker, Sinéad (2017) 'Addressing the Citizens' Assembly, USI Calls for Repeal of Eighth Amendment', *University Times*, 5 March.

Enright, Máiréad (2012) 'Savita Halappanavar: Ireland, Abortion and the Politics of Death and Grief', *Human Rights in Ireland*, 14 November, http://humanrights.ie/gender-sexuality-and-the-law/savita-halappanavar-ireland-abortion-and-the-politics-of-death-and-grief/.

Hesketh, Tom (1990) *The Second Partitioning of Ireland? The Abortion Referendum of 1983*, Dublin: Brandsma Books.

Holland, Kitty (2014) 'Timeline of the Ms Y Case', *Irish Times*, 4 October.

Ingle, Róisín (2017) 'The Ann Lovett Letters: Sorrow, Shame, Anger and Indignation', *Irish Times*, 31 January.

Kingston, James, Anthony Whelan and Ivana Bacik (1997) *Abortion and the Law*, Dublin: Round Hall, Sweet and Maxwell.

McGrath, Dominic and Kathleen McNamee (2017) 'Students Join 30,000 on Dublin's Streets, Calling for Repeal', *University Times*, 30 September.

McKiernan, Ruairi (2015) 'A New Ireland Has Been Born', *Huffington Post*, 26 May, www.huffingtonpost.com/ruairi-mckiernan/ireland-shakes-off-shackl_b_7427264.html

O'Carroll, Sinead (2012) 'Twenty Years On: A Timeline of the X Case', *TheJournal.ie*, 6 February, www.thejournal.ie/twenty-years-on-a-timeline-of-the-x-case-347359-Feb2012/.

O'Toole, Fintan (2014) 'Why Ireland Became the Only Country in the Democratic World to Have a Constitutional Ban on Abortion', *Irish Times*, 26 August.

Union of Students in Ireland (2017) *Paper of the Union of Students in Ireland (USI) Delivered to the Citizens' Assembly*, 5 March, www.citizensassembly.ie/en/Meetings/Union-of-Students-in-Ireland-s-Paper.pdf.

Endnotes

1   O'Toole (2014).
2   Hesketh (1990).
3   Ingle (2017).

4   *Attorney General v X* [1992].
5   O'Carroll (2012).
6   *A. and B. v EHB and C.* [1997].
7   Holland (2014).
8   Enright (2012).
9   Kingston, Whelan and Bacik (1997).
10   *Ibid.*
11   *Ibid.*
12   Union of Students in Ireland (2017).
13   McKiernan (2015).
14   Baker (2015).
15   *Ibid.*
16   McGrath and McNamee (2017).
17   Baker (2017).

One Hundred Years After the Rising We Must Offer Women a Better Answer than Abortion

Niamh Uí Bhriain

When my first child was born, I remember my mother touching my daughter on her soft, tiny newborn head and whispering in the quiet of the hospital ward that she was such a miracle. And she was, not because anything especially out of the ordinary had happened that October day, but because every human being is an everyday miracle.

I don't mean that in a particularly religious sense, because people of all faiths and none understand the sense of awe that is invoked when a new life is brought into the world. There's that last Earth-shattering push as the whole world holds its breath, and then she is in your arms, both of you in tears now at the intensity of it all, at the feeling that nothing this incredible could surely ever have happened before.

It is profound, and extraordinary, and altogether beautiful, and it's how we all came to be. Every person on this earth knew the darkness and warmth of our mother's womb before we emerged to find our unsteady way in the world.

It is, as Kavanagh wrote, the wonder we find 'wherever life pours ordinary plenty', but now we know that the deep connections we make in those first nine months are more remarkable and intense than we ever might have previously imagined.

Recently I learned that during pregnancy cells from the baby stray across the placenta into the mother's bloodstream, and scientists now believe those cells may later be called into service to treat damage to the mother's heart, brain, liver or other organs.[1]

It's as if baby is giving back: a thank you for the morning sickness, and the swollen feet, and the trials of childbirth. A thank you for doing what only a woman can do – carry a child under her heart for the first nine months of life, in a complex, awe-inspiring, truly remarkable partnership which enters a new chapter at birth. It's mind-blowing really, like the stuff of science fiction.

The bond between mother and baby is not just physical or psychological; it's a deep biological connection, a synergy of love and protection.

We're living at a time when our life before birth has never been so well observed, yet it's all too easy to forget our own beginnings in this never-ending debate on abortion, this debate that is hurtling Ireland towards a vote where we will decide which child may live and which child can be killed.

It's easy to forget what every schoolchild now knows: that when you were just three weeks old, for example, your heart began to beat. It was a rudimentary tube, but your pulse was fast, like horses at gallop, and it was determined too: resolute, like all human life, to stay the course, to exist, to remain alive. You were tiny then, of course, we all were, but you were indisputably still you, infinitely more vulnerable, but with incredible, intricate developments rapidly bringing you towards further formation and birth. Of course, the amazing development of the baby in the womb has been known for a long time now – longer than I've been alive – and it always seems odd to me that we can know something to be true and deny it at the same time.

So we are living in a time when we know more than ever about the humanity of the child in the womb – yet millions of preborn babies are aborted every year. How can we live with this cognitive dissonance, where we marvel at the cuteness of a baby captured in an ultrasound, while holding that the same child can be aborted if she is inconvenient or sick or might live in poverty?

Where we say it's a baby when it's a wanted pregnancy, and a disposable foetus when it's not. Where we deny the hurt and harm and heartbreak abortion causes to women even when we see it before our very eyes. Where we believe we can vote to take away the right to life of another human being, on the basis that they are smaller and weaker and more helpless than ourselves.

This is not how a compassionate, progressive society is meant to function. We are obliged to recognise that our human rights belong to us by the very virtue of the fact that we are human. Human rights should be written in stone. Otherwise we can decide that some human beings are less worthy of human rights than others, and that, we should know by now, can bring horrifying consequences. History shows that we are well capable of inflicting the most terrible cruelties on other people under the pretence that they are less human than ourselves. History also has a habit of repeating itself.

Denying the very obvious humanity of the preborn child is a ploy often used to justify abortion. But the truth is, abortion denies the humanity of both mother and baby. Let's be honest here: deep down most of us know that abortion doesn't empower women, and it especially doesn't empower those women who are driven to the abortion clinic by fear and panic. We are failing women when we tell them that they are free to choose abortion. What we are really saying is that we have washed our hands of the problem, and washed our hands too of any regret or sorrow or pain that follows, since granting the freedom to choose also absolves us of any responsibility for that choice.

Think about that, if you will, for a moment. We might pretend to ourselves that we are giving women their 'right to choose' but are we really telling them that they're on their own?

Are we telling them they *have* to choose, that it's all on them: the decision, the anguish, the abortion itself, the dreadful physical reality of what all that means. How is that progress? How is that advancing women's best interests or shaping a better society?

It's much harder, isn't it, to actually help women than to tell them they can have an abortion? The irony is that those who are campaigning for a woman's right to choose haven't provided women with the assistance they need. Pregnancy help centres have always been powered by pro-life people, whose help usually goes well beyond the initial counselling and practical support that is essential in many of these cases.

Sometimes that means being a birthing partner for a woman who has no one else to accompany her into the hospital, or collecting furniture or a pram or nappies and clothes when mother and baby need help after birth. Sometimes it means helping to find accommodation, or seeking mental health support, or simply being a shoulder to cry on. Sometimes that support continues long after baby is born, not just because it should, but because deep and lasting friendships are formed.

In my 25 years of working on this issue, there is one thing that everyone who has been in this situation agrees on: no mother ever regrets her child. In contrast, a lifetime of regret will not bring back your child, and for many women that reality brings real pain.

Imagine, if you will, what supports could be provided if all the energy spent on demanding legalised abortion was poured into actually helping women, into providing a better answer than abortion? It would make for a better world.

Why is too much to ask that we seek positive, life-affirming options instead of pushing women towards abortion and all the darkness and sadness and loss that involves? Some of the richest people in the world, like the investor Warren Buffett, have given tens of millions to funds which pay for poor women to have abortions. Why not spend that in helping women build a future for themselves and their babies?

Women are stronger and braver than what the abortion industry would have us believe. We have the courage to love, despite the expectations or judgements of society. Feminists for Life urge us to 'terminate the crisis, and not the child'. I think that's a worthy aspiration.

Aren't mentoring programmes that help young women to finish school or college while also raising their baby better than abortion clinics who demand upfront payments for ending that baby's life? Isn't it better to empower women so that they can raise their children without fear, instead of letting the abortion industry exploit them for profit?

Why aren't we challenging men to grow up and man up, to accept some responsibilities instead of just walking away and leaving women with the 'right to choose' when very often there is no freedom of choice involved at all, just an abandonment of responsibility which drives women towards abortion.

Abortion is a gift to feckless, careless, selfish men, the kind who think they are being decent if they offer to pay for an abortion – and who think they have the right to feel aggrieved if they are 'forced' to become a father, something they became once that baby was conceived. Studies suggest that a majority of women feel coercion when undergoing an abortion, something I have heard from women repeatedly. Fear of an angry parent, a boyfriend who'll walk, of losing your job, of living in poverty; all these factors and more make abortion the opposite of a 'free choice'.[2] Any suggestion that women are pushed into undergoing an abortion is always robustly denied by campaigners, but the facts speak for themselves.

Look at Marie Stopes, one of the UK's largest abortion chains, which is in receipt of tens of millions of pounds from the British taxpayer each year. In 2016, inspections carried out by the Care Quality Commission for the Department of Health found that practices at the clinics were so shoddy that women's lives were endangered by lack of staff training and falsified safety checks. Perhaps the most shocking revelation concerned a case wherein workers at one clinic performed an abortion on a woman with severe learning disabilities who did not fully understand what was being done to her.[3]

Almost a year later, the Care Quality Commission reported something else about Marie Stopes that made it very clear that abortion is an industry which sells abortion assiduously, not to help women, but to exploit them. The inspectors reported that Marie Stopes' staff – in all 70 clinics across the country – were 'encouraged' to ensure women had abortions because this was 'linked to their performance bonus'. Staff were actually told to phone women who had decided against having an abortion and offer them another appointment. Furthermore, if parents or partners accompanied a woman who had changed her mind, they were seen by the abortion clinic as an 'inconvenience' and 'their presence strongly discouraged', according to the inspectors.[4]

I found this all desperately sad, but the Irish media completely ignored the inspectorate's findings, even though Marie Stopes operates a referral centre in Dublin. It seems as if women don't have the right to be informed when that information might interfere with the relentless media narrative that abortion is a service which assists women.

The Irish edition of the London *Times*, for example, obsessively focuses on the Irish abortion debate, often inflating scraps of information into breathless headlines, and reporting almost exclusively in a way that favours pro-abortion campaigners. However, there was a curious silence from the newspaper on the reports revealing that Marie Stopes was paying bonuses to staff to push abortions, or that the clinic had recorded almost 400 botched abortions.

We don't have Marie Stopes abortion clinics in Ireland because of the Eighth Amendment, which protects the right to life of both mother and baby. We don't have Britain's abortion rate either. In Britain one in every five babies are aborted. The repeat abortion rate is 40 per cent.[5] The reality of the British *Abortion Act* can only be described as carnage. Little wonder that David Steele, the architect of the 1967 Act, recently remarked that he 'never envisaged there would be so many abortions'.[6]

Law changes culture, and a culture that regards human life as disposable becomes adept at ignoring the shocking realities that naturally follow. You could argue that the Eighth Amendment also helped to change the culture; that it demanded we, as a society, provide a better alternative than abortion. All the spin in the world can't change the fact that our abortion rates are much lower than in jurisdictions where abortion is legal. As previously noted, one in every five babies is aborted in Britain, and pretty similar rates are seen across Europe. In Ireland our abortion rate is estimated at around one in twenty. In 2016, for example, there were 63,897 births in Ireland and 3,265 women travelled for an abortion. That means that one in twenty babies were aborted – a quarter of the British abortion rate.[7]

In fact, the Irish abortion rate has fallen from some 7,000 to 3,500 annually in the past 12 years – a 50 per cent decline – which surely is a most welcome development, though it's noticeable that abortion campaigners have never, ever welcomed the steady fall.[8] (Instead they try to claim that thousands of women are accessing abortion pills online, but the fall in our abortion rate began years before the pills began to be pushed online, and clearly those selling the abortion pills have a vested interest in exaggerating the demand. What is truly extraordinary is that elected representatives such as Ruth Coppinger were happy to illegally distribute abortion pills, despite warnings from the master of the Rotunda Hospital that women could die as a result of taking the pills without medical supervision. So much for keeping women safe.)

If Ireland had Britain's model of abortion – and that country's abortion rate of 20 per cent – some 13,500 babies would have been aborted in 2016. An additional 10,000 abortions would have taken place. Surely no reasonable person wants more abortions? It seems to me that only a troubled and disturbing ideology would welcome an additional 10,000 babies being aborted every year.

Law changes culture. It also either saves lives, or leads to many, many lives being taken. The Eighth has meant fewer abortions, and hundreds of thousands of people owe their lives to the law that spelled out the obvious – both mother and baby can and should be protected. That's a lot of lives saved. These are real people, in your GAA club, at school with your kids, on the bus next to you, at the desk beside you in work. None of them, I guarantee you, regret that they are alive. No one regrets that they were not aborted.

That's not to say that carrying a child is always easy, and sometimes where there should be joy there can be fear and panic and unthinkable sorrow. The question facing Ireland right now is what we do to help when things can seem unbearably hard? Do we find a better answer than abortion, do we offer genuine help and support to women and families who face the most difficult circumstances possible? Or do we just follow the failure of Britain and other countries where preborn babies have become utterly disposable, and where women are failed by the contraction of compassion which abortion always brings?

Sometimes I feel that, while there is much lip service given to trusting women, women who want to speak out on this issue are shouted down if they are the wrong kind of feminist – or the wrong kind of strong, feisty opinionated woman. Recently we saw that abortion campaigners in Ireland were willing to shout down rape survivors who wanted to speak publicly about why their experiences had led them to believe that abortion was not the answer.[9] Some of the People Before Profit activists who tore down the rape survivors' posters and threatened the hotel where the women were to speak might have the excuse of being young and foolish, but their TDs in the Dáil have no such defence. Their silence told us all we need to know about their respect for women, and for rape victims in particular.

If they had listened to women like Shauna Prewitt and Jennifer Christie, who became pregnant after rape, they might have learned that these women were told by almost everyone that abortion was their best option. They refused that option because, they said, abortion would not heal their trauma, and because their babies were innocent too. Their courage is inspiring; the insights they shared opened up that crack that Leonard Cohen talked about that lets the light in.[10]

There are other very difficult circumstances. What do we do when baby has a severe life-limiting condition, and may not live for long after birth? Maybe we should start by listening to families who received this diagnosis, to the mothers and fathers who felt their babies alive and kicking even as abortion was the first suggestion made by medics who equate a disability that can't be cured with a life not worth living.

Read the stories on the website of Every Life Counts.[11] See the parents who, in response to the misleading and offensive claim that their babies were 'incompatible with life', replied that they were 'compatible with love' – such a beautiful response from mothers and fathers who know that however severe the diagnosis, their babies' lives are precious and important and have value.

They want other parents to learn how to pour 'a lifetime of love into those hours or days after birth', and how to understand that as long as baby is safe and warm in the womb that time is part of their life together. 'We had nine months together, and we had singsongs, and walked in the park, and listened to the birds, and he was warm and snug and safe inside me and he knew he was so loved', Fiona says about her baby, Andrew, who lived for 27 hours after birth with anencephaly. 'He is carved in my heart forever.'[12]

These are parents who know that, although loss and pain and grief will come, the time shared with baby can also bring joy and love and memory-making and healing. The media wants you to think of these babies as 'fatal abnormalities' or 'doomed pregnancies', but to their parents they are simply their children: children who fought to come to say hello and goodbye, children who deserved a chance, children who were beautiful and important and loved. What strikes me most in knowing so many of these families is that they are so proud of their babies, whose brief lives touched so many people so deeply. One example is Tanya Coonan, who spoke about her daughter Lillie:

> I am so blessed to have carried her and held her and to know that we wrapped her in love for her short life, before and after birth. In a recovery room, I held my daughter and I smiled at her beautiful baby face and kissed her warm, soft cheek and held her tiny little hand. If abortion had ended her life before birth, I would have never received all the gifts Lillie gave to me. She showed me that even the most striking imperfections are beautiful, and she was so beautiful. I'm so proud of her that she fought to come and say hello and goodbye to us.[13]

'All she could feel was me loving her. She was fine and happy and snug where she was. Her life wasn't mine to end. Abortion would have robbed me of that time with my baby' says Vicky Wall about her daughter Líadán.[14]

'If our love could have saved you, you would have lived for ever' is transcribed on Líadán's grave. A little girl gone too soon, but who knew only love in her short life, something very few of us can claim.

It's interesting to note that where good care is given, the vast majority of Irish parents in these circumstances don't look for an abortion. One study from Cork University Maternity Hospital which looked at all pregnancies where babies were diagnosed with Trisomy 13 or Trisomy 18 from 2001 to 2012 found that between 94 per cent and 96 per cent of parents did not abort their baby.[15]

The natural fear and distress that parents feel at this time is horribly manipulated by campaigners – and by the media – who not only do all they can to dehumanise the baby, but also deliberately misinform families. We often hear, for example, that these babies will suffer before or after birth, when it's a medical fact that none of these conditions cause babies to suffer in the womb, and any discomfort afterwards is managed with proper medical and palliative care.

Parents can be misled by medical professionals too, who often suggest abortion repeatedly and do not seem to understand the value of these babies' lives. Dr Fergal Malone, speaking at the Joint Oireachtas Committee on the Eighth Amendment, suggested that parents are told that 'their baby has no head' when a diagnosis of anencephaly is made.[16] These horrifying and misleading words would certainly nudge parents towards abortion.

A 2017 Newstalk radio discussion around babies diagnosed with Trisomy 18 (Edwards syndrome) heard the presenter make the claim that children born with a 'fatal foetal abnormality' would be 'in extreme pain' and stating: 'the terrible quality of that short life, isn't that cruel to the child?'.[17] The presenter was obviously unaware of the research published in *Pediatrics* (2012) which showed that 97 per cent of parents of children diagnosed with Trisomy 13 or 18 reported that their child was happy, with similar numbers saying their child enriched their lives, however long the child's life was.[18]

He was also likely unacquainted with the 2016 editorial in the *Journal of the American Medical Association* by Dr John Lantos, a paediatrician and leading expert in medical ethics, which pointed out that babies with these conditions used to be described as 'incompatible with life', but 'in the age of social media, however, everything changed.' He wrote that 'Parents share stories and videos, showing their happy 4- and 5-year-old children with these conditions. Survival, it turns out, is not as rare as once thought.'[19]

Dr Lantos noted that 'predictions of lethality become self-fulfilling prophecies' and says that:

The concept of quality of life is too vague and subjective to be helpful as a criterion for deciding about the appropriateness of treatment. No one can know with certainty what any infant is thinking, feeling, or experiencing, but what is observed can be interpreted. Children with trisomy 13 and 18 smile and laugh. They are not in pain. They give and receive love. These factors suggest that their subjective quality of life is not so poor that life-prolonging treatment should not be offered.[20]

Now, maybe it's unfair to expect radio presenters to keep abreast of medical research, and RTÉ and other media outlets have been equally misleading in regard to the medical facts around life-limiting conditions. However, you would expect, at the very least, that when the programme had been informed as to how misleading and incorrect it had been, they would abide by the code of broadcasting ethics and move to correct the misinformation. Newstalk didn't do so, and most media outlets in Ireland consistently fail to do so. When it comes to abortion the facts don't seem to matter much, and the media are part and parcel of the well-funded campaign pushing to legalise abortion in Ireland.

However, we're seeing that public opinion is shifting, and becoming increasingly pro-life in regard to protecting preborn children with a disability. Recent polls show there has been a significant fall in support for abortion on disability grounds,[21] something entirely due to the great courage shown by people with disabilities and their families whose inspirational personal stories have clearly struck a chord with the public, as has their message that abortion is the very worst form of discrimination. Parents like Anne Trainer, who wrote powerfully in the mainstream media about her son Kevin, and about the protection offered by the Eighth:

I believe the debate on the Eighth Amendment needs to hear from families like mine. People like Kevin are not here just to give us warm and cosy feelings during the Special Olympics. Their lives matter. Their human right to life matters. Children like Kevin are facing extinction in other countries.

So the question is – will Ireland choose a better path, a path of compassion and love and understanding? A path where we help families to love and raise their children, rather than eliminating people with Down Syndrome before they are born.

I believe we can. The Eighth Amendment protected my son, and he was deserving of that protection. It should remain as a shining light to a world where the best and most beautiful of our citizens are being snuffed out.[22]

These are heroic parents who have been forced by the cruelty in this debate to speak up to say that, yes, their children have a right to life, whatever their disabilities. They bring to mind those other heroes who in 1916 called on the Irish people to protect all of the children of the nation, without exclusion.

When the leaders of the Rising proclaimed a republic they envisaged it as a nation where, in the words of the Proclamation, all the children of the nation would be cherished equally. I'm well aware of the relevance regarding the different traditions on the island, but it's important to remember that the Proclamation and the Rising were underpinned by an inspiring belief in fairness and equality. The Rising was about establishing an Ireland for a people who were not just free themselves, but where the freedoms of others were also protected. A people who had for centuries suffered loss and displacement and discrimination would not deprive helpless children of their right to be born, of the right to have a chance at life.

Pádraig Pearse wrote of a dream that that was built in the heart, and that only the heart can hold. Pearse, who challenged an empire, and who proclaimed our freedom; Pearse, who wrote that law could not be stronger than life or than men's desire to be free; Pearse, I believe, would be a leader today in this historical movement to demand a better answer than abortion, just as would all those who knew that a nation that kills its own children is a nation that cannot endure.

I believe that to be true because the writings and the actions of the leaders of the Rising contain an idealism and an honesty that is very far removed from the weasel words that have constructed an entirely false debate around the issue of abortion today. Behind those weasel words is the truth abortion campaigners wish to hide: that abortion dismembers preborn children who are alive and kicking in the womb – and it is the aim of said campaigners to make this appalling violence legal through all nine months of pregnancy.

Their message is one of despair defeating hope, of cruelty replacing compassion, of fear being allowed to conquer love. There is no desire for real solidarity, or sacrifice, or a coming together of people to find a better answer. There is only the demand to be rid of the child instead of really helping women. Their vision is clearly not of a nation which cherishes all the children of the nation equally.

I do not believe that James Connolly, who was all too familiar with the grinding poverty so many people of that time endured, would support the private-school educated socialists of today in their demand for abortion on socioeconomic grounds. It was evident that the rebels sought a radical departure from a government and culture that was being imposed on the nation. A pressing priority for them was to improve the conditions and lives of ordinary

Irish people, and also to establish an Ireland that was, as Pearse said, not free merely but Gaelic as well, not Gaelic merely but free as well.

That radical departure – that desire to be true to our own nature and identity, rather than accept a culture imposed upon us – is a reminder that the Rising helped to gain us the right to determine and to shape our own laws, our culture and our identity. The heroes of 1916 knew that real freedom is not built in trampling on the rights of the most helpless and vulnerable of all.

Their sacrifice should be a challenge to us to take a bold and radical stand by rejecting the abortion culture which has been accepted by other countries. We can determine that there is nothing progressive or compassionate about abortion, and offer the world a better vision: a society where life is valued and protected.

At this time, we are called, as a nation, to have the courage to cherish all the children of the nation equally, and to see abortion for what it really is – a failure to love and care for our mothers and our babies. Our rebellion should be against the political and media elites, and against the wealthy international abortion industry. It should be a rebellion of the people for the people, where we stand, in the spirit of the Proclamation, for the right to life of every child.

Of course, the push for abortion in Ireland is sponsored to the hilt by powerful, wealthy international abortion funders – with millions coming from billionaires like George Soros and Chuck Feeney to fund abortion campaigners. It's what the Proclamation might have described as an attempt to usurp the sovereign right of the Irish nation by a foreign people and government. Yet our own government, also channelling millions into pro-Repeal the Eighth groups, is riddled with inconsistencies.

We have a Minister for Children, Katherine Zappone, who is constantly arguing that children who are not yet born can be aborted, even though our Constitution recognises the right to life of these children. We also have a Minister for Disability Issues who doesn't seem to have an issue with the tragic reality that, where abortion is legalised, it is being used to eradicate people with Down syndrome before birth.

Our Minister for Health, Simon Harris, says that we should repeal the right to life of preborn babies because Ireland has been found to be a 'cold, neglectful and lonely' place for women with crisis pregnancies.[23] Surely you would expect the Minister then to make progressive and compassionate supports available for women? Instead, his party has presided over savage cuts to single-parent families, including the exclusion of support once children reached the age of seven, a truly heartless measure which, according to a recent report from Indecon Economic Consultants, drove many families into poverty.[24]

It seems to me that it is the cruelty of these and other policies inflicted by successive governments that makes Ireland a cold, neglectful and lonely place for many people, but the Minister seems to be suggesting that we solve this by ending the lives of some of our citizens before they are born. The Eighth Amendment protects both mother and baby. The government should do the same, unless Minister Harris sees abortion as another cost-cutting exercise.

There are very likely those on the right who do have the unspoken view that abortion is a means of reducing the cost to the taxpayer in terms of medical costs or services or welfare costs. It's an abhorrent view, but the irony is that it is almost mirrored in the mantra of those supposedly on the left who argue that abortion needs to be legalised, in particular, to give poorer women access to abortion clinics. It is ludicrous that this needs to be spelled out, but abortion is not a solution to poverty: education, equality of opportunity, fairness and justice are. Are these people seriously saying that babies being born to disadvantaged women are better off dead? It's the worst form of discrimination, and it comes as no surprise that abortion chains like Planned Parenthood in the US disproportionately operate in poor and minority areas. In New York, more black babies are aborted than born now, at a rate of 55 per cent, a deeply shocking and troubling statistic that is rarely discussed.[25]

This brings us to the question as to what kind of a country do we want? One that's fair and equitable, where decency holds sway, where we adhere to the maxim that we should 'first do no harm'? Or one where the most vulnerable amongst us are not protected? One where all the children are cherished equally, or where some are killed before birth because we have voted to strip the most helpless of all our children of their basic human right to life?

Would we have a vote on the right-to-life of Simon Harris? Or Leo Varadkar? Or any of the belligerent abortion campaigners who are shouting that the foetus should have no rights until it is born? Of course not, the thought is preposterous, yet we will shortly vote on whether some children can live and some can be killed. I have never been able to understand the mindset that argues that when we are most vulnerable we should be least protected. But it is easy to be pro-choice, isn't it, when you are not the one being chosen?

REFERENCES

Biggs, M. Antonia, Heather Gould and Diana Greene Foster (2013) 'Understanding Why Women Seek Abortions in the US', *BMC Women's Health*, Vol. 13, p. 29.

Care Quality Commission (2016) 'CQC Publishes Inspection Reports on Marie Stopes International', *Care Quality Commission*, 20 December, www.cqc.org.uk/news/releases/cqc-publishes-inspection-reports-marie-stopes-international.

Care Quality Commission (2017) *Marie Stopes International Maidstone Centre Quality Report*, 2 October, www.cqc.org.uk/sites/default/files/new_reports/AAAF4825.pdf.

Central Statistics Office (2017) 'Vital Statistics Yearly Summary: 2016', *Central Statistics Office*, 31 May, www.cso.ie/en/releasesandpublications/ep/p-vsys/vitalstatistics yearlysummary2016/.

Christie, Jennifer (n.d.) 'Jennifer Christie', *Unbroken Ireland*, https://unbrokenireland. org/stories/jen-christie/.

Coghlan, Andy (2011) 'Fetus Donates Stem Cells to Heal Mother's Heart', *New Scientist*, 21 November, www.newscientist.com/article/dn21185-fetus-donates-stem-cells-to-heal-mothers-heart/.

Coonan, Tanya (2016) 'Stop Cruel Attacks on Mums Like Me – Who Choose to Give Birth to a Baby Who Can't Survive', *Irish Independent*, 30 November, www. independent.ie/opinion/comment/stop-cruel-attacks-on-mums-like-me-who-choose-to-give-birth-to-a-baby-who-cant-survive-35256257.html.

Coonan, Tanya (n.d.) 'Lillie Coonon', *Every Life Counts*, www.everylifecounts.ie/stories/lillie-coonan/.

Department of Health (New York State) (2015) 'Table 23: Induced Abortion and Abortion Ratios by Race/Ethnicity and Resident County New York State – 2013', *Department of Health (New York State)*, February, www.health.ny.gov/statistics/vital_statistics/2013/table23.htm.

Department of Health (UK) (2017) 'Report on Abortion Statistics in England and Wales for 2016', *Gov.uk*, 13 June, www.gov.uk/government/statistics/report-on-abortion-statistics-in-england-and-wales-for-2016.

Dungarvan Leader (2018) '"Abortion Would Have Robbed Me of Time with My Baby" Dungarvan Woman to Tell Pro-Life Meeting', *Dungarvan Leader*, 26 January.

Fiona (n.d.) 'Little Andrew', *Every Life Counts*, www.everylifecounts.ie/stories/little-andrew/.

Health Service Executive (2017) 'Over 50% Decrease in the Number of Women Giving Irish Addresses at Abortion Clinics in England and Wales', *Health Service Executive*, 13 June, www.hse.ie/eng/services/news/media/pressrel/over-50-decrease-in-the-number-of-women-giving-irish-addresses-at-abortion-clinics-in-england-and-wales-.html.

Houlihan, Orla A. and Keelin O'Donoghue (2013) 'The Natural History of Pregnancies with a Diagnosis of Trisomy 18 or Trisomy 13; A Retrospective Case Series', *BMC Pregnancy & Childbirth*, Vol. 13, pp. 209–218.

Indecon Economic Consultants (2017) *Indecon Independent Review of the Amendments to the One-Parent Family Payment since January 2012*, Presented to the Department of Employment Affairs and Social Protection, 4 October, www.welfare.ie/en/downloads/DEASP_OFP_Review.pdf.

Irish Times (2017a) 'The *Irish Times* Poll', *Irish Times*, 26 May, www.irishtimes.com/news/politics/poll/poll-may-26th-2017.

Irish Times (2017b) 'Ipsos MRBI Poll: Abortion, Voters and Nuance', *Irish Times*, 27 May, www.irishtimes.com/opinion/editorial/ipsos-mrbi-poll-abortion-voters-and-nuance-1.3097371.

Janvier, Annie, Barbara Farlow and Benjamin S. Wilfond (2012) 'The Experience of Families with Children with Trisomy 13 and 18 in Social Networks', *Pediatrics*, Vol. 130, No. 2, pp. 293–298, http://pediatrics.aappublications.org/content/early/2012/07/18/peds.2012-0151..info.

Lantos, John D. (2016) 'Trisomy 13 and 18—Treatment Decisions in a Stable Gray Zone', *Journal of the American Medical Association*, Vol. 316, No. 4, pp. 396–398.

Mahony, Rhona and Fergal Malone (2017) 'Health Care Issues Arising from the Citizens' Assembly Recommendations: Masters of the National Maternity Hospital, Holles Street and the Rotunda Hospital', Submission to the Joint Oireachtas Committee on the Eighth Amendment, 11 October, https://beta.oireachtas.ie/en/debates/debate/joint_committee_on_the_eighth_amendment_of_the_constitution/2017-10-11/3/.

Newstalk (2017) 'Tim Jackson on Moncrieff', *YouTube*, 19 September, www.youtube.com/watch?v=lwKxDNfnQyA.

Nolan, Sean (2017) 'People Before Profit Group Defend Removing Posters Advertising Pro-Life Event in Dublin', *Irish Independent*, 28 September.

O'Doherty, Gemma (2012) 'UK Peer Warns on Suicide Clause', *Irish Independent*, 21 December, www.independent.ie/irish-news/uk-peer-warns-on-suicide-clause-28950172.html.

O'Halloran, Marie (2017) 'Ireland "Cold, Neglectful, Lonely" for Women in Crisis Pregnancy', *Irish Times*, 11 November, www.irishtimes.com/news/politics/ireland-cold-neglectful-lonely-for-women-in-crisis-pregnancy-1.3288866.

Prewitt, Shauna (2017) 'Shauna Prewitt', *Unbroken Ireland*, https://unbrokenireland.org/stories/shauna-prewitt/.

Pritchard, Stephanie and Diana W. Bianchi (2012) 'Fetal Cell Microchimerism in the Maternal Heart: Baby Gives Back', *Circulation Research*, Vol. 110, No. 1, pp. 3–5.

Rue, Vincent M., Priscilla K. Coleman, James J. Rue and David C. Reardon (2004) 'Induced Abortion and Traumatic Stress: A Preliminary Comparison of American and Russian Women', *Medical Science Monitor*, Vol. 10, No. 10, pp. SR5–16.

Trainer, Anne (2017) '"Abortion Is Leading Us to a 'Down's Syndrome-Free' World. I Can Barely Type the Words"', *TheJournal.ie*, 4 February, www.thejournal.ie/readme/the-eighth-amendment-protected-my-son-3217231-Feb2017/.

Wall, Vicky (n.d.) 'Líadán Curran Wall', *Every Life Counts*, www.everylifecounts.ie/stories/ladn-curran-wall/.

ENDNOTES

[1]   Coghlan (2011); Pritchard and Bianchi (2012).
[2]   Rue, Coleman, Rue and Reardon (2004); Biggs, Gould and Greene Foster (2013).
[3]   Care Quality Commission (2016).

4   Care Quality Commission (2017).
5   Department of Health (UK) (2017).
6   O'Doherty (2012).
7   Health Service Executive (2017); Central Statistics Office (2017).
8   Health Service Executive (2017).
9   Nolan (2017).
10 Prewitt (2017); Christie (n.d.).
11 See www.everylifecounts.ie.
12 Fiona (n.d.).
13 Coonan (2016); see also Coonan (n.d.).
14 Wall (n.d.) and *Dungarvan Leader* (2018).
15 Houlihan and O'Donoghue (2013).
16 Mahony and Malone (2017).
17 Newstalk (2017).
18 Janvier, Farlow and Wilfond (2012).
19 Lantos (2016), p. 396.
20 *Ibid*, p. 397.
21 *Irish Times* (2017a, 2017b).
22 Trainer (2017).
23 O'Halloran (2017).
24 Indecon Economic Consultants (2017).
25 Department of Health (New York State) (2015).

From 1983 to 2018: *Bunreacht na hÉireann* Was Never the Place to Deal with Abortion

Jan O'Sullivan

I became actively involved in politics in Ireland in the early 1980s after returning from a period of time living in Canada where my first child was born. My first experience of canvassing door-to-door was in the 1983 referendum on the Eighth Amendment to *Bunreacht na hÉireann*.

I could describe it as a baptism of fire. This was an extraordinarily divisive campaign, during which we were frequently banished from doors and told we were baby killers. We argued that the wording that the state would 'defend and vindicate' the equal right to life of the mother and the unborn was unworkable: that it would put doctors in the impossible position of balancing these two rights, and that the Constitution was not the place to deal with such complex issues.

It was the first time I had gone door-to-door with a group of canvassers and, despite the hostility we met, there was a great sense of shared purpose and conviction amongst the team. We argued our case wherever we got the chance. Even though we didn't win in 1983, I became convinced of the importance of going out and talking directly to people in order to bring about social change. As well as competing in electoral politics, I subsequently knocked on doors in Limerick on issues such as divorce (twice), the right to information and the right to travel, and, most recently, marriage equality. During each of these campaigns, I met some great and inspiring people along the way. In truth, I feel privileged to have been part of an opening up of Irish society during my lifetime.

Back in 1983, our campaign in Limerick organised public meetings featuring national campaigners like the late Adrian Hardiman and Monica Barnes. Jim Kemmy, my political mentor, lost his Dáil seat because he advocated for the right to have an abortion in the very limited circumstances of rape, fatal foetal abnormality and a risk to the life of the mother.

I was a member of Jim's Democratic Socialist Party (subsequently merged with the Labour Party), which had adopted a policy of allowing access to abortion in those limited circumstances. It took huge courage for an elected public representative like Jim to take such a stand. Others – like Mary Robinson, current leader of the Labour Party, Brendan Howlin, and then leader, Dick Spring – were also prepared to argue against the proposed constitutional amendment.

Despite our efforts, the referendum was passed and the Eighth Amendment was inserted into the Constitution of Ireland. It was subsequently amended to allow the right to information and the right to travel. The latter was introduced in 1992 after a fourteen-year-old girl was stopped from going to England for a termination of her pregnancy, leading to widespread protests and a memorable Martyn Turner cartoon in the *Irish Times* of a map of Ireland with a barbed wire fence around it and a teenaged girl trapped inside. I believe this powerful image brought home to many people just how extreme the constitutional restriction was. However, public opinion at that time was still largely content to keep the status quo and the pretence that Ireland was an abortion-free zone.

Of course, it wasn't. Irish women continued to be bound by the Eighth Amendment but, confronted with crisis pregnancy, they made decisions, largely in secret and frequently without counselling or medical advice. Thousands travelled each year to the UK in search of the care they were being denied at home, and, despite several appeals to Irish and European courts, little changed.

In 2012, the Eighth Amendment cost a 31-year-old mother her life. The country continues to remember and grieve for Savita Halappanavar, but, six years on, the kind of decisions her medical team had to make in deciding when they could intervene are still faced by obstetricians and the women they are caring for.

Dr Rhona Mahony, master of the National Maternity Hospital, has described during her expert witness testimony to the Oireachtas Joint Committee on the Eighth Amendment of the Constitution the fine line doctors must walk in deciding the point at which a woman's life, as opposed to her health, is in danger. She must wait until she is sufficiently ill that she might die; but how can a doctor be sure? She explains that there is a narrow therapeutic window and her condition can deteriorate very rapidly, for example in cases of sepsis. Doctors are trained to look after the health of their patients. But, in these difficult circumstances, the spectre of the criminal law hangs over them while the pregnant woman herself is denied her voice.

While these restrictions pertain in Irish hospitals and clinics, at least 170,216 women and girls have travelled outside of Ireland for a termination of pregnancy between 1980 and 2016.[1] This staggering figure shows just how many have made the decision to end their pregnancy, despite the constitutional ban.

Information and travel have become much more accessible, and this has aided Irish women greatly. Women can now travel more easily to Britain and, thanks to the internet, information on how and where to book these procedures is much simpler to find than it once was. In recent years, Irish women have also been able to buy pills that induce early termination of pregnancy on the internet. However, although it is an easier process than it once was, that in no ways means it is an easy one and many women are not able to face the challenges this decision entails.

They also have to face considerable costs. Irish women pay anywhere from €410 to €1,670 for the procedure alone, and then must add the cost of travel, accommodation, transportation and often also make arrangements for the children they leave behind at home. It has been estimated that the overall cost of travelling to Britain for an abortion can range from €800 to €4,000 depending on the woman's individual circumstances.

This cost is prohibitive to many women all across the country. And even if we took away the issue of cost, we cannot ignore the situation of many women who are not able travel for immigration reasons, or because their age or other circumstances simply don't allow it. These women are left behind by a system that only caters to those who can find the means to afford it. Sadly, we will probably never hear these women's stories, as they are forced to carry on a pregnancy they do not feel they can sustain. It is impossible to quantify the number of women who have faced this dilemma.

Research suggests that approximately 63 women per week travel from the Republic of Ireland to have a termination of pregnancy, while a further 25[2] per week procure one by taking pills purchased over the internet. That means that, regardless of the law and the Constitution, at least 12 abortions are procured by women living in the Republic of Ireland, every single day.

These figures suggest that Ireland's abortion rate is on a par with other developed countries. It just happens illegally. Professor Sabaratnam Arulkumaran, former President of the British Medical Association and the International Federation of Obstetrics and Gynaecology and author of the report on the death of Savita Halappanavar, recently put it bluntly to the Oireachtas Committee on the Eighth Amendment: we either have legal or illegal abortion in Ireland, but we will always have abortions.

It is also the case statistically that Irish women have terminations at a later stage of pregnancy than EU norms; for example 81 per cent of UK residents access abortion services before ten weeks of pregnancy whereas only 69 per cent of Republic of Ireland residents do so.[3]

International statistics actually point to the fact that abortion rates have reduced in several countries when they legalised abortion. Such was the case in Romania, where abortion rates dropped significantly within years of it being legalised by the state. This was largely because abortion services were provided together with a constellation of other sexual health services, such as sex education, counselling and affordable contraceptive methods.

Overall, figures collected by the World Health Organization and the Guttmacher Institute in fact show that countries where abortion is illegal tend to have slightly higher abortion rates than those where it is legal. Most of the evidence therefore suggests that if we want to see abortion rates drop, legalising abortion and putting in place comprehensive sexual and reproductive healthcare are required steps to achieve this goal. Abortion rates in developed countries, most of which provide abortion services, have nowadays reached a historic low, dropping from 46 for every 1,000 women of childbearing age in 1990 to 27 in 2014.[4]

Ireland and Malta are outliers in Europe in this respect, given how restrictive our laws are. This means that out of the 260 million women that reside in the EU, only 2.5 million don't have access to safe and legal abortions in their own country, with the vast majority of them living in Ireland.

Illegality and criminalisation do nothing to stop abortions from taking place. Instead, they create barriers which prevent women from receiving the care they need. Experts often talk of a 'chilling effect' on both healthcare providers and patients: patients are scared of asking for help, and health practitioners fear providing it. Because we have easy access to Britain and to the internet, we don't have, as far as we know, back-street abortions. Many other parts of the world are not so fortunate in this regard.

The World Health Organization estimates that 22 million unsafe abortions are carried out each year around the world. About 7 million women are admitted into hospital as a result of complications from these unsafe abortions. Approximately 68,000 of those will die trying to terminate their pregnancies. The vast majority of these women live in poor developing countries.[5]

We are lucky that this is not the case in Ireland. But this is not because abortion does not take place – it is simply because we effectively outsource our abortion service to the UK (for those who can afford it), and some women are able to access abortion pills from home. Nevertheless, the fact that women are not dying should not be enough. Women are entitled to more than just being alive.

ANOTHER REFERENDUM: FROM 1983 TO 2018

Public opinion has significantly changed in Ireland since 1983 on the issue of abortion. Recent opinion polls show a large proportion of the population want change. Indeed, polling data published in October 2017 has suggested that 89 per cent of people believe that there should be access to abortion in cases where the health of the woman is at risk, while 60 per cent believe that there should be access to abortion without restrictions as to reasons, at least until specified gestational limits.[6]

In response to shifting public demand, and to continuing public controversy over this issue, the Government established a Citizens' Assembly to hear expert testimony and to make recommendations which would be considered by a cross-party Oireachtas committee which would, in turn, bring proposals to both Houses of the Oireachtas to be acted on by Government. While this process has somewhat delayed any resolution of the issue, the recommendations of the Citizens' Assembly surprised many people, particularly their clear recommendation in favour of access to abortion in the first twelve weeks of pregnancy without restriction.

I was nominated by the Labour Party to serve on the Oireachtas Committee and to work constructively with other members to address the various recommendations of the Citizens' Assembly. I believe the Committee has fulfilled that mandate with dedication. As far as I am concerned, the most important goal we must achieve is to remove the issue from the Constitution. That means repealing Article 40.3.3.

The decision made in October 2017 to recommend that the article not be retained in its current form was an important first step. It means, if implemented, that we will certainly have a referendum in 2018. My view is that the wording put before the people should be to delete Article 40.3.3. It is time to undo the decision of 1983 and deal with the issue of abortion in the context of healthcare, not constitutional prohibition.

During the Committee meetings, expert witnesses have brought forward many testimonies of women contemplating desperate measures when they were not able to meet the requirements travelling to Britain imposed. We have accounts of women exercising excessively, taking boiling hot baths or considering drinking bleach. Many also admitted to considering suicide as an alternative at some point during the process. One woman's story in particular really shook me:

> I was walking up to 20 kilometres every day. I was doing sit-ups, I was doing squats. I was doing anything I could possibly do to make this happen. I don't think I ate for several days because I had read that if you have an extremely low calorie count and [you take] Vitamin C that can cause a miscarriage. I was actually reading pregnancy sites that warn you not to do things and everything they were warning you not to do was

exactly what I was doing; roasting hot baths to the point that I almost scalded myself, and when I think about it I'm an educated woman, do you know, I'm a grown woman. It's just so sad.

While this was being read to the Committee, I was reminded once more of 1992 and the *Irish Times*' cartoon of the trapped girl inside the barbed wire. Only this time it wasn't a girl but an adult woman.

Amongst the most moving testimonies given to the Oireachtas Committee were the personal accounts of representatives of TFMR (Termination for Medical Reasons). They described the sorrow of knowing their wanted baby would not survive after birth, the painful decision to be made on whether to continue the pregnancy or to travel to Britain with no medical referral, just a file under their arm and at the mercy of another country's health service. To me, the most harrowing was the description of having to bring a dead baby home, either in the boot of the car, left there during the ferry crossing, or in luggage on a plane to be collected on the carousel along with the suitcases, or, if the baby was cremated, the ashes sent home by courier.

We are failing these families by not allowing them to access the care they need at a time when they are at their most vulnerable. We are forcing them to leave their country, making them feel like 'medical refugees'. Surely, even those who most oppose abortion in Ireland, would give such families the option of making this difficult choice with the knowledge that, whatever they decide, they can be cared for in their own community?

I understand that people have concerns about 'opening the floodgates', but all the statistics from countries that have legalised abortion show that this simply doesn't happen. Women do not choose abortion as a form of contraception. In fact, one of the reasons abortion rates have gone down after legalisation in some countries has been attributed to information and counselling on the use of contraception after a termination. Legalisation has brought down the numbers of women having a second or subsequent abortion.

Irish women will access abortion whether it is legal or illegal, whether it is criminalised or not, but they will do so at an added cost – not only to their finances but also to their physical and mental health. Expert research has proven that restrictive legislation has no effect on the number of abortions that are carried out. We can either face this reality and allow women to access the healthcare they need and are entitled to at home, or we can isolate, stigmatise and endanger them.

I am proud that we are witnessing a shift in Ireland's beliefs from what they were at the time when the Eighth Amendment was ratified. In 2016 the Citizens'

Assembly was appointed to discuss the Eighth Amendment. It held five meetings between November and April. The members heard and discussed testimonies of many experts in the field and then voted to put forward recommendations for the Oireachtas to legislate. A vast majority of 87 per cent came to the conclusion that the Eighth Amendment should not be retained in full, and 67 per cent of the members expressed the belief that the termination of pregnancy without restriction should be lawful in Ireland. Percentages were even higher when considering specific circumstances when abortion should be allowed, including rape (89 per cent), fatal foetal abnormality (89 per cent), and risk to health of the mother (79 per cent).[7]

A recent study conducted by Ulster University and commissioned by a group of trade unions closely echoes the resolutions of the Citizens' Assembly. Much in accordance with what was decided by the Citizens' Assembly, out of 3,180 respondents, 66 per cent agreed abortion should be available when the pregnancy is a result of rape, 65 per cent when there is a serious malformation of the foetus, and 62 per cent when a woman's health is at risk. Over half of all respondents believe abortion should be available upon request. Amnesty International have also conducted their own independent poll and got similar results, with 60 per cent of the 1000 people polled believing abortion in Ireland should be available on request.

The study conducted by Ulster University took things one step further. They found that despite the range of views on when abortion should be legal, 87 per cent of respondents were against women being criminalised for having an abortion under any circumstance.[8] No matter what people's beliefs are, when the coin is flipped an overwhelming majority would still recognise a woman's right to her own bodily autonomy and decisions. This, I think, says a lot about our society.

These figures and the tone of the discussion at the Citizens' Assembly, the Oireachtas Committee and media debate suggest that, if we went canvassing door-to-door today we would get a much more empathetic, understanding and humane response than we did back in 1983. But we still have a long way to go, and if Ireland wants to do right by half of its population, then we need to repeal the Eighth Amendment now.

I am not in favour of replacing the current wording with an alternative that might permit abortion in certain circumstances. I believe we should simply remove Article 40.3.3 from *Bunreacht na hÉireann*, and that the Oireachtas should subsequently legislate to determine the circumstances in which termination of pregnancy would be permitted and provided within the Irish health services.

A restrictive constitutional framework that would only allow abortions to be carried out in specific scenarios would open a wide set of issues from legal, medical and ethical perspectives. It would perpetuate a cycle of referendums and denial of women's rights.

Whatever legislation the Government proposes to introduce following a potentially successful referendum, it must accommodate a risk to the health of the mother. We in Ireland know this too well, where a legal distinction between risk to life and risk to health cost at least one woman her life.

Access to safe legal abortion should not be a matter of being able to afford to pay either. We cannot put in place measures that systematically discriminate against those most vulnerable and cheat them of their right to access health services. The current status quo, where abortion is only available for those who have the means to access it, cannot be sustained.

This is why we need to repeal, not replace, and remove Article 40.3.3.

I don't believe the Constitution is the place to determine such an issue. The medical and legal witnesses to the Committee agree the Constitution is too rigid a place to legislate working paradigms for medical procedures. We would only be replacing one problem with another.

Medical practice involves constantly making case-based decisions given specific circumstances; it supposes working with everyday changing and evolving techniques and technologies that move forward quickly as science advances. The Constitution is no place to regulate medicine since it is by definition a document that cannot be easily amended or regularly updated. Legislating for good, inclusive and safe abortion practices in the Constitution would be impossible.

INTEGRATING REPRODUCTIVE HEALTH INTO THE HEALTHCARE SYSTEM

In May 2018 the Irish people will have their say in determining the legal, ethical and social parameters within which reproductive health will be provided for in this country. In implementing new policy, we need to strive to design our sexual and reproductive healthcare from a human rights and women-centred perspective. A good, solid and fair healthcare system is one that respects and protects women's right to consultation, dignity and privacy. If this is to be the case for all women, we also have to ensure special protections are put in place for the most vulnerable demographics.

In order to function properly and fairly, abortion services will have to be integrated into the HSE. This will legitimise and destigmatise the procedure, offering women a safe space where they can access care, information and non-directive counselling, should they ask for it. Abortion is an inherently safe procedure, when done under the right circumstances and conditions. From the 190,406 abortions that took place in the UK during all of 2016, only 294 complications were reported. That means 99.8 per cent of abortions in the UK were carried out without any reported complications.[9]

Many experts agree that it is a myth that the resulting costs would be significant, and instead argue that integration of such supports into the existing health system would be relatively straightforward. According to recent studies and projections calculated by the World Health Organization,[10] integrating abortion into a national health system usually only requires small changes to existing facilities and services and therefore its implementation only signifies a modest cost in most cases. Most of the equipment and supplies needed to provide abortion services are the same as those needed for other obstetrician practices, which means there is no reason why legalising abortion should require a large investment.

Similarly, the two main drugs needed to carry out a medical abortion are inexpensive and easy to access. Misoprostol would only cost a few cents per tablet, and Mifepristone would cost €3.30 per tablet if sourced in bulk by the state. These seem minimal when we realise Irish women already spend at least €4 million each year out of their own pockets in order to access abortion in the UK.

Another common concern is Ireland's capacity to deal with abortion services in terms of human resources. Ireland is estimated to have some of the lowest rates of obstetricians within the European Union, which should be double what they are according to international standards. I found Dr Rhona Mahony's analysis of this reality to the Committee especially interesting. She suggested this is due to obstetrics being viewed as a very high-risk profession in Ireland because of our legislation, deterring young people from taking on this specialisation. While this is a much broader issue that will clearly require investment to resolve, setting up a cohesive, workable legislative framework might be one step towards helping to bring more young professionals into obstetrics.

The World Health Organization recommends, in this respect, that first trimester abortions are simple procedures that can be provided not only by obstetricians but by general physicians, clinical officers and nurses. Most abortions are carried out at this stage when available in the country, since women don't have to wait to gather the funds or be delayed by other issues that arise when they have to travel abroad.

These are some of the practical considerations that will arise, whatever decisions the government and future governments make following the referendum.

CONCLUSION

The Eighth Amendment has caused unnecessary suffering to hundreds of thousands of women and families for almost 35 years. I'm happy to see the debate has evolved since 1983, and that women and women's rights, views and experiences are finally being put at the centre of the discussion. The work carried out by both the Citizens' Assembly and the Oireachtas Joint Committee has been exceptional and ground-breaking. So have been the efforts of the many NGOs and agencies striving for change.

I have every hope that come May 2018 Irish people will vote not to retain the Eighth Amendment and to remove Article 40.3.3 from *Bunreacht na hÉireann*. Work will only then start in providing a flexible yet strong legal framework to regulate, facilitate and guarantee the best possible level of medical practice, available to all women equally.

As an elected public representative for most of the 35 years since the Eighth Amendment was inserted in to the Constitution, I want to see it removed before I hang up my political boots and make more use of my hill-walking ones! As one of the minority of women in public life, I want to see humane services for women here in our own country. And I want to see an end to the hardship and hypocrisy of relying on Britain and the internet to resolve crisis pregnancies.

REFERENCES

Amnesty International (2017) 'Amnesty International/Red C Poll Reveals 60% Support Access to Abortion on Request', *Amnesty International*, www.amnesty.ie/itstimepoll/.

Bloomer, F., J. Devlin-Trew, C. Pierson, N. MacNamara and D. Mackle (2017) *Abortion as a Workplace Issue: Trade Union Survey – North And South Of Ireland*, Dublin: UNITE the Union, Unison, Mandate Trade Union, the CWU Ireland, the GMB, Alliance for Choice, Trade Union Campaign to Repeal the 8th.

Citizens' Assembly, The (2017) *The Eighth Amendment of the Constitution*, www.citizensassembly.ie/en/The-Eighth-Amendment-of-the-Constitution.

Department of Health (UK) (2017) *Abortion Statistics, England and Wales: 2016*, www.gov.uk/government/uploads/system/uploads/attachment_data/file/652083/Abortion_stats_England_Wales_2016.pdf.

Ganatra, B. et al. (2017) 'Global, Regional, and Subregional Classification of Abortions by Safety, 2010–14: Estimates from a Bayesian Hierarchical Model', *The Lancet*, Vol. 390, No. 10110, pp. 2372–2381, www.thelancet.com/journals/lancet/article/PIIS0140-6736(17)31794-4/fulltext.

Guttmacher Institute (2017) *Induced Abortion Worldwide: Global Incidence and Trends*, September 2017 Fact Sheet, www.guttmacher.org/fact-sheet/induced-abortion-worldwide.

World Health Organization (2012) *Safe Abortion: Technical and Policy Guidance for Health Systems*, second edition, Geneva: WHO Publications, http://apps.who.int/iris/bitstream/10665/70914/1/9789241548434_eng.pdf?ua=1.

ENDNOTES

[1] Figure obtained from Department of Health (UK) (2017).
[2] This number is an estimate calculated from the number of women who ordered pills online from Women on Web in 2016. It includes women from Northern Ireland and Republic of Ireland, since it is impossible to measure them separately under the current circumstances. It is a calculated approximation that could vary slightly, given there could have been women who ordered the pills but didn't go through with the procedure, women who got hold of the pills through unknown and unregistered sources, and so on.
[3] Department of Health (UK) (2017).
[4] Guttmacher Institute (2017).
[5] Ganatra et al. (2017).
[6] Amnesty International (2017).
[7] Citizens' Assembly, The (2017).
[8] Bloomer, Devlin-Trew, Pierson, MacNamara and Mackle (2017).
[9] Department of Health (UK) (2017).
[10] World Health Organization (2012).

KATHLEEN ROSE:
A BEAUTIFUL AND UNEXPECTED JOURNEY

Tracy Harkin

It was a warm September evening in 2006. Washington State is particularly beautiful at this time of year, the landscape transforming into an amazing patchwork of colour. I had taken our four children leaf-collecting in a local park. As we entered, a young woman, noticing my obvious bump, held open the gate and asked me when I was due. As we chatted the conversation turned to politics. She told me of the 'right-wing element' emerging in the country and that even women's' right to choose' was under threat. 'I mean', she said with intensity, 'what if the child is disabled for heaven's sake?' Before I could respond, her lift had arrived and with a 'nice meetin' ya' she was gone. Her words, however, rang in my ears long after her departure. So *what* if the child is disabled?

'How could she think like that?' I asked my husband, bemused, that evening. In my student years I had worked with special needs children in Saturday clubs and summer schemes and had thoroughly enjoyed the work. I thought of my younger cousin with spina bifida and how her local community had rallied round to fundraise for her new wheelchair; the friendly and efficient wheelchair-bound cashier at my local Tesco's back home; the little girl with Down syndrome who had given me a high five yesterday morning at my local parish. I couldn't fathom how their disability made them any less worthy of life than those insisting this was the case.

The obstetrician had assured my husband, Tom, and I at our twenty-week scan that the baby looked perfect. During the entirety of the pregnancy there was no cause for concern whatsoever. I remember watching with awe as the 3D image of this new baby appeared on the screen. It was fascinating how through this new technology we could clearly see even her nose and lips.

I remember his parting words: 'Well Mam, it's number five so should be plain sailing for you!' His statement inspired so much confidence that I decided to literally take the plunge with this baby and have my first home water-birth. We had visited the midwife centre some months before and I had observed with amusement the panic-stricken look on Tom's face as he looked at the photographs displayed in the waiting room. They had beautifully captured the joy of several couples holding their newborn baby in the birth pool moments after birth. I quickly assured him that *he* at no time would be required to strip off and get into the pool.

Kathleen Rose was born at 6.15 a.m. on 2 November 2006, weighing in at 6lb 7oz . She had been my shortest labour and quickest birth yet. I will always remember seeing her as a beautiful, tiny newborn floating upwards into my arms. Her skin felt so soft and silky against mine. We had a wonderful first hour together as a family. I watched as the other children's tiredness turned into excitement as they admired their new baby sister. Relieved, I closed my eyes. She was here, safe and well. The midwives had been wonderful and I was so glad I had finally had the courage to choose a home birth, avoiding all of the anxiety of leaving the children and rushing to hospital.

My relief was short-lived, however, as two hours later our baby girl still hadn't fed. When the midwives finally took Kathleen from my arms, I noticed them running their fingers up and down her back as they spoke in hushed tones. When Veronica, the lead midwife, gently suggested we take Kathleen to hospital for observation, I knew something was seriously wrong. Exhausted as I was, within minutes Tom and I were on the freeway en route to the children's hospital. When we got to the ER, no one seemed in any panic. Doctors came and went. One nurse came in and handed me a little syringe of milk. I administered a couple of drops on the corner of her mouth, but she still didn't seem interested. 'What's wrong with her?' I asked Tom, completely exasperated.

Nothing could have prepared us for what happened next. A horrible blue colour began crawling across her body. I screamed as doctors came out of nowhere, pushing tubes down her throat and pummelling her chest again and again. Then out they flew, racing down the corridor towards the Intensive Care Unit as we followed helplessly behind.

Kathleen didn't die that day. Against all the odds she survived.

When we next saw her she was ventilated and on a drip. My yearning to hold and feed her was overwhelming. Having said goodbye to Tom that night, I collapsed, exhausted and disorientated, into my little room beside ICU and finally succumbed to the shock and grief that had been welling up inside me. How could everything have gone wrong so quickly? I was so looking forward to this baby. I was supposed to be at home, in my beautiful, comfortable American home. I had planned it all so well. Everything was supposed to be perfect.

The days that followed were a whirlwind of endless tests. The results came back in quick succession, each one more depressing than the last. It seemed every part of Kathleen's little body was imperfect in some way or another. Her heart, her lungs, her kidneys, her digestive system, her spine, her swallow, her eyes. Within a week we were called to a meeting. I took one look at the box of tissues and another at the grim faces of the two doctors and my heart sank. The geneticist handed us two sheets of paper and exhaled heavily before she began. 'I'm so sorry to tell you that we have received a diagnosis. Your baby has a rare chromosome condition that affects around 1 in 10,000 children called Trisomy 13, also known as Patau syndrome. It is usually a lethal condition. I have to tell you around 90 per cent of these babies don't survive beyond their first birthday.'

I looked at the sheet in my hand and winced at the words 'incompatible with life' and 'severe mental retardation' in bold print, followed by a lengthy list of medical complications associated with this condition. Tom and I sat quietly as we processed this new information. The two doctors probably thought we were both in shock. In truth, at this stage we had suspected there was some underlying condition and were glad at the speed with which her diagnosis was confirmed. We had watched our baby dying before our very eyes. We had seen her turn blue from head to toe. But she was still here and she was now surviving off the ventilator. We could only be grateful for that. Despite this devastating diagnosis we continued to insist that Kathleen be given appropriate medical intervention and every opportunity to reach her full potential, whatever that may be.

In the five weeks of her hospitalisation that followed, there were many dark moments when we didn't know if she would pull through. We continued to have a deep peace, however, that at least we were giving her the best chance possible.

Fortunately, we were surrounded by a fantastic network of families whose kindness, generosity and sheer determination to do whatever it took to help us was remarkable. From a daily delivery of meals to our home to raking our lawn, word had spread about this Irish family in Seattle and baskets of practical items like toiletries, disposable cameras, knitted blankets, hats and beautiful devotional items were left at our door. Time and time again we were reminded that even though we were far from family and friends back home, we were surrounded by kindness and support during this difficult time.

One family put us in touch with a centre for bioethics. The conversations we had reassured us that the decisions we were making for Kathleen were the right ones. The importance of proceeding with life-saving intervention such as ventilation or surgery if it will act as a 'bridge to healing' was explained to us. The term 'bridge to healing' was particularly important for us to articulate to the medical team when deciding on appropriate surgery after Kathleen's diagnosis.

One night after the surgery to address her reflux and insert a feeding tube, I was back at her bedside. A young doctor entered the room and stood beside me. 'Mrs Harkin', he said softly, 'you don't need to do all this you know.' Weary as I was, I knew immediately what he meant. A chill snaked its way down my spine as I thought of how, with just one word from Tom or me, we could give up on our little girl and let her die. Unlike other more 'perfect' babies in the unit, Kathleen's diagnosis meant she had no 'right' to care whatsoever. *Doctor, how so? I thought. How could we do away with her? Maybe take down her drip, turn off her oxygen? Or perhaps,* I thought sarcastically, *we could just take her out of the incubator and let her freeze to death!*

I swallowed the bitterness in my mouth, mustered up all the dignity I could and just stared at him silently. He made a very hasty exit.

However, many doctors at this stage were more positive and continued to follow our directives without question. We were the ones setting the standard and, because of that, they treated Kathleen as an individual and not as a fatal diagnosis. Although she had many anomalies, on closer examination none of her major organs were found to be *fatally* affected. Three weeks after surgery she was off oxygen, stable and ready for home.

We were delighted to be at this stage. I was eagerly looking forward to sleeping in my own bed again and being with the other children. We would never again take being together as a family for granted. We were obviously a little too upbeat and positive though, as the medical team decided we were in need of a reality check. The day before her planned discharge from hospital, Tom and I were called to a meeting.

Around a dozen or so medical personnel, social workers and palliative care specialists were waiting on us as we entered the room. I noticed there weren't enough seats for everyone and some people were uncomfortably perched on the arm of several chairs. The box of tissues had returned, placed conspicuously on the coffee table in front of our two reserved seats. Bemused, we both sat down tentatively and waited. The meeting began with an overview of Kathleen's diagnosis. A long list of her medical anomalies was read out and then we fielded one question after another. How would we cope with this child? Were we really aware of how serious her condition was? She would never be able to *do* anything! She would never be able to go to school, she would never walk, never talk and would need 24-hour care. What was our plan? Had we thought of how this would negatively impact our other four children? Had we thought of how resentful they might become, having to help care for their sister?

Tom and I were dumbfounded. What was happening? Why were they being so negative about our baby girl after all we had been through? After six weeks of hospitalisation she was stable and ready for home. Surely that was something to celebrate.

We calmly assured the team that we were very aware of Kathleen's diagnosis, her medical anomalies and fragile health. We had read all the reports from cover to cover. We were completely realistic, but she had taught us one important lesson in life so far: Take each day as it comes and celebrate life for as long as we have it. We told them we would continue to love and help our daughter reach her full potential, whatever that may be. Tom summed up our approach in his usual straightforward style. 'Look Doctor', he said, 'we will continue to expect the worst but hope for the best.'

We thanked them for the excellent care that had been provided by the hospital and asked them about any necessary equipment we should have at home for her. We had already arranged for a feeding pump and supply of special milk. I asked for a basic monitor that would alert us if she stops breathing at night due to her history of sleep apnoea and a supply of home oxygen to make her more comfortable if her saturations got low. They repeatedly denied she would need these items. 'We wouldn't discharge her if she needed these', one doctor said, firmly bringing the meeting to a close. We realised later of course that the medical team was drawing a line under this episode of care. If we needed anywhere near this level of intervention again we knew we would probably have a fight on our hands. It was a bittersweet end to our hospital stay.

The day of her homecoming we literally went from one storm to another. We were home only hours and totally dependent on electricity to power her feed pump when our entire neighbourhood went into blackout. The worst storm in decades had hit Washington State. Power lines were down for days; the Red Cross erected tents and provided warm food and heat. Thankfully, we could take refuge in a friend's newly furnished basement, one of the few homes that still had power in the region. After this little adventure, things settled down and for the first year Kathleen did amazingly well.

Both she and her feed pump came everywhere with us. It was our new normal. I had even mastered using the little syringes to administer her medicines and no longer had to wipe the red and yellow stains from the ceiling. She was an interactive baby who was responding well to us and making mighty attempts to crawl. I continued to take her to outpatients' clinics and all the doctors agreed her progress was much better than expected. She had a successful day procedure to address her kidney reflux and even her myoclonic epilepsy was stabilised as the dedicated neurologist persevered in trying different medicines and dosages and eventually got the right mix. It was a happy first year.

Our family paediatrician, though, was concerned that we had been sent home without a basic suction machine in case she became unwell and wasn't able to swallow. At this point I had never even heard of a suction machine before, never mind knowing to ask for one. The doctor informed us how common they were in the community and that they were used by patients with much fewer complications than Kathleen. I was mortified. He spoke as though we were deliberately trying to hasten her death. Indignantly, I quickly assured him of the contrary.

Concerned about Kathleen's stridor (noisy breathing) and the fact that the hospital had not prescribed us an apnoea monitor, he referred her for a sleep study. The results were startling. Kathleen, at one year old, was found to have severe obstructive sleep apnoea, meaning she stopped breathing multiple times during the night. The consultant was astounded she was still alive.

Around this time I also noticed little brown coffee-like granules appearing in her feed tube. As it was a Saturday evening we took her into the ER to get her checked out. We were ushered into a cubicle and two doctors appeared, holding a thick wad of notes. One of them, a young woman, told us, 'I have read the notes on Kathleen and I'm sorry we can't help you here any further.'

'It's just these granules have appeared in her feed tube and I'm thinking perhaps she needs something to settle her stomach', I replied quickly. The two doctors continued to stand at the entrance of the cubicle. I went on, assuring them that our insurance was in order. 'I'm sorry ma'am', one repeated, 'we can't help you today.' The curtain was closed and they briskly moved onto the next patient. Tom, who had copped on to the situation before I did, was already gathering up our things. We drove home that evening in silence. How I wished I could have taken those notes with that stupid diagnosis and burned them. *They wouldn't even examine her*, was all I could think. She's just a fatal diagnosis to them now. Not even a person. They are all just waiting. Waiting for her to die. I had never in my life felt so powerless.

It was at this point that we decided to take time out and return to Ireland. Our American dream had come to an abrupt end.

Travelling by coach from Seattle to Vancouver airport with four children under ten, twenty suitcases, Kathleen Rose and her equipment was no easy feat. We must have looked a rare sight. When we arrived in Vancouver the coach driver thoughtlessly drove a hundred yards beyond the hotel stop. 'How on earth', Tom asked him incredulously, 'are we to transport twenty suitcases, four children and a special needs baby back up that hill to the hotel?' He shrugged his shoulders and waited while a fuming Tom lifted each suitcase from the hold and piled them up along the roadside before heading down to the hotel to get a baggage cart. To this day I can still see him wheeling that cart piled high with our suitcases back and forward from that hotel while I sat on a suitcase at the roadside, Kathleen in my lap and the other children huddled around, terrified as the traffic whizzed by. Nothing about this journey home was going to be easy.

The next day at the airport we went through the complicated process of getting permission to have a portable oxygen cylinder on board in case the altitude affected Kathleen's breathing. Having finally got our paperwork approved, we boarded the plane. An hour into the flight, however, I gave up on this completely. Kathleen kept pulling the mask off her face repeatedly, as if to say, 'Mum, I'll be fine.' Indeed, her breathing remained completely stable for the whole of the journey and I even managed to doze off instead of scrutinising her face the entire journey. Exhausted and bedraggled, we arrived into Belfast airport for what was to be the beginning of a rollercoaster of a year back home.

Thanks to a highly dedicated team of experienced community nurses and the support of family and friends, we settled into a routine with Kathleen and the other children relatively quickly. The support of home visits and on-call medical advice at a community level was something I was incredibly grateful for and hadn't experienced in the United States.

Around three months into our return Kathleen began to develop a series of chest infections. Due to her diagnosis, the inevitable encounter with hospital consultants had to take place, now on this side of the Atlantic. Did we desire intensive care for her if she should need it? Did we want her resuscitated? 'Doctor', I would say, 'she has a chest infection at present; how would you treat a child with such a complaint if she didn't have Trisomy 13? Please just give her the standard treatment that any child would be given and we will cross that other bridge if we come to it.'

Despite several hospitalisations for chest infections that year and two occasions when her oxygen levels dropped so low we were preparing to say goodbye, Kathleen Rose just kept bouncing back, consistently responding well to the standard treatment of IV and oral antibiotics and physiotherapy. After each episode she was usually back home and on the mend within one to two weeks.

By the time she was three years old she was defying all medical expectations. Her health had stabilised remarkably and she was going from strength to strength, no longer requiring oxygen at night or even a monitor. Her sleep apnoea had even gradually rectified itself.

At four years old she started special school and became quite a character. She was so active that staff had to let her out every day with her 'wheelie walker' to whizz up and down the corridor and even had a large trampoline placed just for her in the classroom.

As time went on and I began searching the internet for other parents' stories I soon realised what a miracle it was that she was still here at all. Through the Every Life Counts charity and One Day More initiatives here in Ireland I have had the privilege of meeting many of these parents. Their stories are both uplifting and profoundly disturbing.

It was clear that many parents whose babies were diagnosed prenatally with these conditions were coming under immense pressure to abort, especially in countries like the US and the UK. Terms like 'incompatible with life' and 'fatal foetal abnormality' were routinely used in reference to their child while still alive and kicking at the time of diagnosis. Parents talked about the fear these dehumanising words had drove into their hearts at such a vulnerable time. Some parents whose babies had been diagnosed with anencephaly had even been told their baby didn't have a head! It was clear that even with the same official diagnosis these babies were all affected in different ways.

Even with the most severe condition, anencephaly, there was a spectrum. In fact, 72 per cent of babies with anencephaly do live for some time after birth, ranging from minutes to days to months.[1]

Following a prenatal diagnosis, a medical examination or intervention was not routinely offered to these babies after birth. Parents talked about being discharged from hospital and taking their babies home to die. In some cases, no fluids were being given as the baby's inability to feed orally was understood by parents to be untreatable.

Some parents were talking about the need for a new type of care called perinatal hospice and palliative care, which wasn't yet routinely available in all maternity hospitals. This care includes referring a family from the point of diagnosis to a specialist team who will provide accurate up-to-date information on their child's condition, counselling and support during and after pregnancy, and linking parents to specialist support services available.

This care is not expensive to provide. When baby is born parents can have their own room with a specialist photographer, chaplain and other family members present if that is desired. They can make handprints, footprints and memories which help sustain them after their child's passing. Any discomfort is managed by palliative care specialists. This pathway of perinatal care gives parents the gift of time with their children in a loving, supportive environment. As one parent so powerfully and poignantly told me, 'you learn to pour a lifetime of love into those hours or days.' With the loss of any child, grief and suffering cannot be avoided. But these mothers described the immense comfort they gained from their precious memories of holding and loving their babies in their arms. As their photographs posted online had beautifully captured, there were moments of joy and peace amidst the sorrow of their child's passing.

Their child was born, their child was loved, their child was named, and their child was laid to rest with dignity. It is no wonder then than emerging research such as that from Duke University[2] shows women who undergo abortion after a diagnosis of anencephaly for example are more likely to suffer depression and despair than mothers who bring their babies to term.

Over the last couple of years many bereaved parents have been heroic in speaking out publicly and sharing their stories online in an effort to improve care standards for other families. It has been particularly difficult to hear children like ours repeatedly described in media discussions as a 'fatal foetal abnormality' or 'incompatible with life'. It is a medical fact that these terms are not a medical diagnosis.[3] Hundreds of doctors have signed the Geneva Declaration on Perinatal Care, calling for an end to this misleading label. In December 2015, Professor Jim Dornan also told the BBC that the phrase has no medical meaning[4] while the Royal College of Obstetricians and Gynaecologists has already stated that it was unhappy with this term.[5]

Most of these babies do live beyond birth, if only for a very short time – and this time means everything to parents. Some, like Elaine Fagan, who lived with Edwards syndrome until she was 25 years old, have defied all the medical odds. In a 2012 study published in the *British Journal of Obstetrics and Gynaecology*, doctors recommended this term should not be used in counselling.[6]

Following an extensive consultation with parents, the Health Service Executive has issued new guidelines which use the correct term 'life-limiting conditions'. This is because the medical literature and the lived experience of parents like myself point to the fact that the blanket label 'fatal foetal abnormality' can prevent best care for baby before and after birth.

Our children may have profound disabilities, their lives may be all too short, but they are sons and daughters, grandchildren, brothers and sisters; they are members of our human family and their lives deserve to be protected and cherished. It would be inspiring to see those within positions of influence come up to speed with progressive developments in caring for these babies and give even a fraction of this time and energy to exploring the proven benefits of perinatal hospice and palliative care.

Every parent wants a healthy child but how we care and support parents and their babies who find themselves in this heart-breaking situation defines us as a culture. Changes in law radically change medical culture and increase pressure and expectation for parents to go down the path of abortion, especially when any disability has been detected.

It has been inspiring for me to have met people like Barbara Farlow from Canada, a published researcher on these conditions, who has shared her own powerful story about her daughter, Annie, who was born with Trisomy 13. Neonatologists like Dr Martin McCaffrey are also making a huge difference in continuing to support babies born with these conditions by appropriate medical intervention and medical research. In this age of modern medicine surely it is startling and inexcusable that the biggest factor impacting on lifespan for babies with life-limiting conditions is a prenatal diagnosis.[7]

I often think back to my twenty-week 3D ultrasound scan with Kathleen and thank God her diagnosis was undetected before birth. If one of the most advanced children's hospitals in the world had refused to even examine my daughter at one year old, they would have hardly rushed her to the ICU unit the day of her birth had they known in advance of that extra chromosome.

At a time when we have such made such admirable medical advances in other areas, why is research into these little ones and better care not available? If Kathleen Rose hadn't survived off that ventilator or had passed away as a result of untreatable sleep apnoea or an epileptic seizure, devastating as that would have been, Tom and I would still have had a tremendous peace in knowing we had done absolutely everything we could. My heart breaks for babies who after a prenatal diagnosis weren't given that chance and the many parents who didn't know to ask for it. Children like Seán Caden Hynes from Dublin, who at twenty weeks was diagnosed with Edwards syndrome (Trisomy 18). Seán lived for two days after birth. His mum, Sarah, has bravely spoken out publicly about her experience of continuing her pregnancy and meeting Sean: 'We just wanted to give him the best possible chance to meet his family, his big sisters, aunts, uncles, cousins and grandparents.'[8]

While Sarah describes her own medical care as being good, she believes that her son, Seán, was medically abandoned after birth. In particular, Sarah has highlighted her distress that Seán's inability to feed properly wasn't addressed by the medical team at the time.

Here in Ireland we have the huge benefit of knowing the chilling effect legalised abortion has had in other countries. Abortion law worldwide has facilitated a flourishing culture of eugenics. How can we call the virtual extinction of the Down syndrome population, for example, anything else? Some within our society are very good at talking about 'choice' but very bad at acknowledging the consequences of this ideology in practice, especially for disabled persons. Law is a powerful tool in any society. Law creates and maintains standards and sends a poignant message to society as to how we should treat one another as human beings.

When any state allows for abortion on grounds of disability right into the third trimester what message does this send about the value of a disabled person's life to wider society? This is surely the very antithesis of equality and authentic human rights. At a time when we have the technology to detect disability in a growing baby in the womb, we are also able to see his or her undeniable *humanity*. What a chilling culture of contradiction abortion law creates. On the one hand, we rightly celebrate the achievements of our special needs citizens, whether it be in the Special Olympics or other areas of life. We have progressive laws regarding access for wheelchair users and fair employment legislation. On the other hand, we would allow abortion on grounds of disability or selected disability up to birth. Where is the outcry from human rights groups about this undeniable reality?

Parents like myself are often criticised for daring to want the best for other babies in Ireland rather than just our own. Can you imagine applying this illogical thinking to other child-related policies? In every area of childcare, we are inundated with a plethora of leaflets and advice – breastfeeding, vaccinations, dietary choices to name but few. In pregnancy we are repeatedly told to stop smoking and limit our intake of alcohol in the interests of our preborn babies' health. Yet when it comes to whether a living baby in our womb should be deliberately killed because of his or her disability or terminal illness we are told it's simply a matter of 'parental choice'.

Today I am delighted to say that Kathleen Rose is an amazing eleven-year-old little girl with a beautiful distinct personality and is known most for her mischievous laughter and *enormous* hugs. Although a wheelchair user, she is extremely mobile and enjoys the rough and tumble of normal family life. Caring for Kathleen has challenges of course. I will never attempt to sugar-coat the inconvenience of tube feeding, nappy changing and cancelled plans. As all parents will know though, every child, from tots to teens, can be highly challenging at times. I know many parents who have suffered immense anxiety and grief because of their child's addiction, suicide or other destructive life choice. Children like Kathleen, however, are pure souls who give and receive love in abundance and will never cause this type of anxiety or distress.

As a family we are so grateful for this gift of time with this unique and precious little girl. She has taught us much about what's truly important in life and helped us overcome our spirit of independence and self-sufficiency. She has challenged us to be flexible and open to changing our course in life. A few months ago our family watched with joy as this special little daughter, sister and grandchild sat smiling on stage during her school's concert at Belfast's Waterfront Hall. She, like all the other children performing that night, is a pupil of a very special school in my local town – a wonderful school that caters for children with profound learning difficulties. Music is an integral part of the school curriculum and Kathleen, like all the other children, absolutely loves it. The eagerness and excitement of the pupils to showcase their talents on stage that night was palpable. This was truly an extraordinary celebration not only of music but also of children with very obvious imperfections being given the dignity, respect and opportunity to reach their full potential that they deserve. As I watched each child perform with such innocence, excitement and joy I was more convinced than ever that we become better parents, more loving people and richer communities by having these pure souls in our midst. Surely all children, no matter how profound their disability, are precious jewels within our society because they give love in abundance and they teach *us* how to love.

It is my fervent hope that here on this island of Ireland we will continue in law and practice to recognise the immense dignity and value of *every* member of our human family, regardless of life expectancy or disability. It is my hope that parents like me will be given every opportunity and the support we deserve to help these special children reach their full potential as valued members of our families and communities. That can only happen if the Eighth Amendment to the Irish Constitution stays firmly in place.

REFERENCES

BBC (2015) *The View*, 3 December, http://www.bbc.co.uk/programmes/b06qmp7d.

Cope, H., M.E. Garrett, S. Gregory and A. Ashley-Koch (2015) 'Pregnancy Continuation and Organizational Religious Activity Following Prenatal Diagnosis of a Lethal Fetal Defect Are Associated with Improved Psychological Outcome', *Prenatal Diagnosis*, Vol. 35, No. 8, pp. 761–768.

Hynes, Sarah (n.d.) 'Seán Caden Hynes', *Every Life Counts*, www.everylifecounts.ie/stories/sen-caden-hynes/.

Janvier, A., B. Farlow and K.J. Barrington (2016) 'Parental Hopes, Interventions, and Survival of Neonates with Trisomy 13 and Trisomy 18', *American Journal of Medical Genetics*, Vol. 172, No. 3, pp. 279–287.

Jaquier, M., A. Klein and E. Boltshauser (2006) 'Spontaneous Pregnancy Outcome after Prenatal Diagnosis of Anencephaly', *British Journal of Obstetrics and Gynaecology*, Vol. 113, No. 8, pp. 951–953.

Lantos, John D. (2016) 'Trisomy 13 and 18—Treatment Decisions in a Stable Gray Zone', *Journal of the American Medical Association*, Vol. 316, No. 4, pp. 396–398.

McCaffrey, M.J. (2016) 'Trisomy 13 and 18: Selecting the Road Previously Not Taken', *American Journal of Medical Genetics*, Vol. 172, No. 3, pp. 251–256.

Wilkinson, D., P. Thiele, A. Watkins and L. De Crespigny (2012) 'Fatally Flawed? A Review and Ethical Analysis of Lethal Congenital Malformations', *British Journal of Obstetrics and Gynaecology*, Vol. 119, No. 11, pp.1302–1308.

ENDNOTES

1   Jaquier, Klein and Boltshauser (2006).
2   Cope, Garrett, Gregory and Ashley-Koch (2015).
3   Wilkinson, Thiele, Watkins and De Crespigny (2012).
4   BBC (2015).
5   *Ibid.*
6   Wilkinson, Thiele, Watkins and De Crespigny (2012).
7   McCaffrey (2016); Lantos (2016); Janvier, Farlow and Barrington (2016).
8   Hynes (n.d.).

Repealing the Eighth: Easing Female Pain

Eóin de Bháldraithe

In June 2017 the Citizens' Assembly (a gathering of 100 citizens) asked that the people be allowed to vote again on the Eighth Amendment to the Constitution, which prohibits abortion. Ms Justice Mary Laffoy said, when presenting the findings, that for herself as for all the other women present this was a terribly serious issue. A Committee of the Oireachtas is now discussing what text should be put before the people in a referendum to be held in May or June 2018. As I write the discussions are still in progress.

In this essay I would like to support the call for another vote on the abortion issue, leading to a repeal of the current wording, as I feel strongly that the skulduggery that went on prior to the first vote makes it necessary that it be voted on again in a calmer atmosphere. I will begin by describing the making of the Eighth Amendment. Then I will present Catholic teaching and thinking on the matter. Next I will outline some present attitudes. But we are not in position to achieve the ideal at present, so I will say what I think the Dáil should do. But first a little bit about myself.

In 1956 I entered the Cistercian monastery near Roscrea. I was very lucky to arrive just after major reforms at the time; instead of 'intervals' we now were to have *lectio divina* – that is a prayerful reading of the scriptures. As I begun theology a few years later, I became fascinated by the Sermon on the Mount and spent some months at it. By the end of that time, I had come to believe in the words of Jesus on loving our enemies and this modified the rabid republicanism of my upbringing.

Garret FitzGerald

When Garret FitzGerald came to power in 1981 he announced a constitutional crusade. This involved allowing civil divorce, limited abortion and the removal of Articles 2 and 3 of the Constitution. His proposal to allow civil divorce was rejected in 1986. He did live to see the two offensive articles removed but it seems that returning power over abortion legislation may not be returned to the Dáil any time soon.

It was in the early 1980s that the Society for the Protection of the Unborn Child (SPUC) approached Fianna Fáil, in government at the time, asking that it propose an amendment to the Constitution to protect the life of the child in the womb. The following text was proposed:

The State acknowledges the right to life of the unborn and guarantees in its laws to respect and, so far as practicable, by its laws to defend and vindicate that right.

Not to be outdone, Garret FitzGerald soon promised that Fine Gael would support the project. He became Taoiseach for six months in 1981, to be succeeded by Charlie Haughey for eight months and then FitzGerald again for four years.

Ms Justice Catherine McGuinness (Church of Ireland) gave a lecture at the Glenstal Ecumenical Congress where she criticised the text for neglecting the rights of the mother, as Catholic theology tends to do. As a result the phrase 'equal right to the life of the mother' was added and the Church of Ireland archbishop of Dublin said this was 'satisfactory and adequate'.

At this stage I wrote to the *Irish Times* on the issue. I made reference to the novel *The Cardinal* by H.M. Robinson, published in 1950. It received widespread attention in the United States as it was made into a film starring John Huston in 1963. At one point in the book, the Cardinal's sister is in labour but the child's head is too big to be born alive. According to Catholic teaching at the time the Cardinal had no option but to let his sister die rather than perform direct killing of the infant. That was the principle: direct killing is never allowed. One stood before the principle rather than before Christ. I indicated in my letter that this was now antiquated thinking and it did alert some people to another way of thinking.

As a kind of digression I would say that the US responded to the Catholic position by the extreme law allowing abortion during the second trimester, usually called 'partial birth abortion'. We know now from our experience in Northern Ireland that one extreme evokes another, perhaps with an equal and opposite reaction. And as Catholics became less extreme so it may be significant that partial birth abortion was banned by law in 2007.

When he first became Taoiseach, FitzGerald received advice from Peter Sutherland, his attorney general, that the text was dangerous and ambiguous. As a lawyer he could guess at the results of strict interpretation of the text. FitzGerald then tried to do something about the text while Haughey ridiculed him as a turncoat. FitzGerald did not retaliate; he was like that: when insulted he did not retaliate with insults (1 Peter 3:9). Later I remember hearing Dick Spring, Tánaiste at the time, say on the RTE Radio One news that Haughey acted like this 'for base political gain'. Fine Gael produced a new text which went as follows:

> Nothing in this constitution shall be invoked to invalidate, or to deprive of force or effect, any provision of a law on the ground that it prohibits abortion.

The legal effect was to allow change to be made in the Dáil rather than by referendum. The wisdom of this is now obvious as we have had four referenda on the issue since then.

Normally bishops would not intervene between political parties yet Dermot Ryan, Archbishop of Dublin at the time, pounced on the Fine Gael text, saying that only the first proposed amendment was acceptable. This incident made many clergy feel that we were all Fianna Fáil now. For the rest of his short life Ryan opposed FitzGerald on everything. A senior Dublin priest said to me that he was like a dog defending his territory.

Kevin McNamara was soon appointed Catholic Archbishop of Dublin. Nuncio Alibrandi is said to have engineered this appointment in order to get him to oppose FitzGerald.[1] A bishop of the time describes the Nuncio as a 'pure Provo'. FitzGerald, with great loyalty and ingenuity, highlighted the two exceptions allowed by the Catholic Church: ectopic pregnancy and cancer of the womb. Roman Catholics say they are not exceptions; rather in those cases there was a double effect and the inevitable abortion was not directly intended. FitzGerald said that those were the only exceptions allowed by Catholics, saying that other exceptions were allowed by other churches. Thus FitzGerald adhered to the Catholic position even while criticising it. This made sure that McNamara could not denounce him as he would have been criticised for getting into a mere war of words.

FitzGerald was again Taoiseach when the referendum was conducted. He spoke to the nation on television just before the voting, saying it was the hardest speech he had ever made: having proposed the referendum he was now asking people to vote against it. However, it was carried by a majority of 70 per cent of the electorate. On the night of the count, former Minister Michael Woods said that Fianna Fáil was the party that delivers. He seemed to be saying that they would deliver anything, true or false, and the rest of Haughey's career bore that out.

In February 1981, after the referendum was signed into law, High Court Judge Declan Costello gave the first order based on the text: a fourteen-year-old girl was not allowed to travel abroad for an abortion in an incident that became known as the X Case. The whole country was deeply upset by the episode and nobody knew what to do about it. It was appealed to the Supreme Court, so everything depended on them. As usual, they relied on public opinion rather than strict justice and responded to the status quo by saying that being suicidal put 'the equal right to life of the mother' at risk.

The girl was allowed to travel to England to avail of an abortion but suffered a miscarriage before the procedure could be carried out. Three more referenda were held to try to adjust the law as it could not be changed in the Dáil, and that is still the situation today. The main proposer was a woman, Mary O'Rourke, Minister for Health at the time. The first was that suicidal ideation be reversed and that was rejected. Two others – the right to travel and the right to seek information on abortion – were passed.

Bertie Ahern as Taoiseach later brought in another referendum. This would have rescinded the judgement on suicidal ideation being a reason for abortion. An Act to follow would have allowed abortion 'necessary to prevent a real and substantial risk of loss of the woman's life other than by self-destruction'. This would have been a generous liberalising of the law. The referendum was defeated with just over 50 per cent of the electorate voting against it. The intervention of Dana (Rosemary Scallon) made all the difference. Ahern blamed the defeat 'on a low turnout on a wet day'. He stated that 'whoever tackles it next won't have Dana ranting away during the campaign'.[2]

CATHOLIC TEACHING

In producing this essay I go before the public as a loyal Catholic, so I will need to explain my position. Firstly there is contraception. Pope Paul VI famously forbade it as 'intrinsically evil' in *Humanae Vitae*, 1968. A number of priests in the diocese of Washington dissented and they were immediately suspended by Cardinal Boyle. Paul set up a committee of American priests working in the Vatican. They issued an interpretation of *Humanae Vitae* saying that contraception was 'objectively evil'; that means that it could be used for serious reasons whereas the letter of *Humanae Vitae* would never allow it to be used for any reason. The Pope accepted this as an official interpretation.[3] That means that the desire to avoid unwanted pregnancy would be sufficient reason to use contraception inside marriage.

Next is the Catholic doctrine on killing, which in fact is not very consistent. Cardinal Bernardin of Chicago tried to give leadership on this matter. All who are against abortion should be equally opposed to the killing involved in war and in capital punishment. The Cardinal was widely hailed as a leader and consensus-builder among American bishops yet some claimed that he was bent on undermining the Vatican's authority.

About 1985 Bernardin had developed the Consistent Ethic of Life ideology, which expressed his response to living in an age in which he believed modern technologies threatened the sanctity of human life. He held that issues such as abortion, capital punishment, militarism and euthanasia all demand a consistent application of moral principles that value the sacredness of human life (as defined by the Catholic Church). In response to critiques from some pro-life activists, Bernardin pointed out that the ethic did not describe all threats to life as equal but all were related. He had not arrived at a position that would allow killing the embryo but his enemies did accuse him of weakening the Catholic opposition to abortion.

> 'A *systemic* vision of life seeks to expand the moral imagination of a society, not partition it into airtight categories. ... A *consistent* ethic of life seeks to present a coherent linkage among a diverse set of issues. It can and should be used to test party platforms, public policies, and political candidates [emphasis added].'4

However, John Paul did not like Bernardin personally and promoted many of his critics inside the hierarchy.

The Pope was himself not quite consistent on this matter. He began a series of condemnations of violence in his speech at Drogheda during his visit to Ireland:

> Violence is a lie, for it goes against the truth of our faith, the truth of our humanity. Violence destroys what it claims to defend: the dignity, the life, the freedom of human beings. Violence is a crime against humanity, for it destroys the very fabric of society. I pray with you that the moral sense and Christian conviction of Irish men and women may never become obscured and blunted by the lie of violence.5

I fear that our conviction was indeed blunted for when he asked the IRA to stop the violence it refused to do so and it was another fifteen years before the group called a ceasefire.

Later, in Vienna for the third centenary of the lifting of the siege of 1683, John Paul said, 'We understand that the language of arms is not the language of Jesus Christ ... armed combat is, at best, an inevitable ill in which even Christians may be involved. Christ turns every one of my enemies into a brother.'6 Later he opposed capital punishment. It was amusing that at the same time Cardinal Ratzinger, later to become Pope Benedict XVI, was saying in his *Catechism* that such punishment was permissible.

In 1995 John Paul published an encyclical, *Evangelium Vitae*, claiming that it was 'gospel' to preserve human life from the first moment of existence. With respect, I think the Pope was mistaken in applying this term to the human embryo. St Paul writes in poetic style telling us what the gospel is:

Christ died for our sins
according to the scriptures
and was buried.

He was raised on the third day
according to the scriptures
and he appeared (to Peter and the twelve) (1 Cor 15:3–5).

This is too sacred a concept to extend it as the Pope did. All Christians agree that no human and not even an angel from heaven can change the gospel (see Galatians 1:8). The Pope 'proved' his point saying that it is the same embryo that will develop into a fully human person. Also, even if it does not, he said, we run the risk of killing a human being by, for example, experimentation.[7]

So to sum up: contraception inside marriage is allowed nowadays. Those who oppose abortion should also oppose the killing involved in warfare and capital punishment. We cannot regard killing the embryo as being against the gospel precept: 'You shall not kill'. Rather it is on a much lower level than killing a fully formed baby or adult.

Some Present Attitudes

Our GP told me a few years ago that we were second only to the US in the amount of complaints we make against doctors and hospitals. But now we are far ahead of them in bringing court cases against medical staff. Rhona Mahony and Fergal Malone, masters of two Dublin maternity hospitals, lay before us the problems caused by the Eighth Amendment.[8] It comes as a surprise that 2–3 per cent of all babies in the womb have significant abnormalities. For example, more than 100 women from those two hospitals with those anomalies went to England for abortion in 2016. This is unsatisfactory. The women must get different doctors to handle their case. The hardest of all is that there is a four-teen-year jail sentence for an Irish doctor who gets it wrong about the risk to life of the foetus even though it is sometimes impossible to decide whether it is a risk to the health or to the life of the mother. The writers ask for two things which seem reasonable. First, the law that it is a crime to perform an abortion in case of foetal abnormality should be changed. Second, doctors in Ireland should be allowed to deal with those anomalies rather than sending patients off to England. It is only a matter of time until someone brings a case against a doctor for mishandling a foetus, so change would be desirable before that happens.

Another master, Chris Fitzpatrick, formerly of the Coombe, tells us that he grew up in the Ireland of Éamon de Valera and John Charles McQuaid.[9] He accepted infallible Catholic dogma but he has been thinking for himself of late and now he holds views he would not have espoused ten years ago. According to the Constitution at present the embryo has the same right to life as the mother. However, we must not describe all threats to life as equal. If a pregnancy threatens the life of the mother, it should be terminated as has been standard practice. He refers to cancer of the womb and ectopic pregnancy, Garret FitzGerald's two exceptions. If it threatens the health of the mother it is more complex but any new legislation should allow doctors room to manoeuvre. We should allow abortion for rape or incest. The same would hold true for fatal foetal abnormality. Education is needed to help people avoid unwanted pregnancy and this should include teaching about contraception.

The situation is further described by solicitor Caoimhe Haughey.[10] As a teenager she was indoctrinated by the Dominicans 'to believe that an unwanted pregnancy would ruin my life'. There was a case where doctors decided they could not withdraw life support from a clinically dead young mother, to protect her unborn child. Sometimes she wept with her clients as she sees no solution to their predicament; surely a situation little short of cruelty. She reasonably asks to allow us to vote again soon and install a system that will allow abortion 'in the State in a wide range of circumstances'.[11]

An argument on the other side is put by Breda O'Brien.[12] She tells us about Edwards and Patau syndromes, which are more severe than Down syndrome. We must always allow for a mother who wants to let nature take its course. She also tells the story of Marty McCaffrey, professor of perinatal care in North Carolina, US, who was trained to regard those conditions as fatal. Yet, 'these children had very severe disabilities, but they were alive, and very much loved and cared for.'[13] He discovered that recent research had shown that if discovered before birth, medical help was generally very limited, whereas if discovered after birth much more help was given and only 1 per cent died in the first 24 hours. A week later, Amy Walsh, in a letter to the editor, told how her daughter was still-born because of a condition called triploidy.[14] Prenatal testing is harmful, she said, because it gives false hopes to parents and undermines medical decisions if the diagnosis is 'fatal'. Not to be outdone, McCaffrey came back on 9 October to defend his approach and had some advice on our referendum.[15] He supports families of 'children with life-limiting conditions'. This is better terminology than 'fatal'. Parents are often pressurised to terminate the pregnancy. Even if a baby with anencephaly, for instance, were to survive for only a few minutes, the parents would have 'the possibility of meeting their child alive'. On the other hand, women who terminate pregnancy have 'significantly more despair, avoidance and depression'. 'Fatal foetal anomalies' are a false narrative. Ireland should learn from the 'tragic errors of other nations' and realise 'that there will be an insatiable call for abortion services to expand'. I think that we must agree with Fitzpatrick rather than McCaffrey because Fitzpatrick says that the difference between the health of the mother and the life of the mother is so complex and he asks that doctors have 'room to manoeuvre'.

Will the desire for abortion get ever broader, as McCaffrey says? On this matter we must trust the innate goodness of the Irish people. In 1995 when the prohibition of divorce was removed from the Constitution some people felt that the floodgates would be opened and marriages would be dissolved wholesale. But this has not happened. At the time Bishop Cassidy of Clonfert wrote a pamphlet, *When the Wind Died Down*.[16] He claimed that things would go well for the first ten years because our tradition of no divorce would support us: the wind would be at our backs. But when the wind died down in fifteen years' time we could expect to see much more divorce. Archbishop McNamara of Dublin recommended everybody to read this pamphlet to convince themselves that they should vote against divorce. Yet Cassidy's deadline of 2010 has come and gone and the situation has got no worse despite the predictions of himself and McNamara. It would be foolhardy of me to prophesy that the same will happen with abortion but at least I can say the dire forebodings about divorce did not materialise.

O'Brien is right in saying that for many people with a deformed foetus the best solution is to let nature take its course. Further, some nurses tell me that with an abortion there always comes a point at which the foetus must be killed and this can be traumatic. However, if, for example, 10 per cent would wish to take this course, there would be 90 per cent who would wish for an abortion. My view is that we must not try to stop them as I will now try to explain.

MUTUAL OBEDIENCE

In Romans 15 Paul tells us to advise, accept and agree with one another. As the tradition developed this became 'mutual obedience', famously in the good zeal of the *Rule of Saint Benedict*. In the fourth century the Emperor Constantine offered and the Church accepted legal and military protection. This was retained by all the mainline churches until our own day. When we read John Whyte's book[17] on the early efforts of the Irish Free State to enshrine ecclesiastical attitudes in the law of the land it reads very similarly to the history of the early Church. It would be hard to blame the bishops of the time as that was the general consensus. However things have suffered a sea change since then, so this would be my advice.

We need to respond to trauma and certainly need to take serious the pain suffered by Ms Haughey's clients, a situation little short of cruelty. Then we need to listen to the experts. The three masters sound to me like 'good Catholics'. They obey us and we have a duty to obey them as they know best and we must allow them full freedom to help patients as best they can. We should even be able to use them to quell the turbulence that is out there. If this leads to large numbers and even to abortion on demand, so be it. We must not use the law of the land to force people to be good; that has happened too often in history.

THE SLOW LEARNER

On 11 October 2016 I wrote in the *Irish Times* on 'The Making of the Eighth Amendment'.[18] At least that was the headline I wanted but they changed it to 'Legislation Would Clear the Way for a Repeal of the Eighth Amendment', as they were entitled to do. Firstly, I presented a time sequence from the first promise of an amendment to the final enactment of the law. That would have rectified Gene Kerrigan's confused sequence as he was up on his soapbox on Christmas Eve.[19] Secondly, I had discovered that in France 'multidisciplinary diagnostic centres' were used to decide when abortion would be legal. I said this would be an excellent route for Ireland to follow.

The day after my article appeared, Ciarán MacGuill wrote from France.[20] Next day Barry Walsh of Clontarf presented a plethora of statistics.[21] Both showed that I had got it wrong. Walsh said that I was right about the laws involved; they were more restrictive than those in the UK. However, the legal protection I had suggested does not work in practice. Despite some additional restrictions, abortion in France (22 per cent of pregnancies) is now more frequent than in the UK (21 per cent).

I must now withdraw my suggestion. I am no match for Walsh on statistics. Likewise, I would need to say that I am neither a legal or medical expert. The last thing people want today is a cleric with all the answers. I am grateful to those two gentlemen for dragging me through the learning process, be it ever so slowly. However, this does not change my underlying conviction, already outlined above, that we must show mercy and allow our medical doctors to treat their patients as they see best, without interference.

LEGISLATION

Decisions 'about abortion are often complex and riddled with ethical inconsistencies and contradictions', says Chris Fitzpatrick.[22] Like so many other things we often have to live with contradiction. *Summum ius, summa iniuria*, they taught us in moral theology long ago. To insist always on the letter of the law would result in doing great injury. So in this case of abortion, things are not going to be black and white.

In his book *Church and State in Modern Ireland 1923–1978*, John Whyte shows that the new state in its early years embarked on a process of enshrining Catholic attitudes in its laws.[23] That was the case with contraception: illegal here until it became available for married people only according to Haughey's 'Irish solution for an Irish problem'. This was also the case with civil divorce until a referendum narrowly decided that the prohibition of divorce would be removed from the Constitution. This was achieved by John Bruton, Taoiseach at the time, arguing the case on radio and convincing the undecided middle.

The *Irish Times*, on 6 October 2017, reported that a referendum giving general access to abortion would lose.[24] It claimed that 70 per cent of the electorate would vote for abortion in limited circumstances, while a vote to allow abortion in all circumstances up to the twenty-second week of pregnancy (as the Citizens' Assembly recommended) would have only 35 per cent support. Pat Leahy says this is 'a hell of a lot' more than it was a decade ago. This political correspondent says that 'if the proposal is along the lines suggested by the Citizen's Assembly and favoured by many repeal campaigners, the referendum will be voted down'.[25] According to Mary Minihan in the *Irish Times*, 'the consensus in the Dáil is that the Assembly's recommendations were an overly-liberal interpretation of the current thinking of middle Ireland on the issue'.[26]

Maeve Taylor, writing on behalf of the Irish Family Planning Association, thinks differently.[27] She asserts that there is 'strong support for abortion access based on the health needs of pregnant women'. She says that the limited poll proposed is 'highly restrictive, unworkable in practice and harmful to women's health'. In almost all European countries reproductive healthcare policies have been implemented. This is 'the sensible, constructive and pragmatic approach'.

Not very sensible, I would say: a good way to go if you want to lose everything!

Barrister Nuala Butler offers expert legal advice to the Dáil Committee on six different possibilities.[28] Her sixth proposal was to confer exclusive power on the Dáil to legislate. This would be FitzGerald's dream realised but I fear that it is not possible just yet. So we would have to go with her second option – that is legislation entrenched in the Constitution. This would 'provide the greatest degree of legal certainty' and it could not be changed without another referendum. On the negative side, she says that this kind of thing does not suit our Constitution very well. We see that if we try to get too much we will end up getting nothing at all.

To have a chance of passing, the pre-referendum legislation would need to name the cases in which abortion would be allowed: threat to woman's health, fatal foetal abnormality, rape and incest. This would not be very satisfactory as Butler points out in her fourth option but it is where we stand at the moment. It may need another referendum to get to the optimum state but that will be the task of a future generation. It seems that we will have to wait for some years longer before we get to FitzGerald's utopian aspiration in his constitutional crusade with the Dáil having power to legislate.

Many churchmen chose Charlie over the saintly Garret just as some people long ago chose Barabbas. I am not saying that he was another Christ but the choice was similar.

REFERENCES

Ahern, Bertie (2009) *Bertie Ahern: The Autobiography*, London: Hutchinson.

Cassidy, Joseph (1995) *When the Wind Died Down*, Dublin: Veritas.

de Bháldraithe, Eóin (2016) 'Legislation Would Clear the Way for a Repeal of the Eighth Amendment', *Irish Times*, 11 October.

Fitzpatrick, Chris (2017) 'In the Media Everyone Is Pro-Choice or Pro-Life. I Am Both', *Irish Times*, 16 September.

Haughey, Caoimhe (2017) 'Courts Should Not Decide Complex Abortion Cases', *Sunday Independent*, 8 October.

John Paul II (1979) *The Pope in Ireland: Addresses and Homilies*, Dublin: Veritas.

John Paul II (1983) 'Address in Vienna', *L'Osservatore Romano* (English edition), 19 September.

Kerrigan, Gene (2017) 'Soapbox: Fear, Guilt, and More Empathy than Ever ...', *Sunday Independent*, 24 December.

Leahy, Pat (2017a) 'Voters Would Reject Referendum on Full Access to Abortion', *Irish Times*, 6 October.

Leahy, Pat (2017b) 'The Six Options Being Considered by the Oireachtas Abortion Committee', *Irish Times*, 12 October.

Longley, Clifford (2017) 'A Newly Fertilised Embryo Is Not, in any Common Sense View, a "Person" as You and I', *The Tablet*, 19 August.

MacGuill, Ciarán (2016) 'Letters to the Editor: The Eighth Amendment', *Irish Times*, 12 October.

Mahony, Rhona and Fergal Malone (2017) 'We Face the Reality Every Day – We Know Why Change Is Needed', *Sunday Independent*, 15 October.

McCaffrey, Martin J. (2017) 'Letters to the Editor: The Eighth Amendment and Life-Limiting Conditions', *Irish Times*, 9 October.

Minihan, Mary (2017) 'Was Citizens' Assembly Best Way to Deal with Abortion Question?', *Irish Times*, 29 April.

O'Brien, Breda (2017) 'Breda O'Brien: When "Fatal" Foetal Abnormalities Are Not so Fatal', *Irish Times*, 23 September.

Sacred Congregation of the Clergy (1982) 'The Washington Case' in A. Flannery (ed.), *Vatican Council II: More Postconciliar Documents*, Dublin: Dominican Publications.

Taylor, Maeve (2017) 'Letter to the Editor: Public Opinion and Eighth Amendment', *Irish Times*, 10 October.

Walsh, Amy (2017) 'Letters to the Editor: Fatal Foetal Abnormalities', *Irish Times*, 29 September.

Walsh, Barry (2016) 'Letters to the Editor: The Eighth Amendment', *Irish Times*, 13 October.

Whyte, John (1971) *Church and State in Modern Ireland 1923–1979*, Dublin: Gill & Macmillan.

Wikipedia (2017a) 'Kevin McNamara (Bishop)', *Wikipedia*, https://en.wikipedia.org/wiki/Kevin_McNamara_(bishop), last edited 14 October 2017.

Wikipedia (2017b) 'Joseph Bernardin', *Wikipedia*, https://en.wikipedia.org/wiki/Joseph_Bernardin, last edited 4 December 2017.

ENDNOTES

[1] Wikipedia (2017a).
[2] Ahern (2009), p. 252.
[3] Sacred Congregation of the Clergy (1982), p. 417.
[4] Wikipedia (2017b).
[5] John Paul II (1979), p. 21.
[6] John Paul II (1983).
[7] Longley (2017).
[8] Mahony and Malone (2017).
[9] Fitzpatrick (2017).
[10] Haughey (2017).
[11] *Ibid.*
[12] O'Brien (2017).
[13] *Ibid.*
[14] Walsh (2017).
[15] McCaffrey (2017).
[16] Cassidy (1995).
[17] Whyte (1971).

18   de Bháldraithe (2016).
19   Kerrigan (2017).
20   MacGuill (2016).
21   Walsh (2016).
22   Fitzpatrick (2017).
23   Whyte (1971).
24   Leahy (2017a).
25   *Ibid.*
26   Minihan (2017).
27   Taylor (2017).
28   Leahy (2017b).

Biblical Arguments for Retaining the Eighth Amendment

Mark Fitzpatrick

Introduction

What has shaped my heart and mind as I come to this subject?

Firstly, I am a father of four daughters and four grandchildren. Being at the births of my own children gave me a profound sense of the beauty and majesty of life as a gift of God.

Secondly, I write from the perspective of being human. What is it to be a human being, and what is it to protect the lives of other human beings? This is one of the great responsibilities we have in this world; to protect, to defend and promote the welfare and good of one another.

Thirdly, as a citizen of this country, I feel the weight of responsibility that is on all our shoulders regarding this subject.

Fourthly, as a pastor I write with a sense of the calling of God. Not so much to state my view, although all I will write I fully believe to be true; but more importantly, I am going to set before you God's Word on this subject.

There are many with their own opinion on this. Does God have a right to an opinion? Does his opinion matter? Not only does his opinion matter, but his will and word is all that matters. If we are out of step with him then the problem is not with him but with us.

Outline

In the first part I will seek to present what I believe to be the main biblical arguments in reference to abortion and the preservation of the Eighth Amendment. In the second part I will seek to answer objections from those who believe in a pro-choice position.

TRUTH

My purpose is to present the Biblical view on this subject with the firm conviction that there is such a thing as ultimate right and wrong. There is truth. Consider the following.

1. Truth does not change. It is always the same.
2. Truth is not meant to be comfortable. It is not meant to suit our feelings.
3. Truth, by its very nature, is unbending and unyielding.

Truth was central to the life and ministry of Jesus Christ. We read that 'truth came by Jesus Christ' (John 1:17). He himself said, 'And ye shall know the truth, and the truth shall make you free' (John 8:32). He said to those who wanted him dead, 'But now ye seek to kill me, a man that hath told you the truth, which I have heard of God' (John 8:40). 'And because I tell you the truth, ye believe me not' (John 8:45). 'And if I say the truth, why do ye not believe me?' (John 8:46).

We see this principle most vividly in his trial when he stood before the Roman governor; 'Pilate therefore said unto him, "Art thou a king then?" Jesus answered, "Thou sayest that I am a king. To this end was I born, and for this cause came I into the world, that I should bear witness unto the truth. *Every one that is of the truth heareth my voice*"' (John 18:37) (emphasis added).

What is the point here? The point is – truth matters! This issue is not to be settled on the grounds of emotion or indifference. This must be decided on the grounds of what is right and what is wrong.

We must be convinced that there is such a thing as truth. There is such a thing as right and wrong. That we will all stand before God one day and give an account for our lives and the decisions and choices that we made. I am not saying this to frighten or anger anyone but because it is the truth.

If there is no truth then nothing matters. In that case, anything goes. Do what makes you feel better, etc. If there is no right and wrong then this book is pointless. Just go with your feelings. But the reality is that you know in your conscience there is a God. We have not been left to ourselves to decide what is right. He has told us in his Word, the Scriptures. The great tragedy is that for generations the Scriptures have remained a closed book in many churches and therefore we are now at a stage when we think we are in control. We decide. We are sovereign and not God.

Let's begin with our arguments.

Argument #1: God Is the Creator – We Did Not Evolve

'In the beginning God created the heaven and the earth' (Genesis 1:1).

This is the very first statement in Scripture and it becomes *the ruling principle* for all that follows in the Word of God. God's rights and authority are all built on this truth that God is the creator and indeed the sustainer of life.

Atheism and Evolution

It is no coincidence that many of the advocates of abortion do not believe in a creator, but in fact believe that we are here as the result of evolution. Now let us be clear about this, if evolution is true then there is nothing wrong with abortion. In fact, if evolution be true then there is no such thing as right and wrong at all.

But the Bible declares that we are not the result of some cosmic accident of chance but we exist because of the will and purpose of God. Therefore, that being so, God is the author of life and only he has the right over its termination.

Evolution and the Nazis

Evolution provided the justification for the ideology of the Nazis, who believed in a master race. It was taught that the Jews and many others were a lower form of human life. This is the exact argument behind abortion. We are told that the foetus is a lower level of development of human life and therefore can be terminated.

Consider what Joseph Goebbels said regarding the Jews and how he defended the Nazi position in terminating them:

> 'Of course the Jew is a human being too. None of us has ever doubted it. But a flea is also an animal. But not a very pleasant one. Since a flea is not a pleasant animal, we have no duty to protect and defend it, to take care of it so that it can bite and torment and torture us. Rather, we make it harmless. It is the same with the Jews.'[1]

This de-humanising of the child in the womb is a central plank in the argument of the abortionists. If they can convince us that the unborn child is something less than human, then they have gone a long way towards making abortion acceptable to society.

Human Rights

What about rights? We often hear this word being used. Consider for a moment, who has the right to end a life? Who has the right, frankly, to play God and say this life is to be terminated?

You see, if evolution is true then all of this is meaningless. As previously stated, there is no right and wrong. There is no standard. It all becomes relative. Everything then becomes what is acceptable or more comfortable for the individual and society in general.

This is the real issue. What suits me has replaced what is right. Rights have replaced Right! We live in a post-Christian culture which has lost its moral compass and does not care about anything but what makes us feel good.

Argument #2: Made in the Image of God and the Nature of the Unborn

And God said, Let us make man in our image, after our likeness: and let them have dominion over the fish of the sea, and over the fowl of the air, and over the cattle, and over all the earth, and over every creeping thing that creepeth upon the earth.

So God created man in his own image, in the image of God created he him; male and female created he them.

And God blessed them, and God said unto them, Be fruitful, and multiply, and replenish the earth, and subdue it: and have dominion over the fish of the sea, and over the fowl of the air, and over every living thing that moveth upon the earth (Genesis 1:26–28).

Human life is not just precious, it is the most precious thing that exists in this world and the reason is that it is made in the very image of God. We live in a strange time indeed when the value of human life is being diminished and considered to be no different than animal life.

Evolution Is Just a Theory

This is another consequence of the evolution theory. It is just a theory, for it has never been shown to be scientific. It is a belief system that rules the morality of the atheist and much of society. It is no more scientific than Santa Claus and the Tooth Fairy.

The Reality of Abortion

Pause for a moment and consider that over 3,000 abortions are carried out each day in the United States of America. Friends, this is the holocaust of our times. The German people, with the exception of a few, remained silent while the Nazis were murdering the Jews. We cannot remain silent while such horror is taking place in the world. We cannot remain silent while the possibility of such horror is considered even a possibility in our nation.

> The number of abortions carried out in England and Wales last year was the highest in five years, driven by growing numbers of women in their 30s and 40s who are terminating a pregnancy, official figures show.
>
> More women are having multiple abortions, according to the annual statistics released by the Department of Health. Almost four in 10 terminations are now carried out on women who have undergone the procedure before. Fifty women had each had eight terminations, the figures revealed.
>
> In all, 185,824 abortions were carried out on women and girls in England and Wales last year. That was 1,253 (0.7%) more than the 184,571 performed in 2014, and the largest number since the 189,931 carried out in 2011.'[2]

Be in no doubt that if abortion comes to this nation that this will be the story here also. Some will use the extreme arguments of rape and abnormal foetal development, etc. The reality is that in the two nations mentioned abortion is used as another form of contraception. Consider 'fifty women' had eight abortions each! *Four hundred lives ended by fifty women!*

The responsibility here is twofold. *Firstly*, on the fifty women who are indifferent to the murder of their unborn children. *Secondly*, on a society that provides the circumstances and facilitates and indeed, carries out such barbarity.

'Righteousness exalteth a nation: but sin is a reproach to any people' (Proverbs 14:34).

It is indeed a reproach to any nation when such facts are revealed. The UK and the US were once nations that honoured God and his Word. Now they have become nations that fear the anger and wrath of the sinful desires of the ungodly who wish to promote wickedness and selfishness as acceptable and even good. Therefore the Word of God also speaks to such when it states, 'Woe unto them that call evil good, and good evil; that put darkness for light, and light for darkness; that put bitter for sweet, and sweet for bitter!' (Isaiah 5:20).

Argument #3: The Law of God Forbids the Unlawful Taking of Life

'Thou shalt not kill' (The Sixth Commandment, Exodus 20:13).

God has not given us the right to take life at will. We are forbidden by God's positive and moral law to end the life of another that he has created to live.

A Twisted Morality

We find here a contraction and indeed an enigma in our generation. There was a time when the state would put to death those who were guilty of murder; as is stated in the law of God. Now we have a scenario in Western Europe where the guilty are set free and the innocent are slaughtered. What is wrong with us? How twisted we have become in our minds when these things are so. We have perverted the image of God beyond recognition when these things are done. In Scripture we read that God loves righteousness and hates wickedness. But we have reversed the order. We have mutilated the image of God by our practices and desires. When we protect the innocent and condemn the wicked we are like God. When we do the reverse we become like devils.

When the issue of rape is raised it is often said that it is justifiable to end the life of the foetus. What Scripture states is that the rapist is to be put to death, not the child. Our generation reverses the order and defends the right to life of the rapist but not the innocent child.

On 3 June 2002, the *Daily Mail* reported an all too familiar story line:

> A serial rapist freed early by judges because he was 'not a long-term danger to women' subjected another woman to a horrific sex ordeal.
>
> Less than two years after being let out of jail, Errol Henry broke into a 22-year-old student's home, overpowered her and tied her up.
>
> After he was found guilty of the latest offence, a senior police officer called the decision to speed his release: 'A travesty, a real miscarriage of justice.'[3]

This is what happens when society has twisted views of morality. Rapists are freed and the unborn are torn apart in the womb!

Argument #4: How the Unborn Is Described in Scripture

What do you call the unborn child in the womb? Do you refer to it as a foetus? It is much easier to be at ease with abortion when we use such terminology. I remember as a child hearing the term 'mongols' being used with reference to people with Down syndrome. This had the effect on me of not seeing them quite as human. They were something different. That was a wrong view based upon a use of language which was, to say the least, unhelpful.

Today it would be completely unacceptable to use this term as it is recognised that it dehumanises those with Down syndrome, and yet this condition is considered a legitimate reason for ending the life of the child. Now which is worse, using the term or killing the child? I know what I would choose. How about you? In Iceland they boast of being Down-syndrome free. How so? They simply end the lives of all Down syndrome babies in the womb. What sort of boasting is this? This is vile and evil boasting. Be in no doubt that this is where our nation will go if we vote to repeal the Eighth Amendment.

But how does God in Scripture describe the relationship between the mother and the unborn? Twenty-six times the Scripture uses the term 'with child' to describe this relationship. It does not say 'with foetus'. According to Scripture, what is in the womb of the woman is a child. To end the life of that child is murder in the sight of God.

OBJECTIONS ANSWERED BIBLICALLY

Let us now turn our attention to the objections and arguments raised by those who want to repeal the Eighth Amendment.

Objection #1: What About the Victims of Rape Who Become Pregnant as a Result?

Rape is a horrible and wicked act and leaves its awful legacy of trauma and pain on its victims. But what about the argument that abortion in such circumstance is not only permissible, but may even be desirable?

What is astounding to the present writer is that many who would advocate the death of the unborn child, would just as forcefully argue that the rapist should be spared! The view of Scripture is exactly the opposite. What does the Scripture say regarding the rapist?

We read in Deuteronomy 22:25–27:

> But if a man find a betrothed damsel in the field, and the man force her, and lie with her: *then the man only that lay with her shall die:*
> But unto the damsel thou shalt do nothing; there is in the damsel no sin worthy of death: *for as when a man riseth against his neighbour, and slayeth him, even so is this matter:*

> For he found her in the field, and the betrothed damsel cried, and there was none to save her [emphasis added].

The Scripture is clear, the rapist is to be put to death. He has committed an act akin to murder. That is God's view of rape. But in society many believe the rapist should not die and the innocent child should. What twisted morality is this? Why does society treat the child as the guilty one and the rapist as the innocent? *To preserve the life of the rapist and take the life of the child is a monstrous form of morality.*

What about the argument that the woman cannot deal with the trauma of having the baby? That is a very understandable and real concern. Many think the response should be to kill the baby. Scripture says, kill the rapist.

We must go back to the principle, is it ever right to take the life of an innocent human being? For example, if a woman who had been raped found out afterwards that her one-year-old child was the child of the rapist, would that make it acceptable for her to have the child terminated? Now, if this be unacceptable in our minds, what is the difference between this scenario and the first? The only difference is the level of development of the life and the environment it is in.

Another important Biblical principle here is that of personal responsibility for sin. Therefore we read:

> The soul that sinneth, it shall die. *The son shall not bear the iniquity of the father*, neither shall the father bear the iniquity of the son: the righteousness of the righteous shall be upon him, and the wickedness of the wicked shall be upon him (Ezekiel 18:20) [emphasis added].

When we save the life of the rapist and take the life of the unborn child we are liberating the guilty and slaying the innocent. Do you see what happens to a society that forsakes God and his laws?

I personally know of situations where children who were conceived in such circumstances have grown to have a wonderful life and relationship with their mothers. God can and does give these blessings even in the context of an awful beginning.

Objection #2: The Foetus Is Not a Fully Developed Human Being and Therefore It Is Acceptable to Terminate

This is a very weak argument used by abortionists. They say that the unborn child at five months could not survive without the mother. Could a six-month-old infant survive without its mother? Would that make it okay to end its life?

Reliance and dependence are not arguments for killing but rather protecting. The womb of a mother should be the safest place in the world for a baby. Instead it has become the death chamber for millions of babies. Let me ask you a question, have you ever watched an abortion? It is the view of the present writer that no one should even consider voting for abortion until they know exactly what it involves.

The following is a description of an abortion procedure in the second trimester from Dr Anthony Levatino, who was a guest speaker at the Citizens' Assembly on the Eighth Amendment. He is a board-certified obstetrician-gynaecologist with 40 years of medical experience. He is a physician and lawyer, and taught as associate professor of OB–GYN at Albany Medical Center, where he also served as the medical student director and residency program director. In the early part of his career, Dr Levatino performed over 1,200 abortions in the first and second trimesters. Dr Levatino has practiced obstetrics and gynaecology in Florida and New York, and currently practices in New Mexico.

A dilation (dilatation) and evacuation abortion, D&E, is a surgical abortion procedure during which an abortionist first dilates the woman's cervix and then uses instruments to dismember and extract the baby from the uterus. The D&E abortion procedure is usually performed between thirteen and twenty-four weeks LMP (that is thirteen to twenty-four weeks after the first day of the woman's last menstrual period).

To prepare for a D&E abortion, the abortionist uses laminaria, a form of sterilized seaweed, to open the woman's cervix 24 to 48 hours before the procedure. The laminaria soaks up liquid from the woman's body and expands, widening (i.e. dilating) the cervix.

When the woman returns to the abortion clinic, the abortionist may administer anesthesia and further open the cervix using metal dilators and a speculum. The abortionist inserts a large suction catheter into the uterus and turns it on, emptying the amniotic fluid.

After the amniotic fluid is removed, the abortionist uses a sopher clamp – a grasping instrument with rows of sharp 'teeth' – to grasp and pull the baby's arms and legs, tearing the limbs from the child's body. The abortionist continues to grasp intestines, spine, heart, lungs, and any other limbs or body parts. The most difficult part of the procedure is usually finding, grasping and crushing the baby's head. After removing pieces of the child's skull, the abortionist uses a curette to scrape the uterus and remove the placenta and any remaining parts of the baby.

The abortionist then collects all of the baby's parts and reassembles them to make sure there are two arms, two legs, and that all of the pieces have been removed.[4]

How can anyone read the above and still believe that abortion is acceptable? Societies of the past turned a blind eye to horrific practices in the name of the state and its people. Slavery was considered acceptable in America and Britain. The Holocaust was conducted by the German nation, with the acceptance of the German people, as a normal and acceptable thing. Are we in Ireland going to follow the bad examples of history and the equally bad examples of these nations in the present day by participating in a modern-time holocaust?

In looking back at the Troubles in Northern Ireland the BBC notes:

> When a huge car bomb exploded in the market town of Omagh on a busy Saturday afternoon in August that year, the shockwaves were felt across Northern Ireland and the world. It was the single worst atrocity of a conflict many had thought was over, *claiming the lives of 29 people and two unborn babies*. [emphasis added].[5]

Was the Real IRA responsible for taking the lives of two unborn babies? Of course the answer is yes. But ultimately what is the difference between this and the government-sanctioned regime of a systematic murder of the unborn?

Objection #3: The Woman Is Not in a Position to Raise the Child

Could we apply this type of argument to a six-month-old baby? If the mother cannot afford to look after the six-month-old baby, should she terminate its life? You say this is ridiculous. I say so is the similar argument used to support abortion. If a pregnant woman is genuinely not in a position to raise the child, are there not many, many people out there who would love to adopt such a child, rather than see it killed? I know of one family in the US who offer to adopt the children of those who are entering the abortion clinics. There are many out there who are crying out for children to raise and love. Abortion is never the answer! Killing a baby must never be the solution. If a woman killed her two-year-old and her defence was that she could no longer raise him, what would happen? She would rightly end up either in prison or a mental asylum. The Biblical answer here is to seek the God who promises to bless and provide for all those who put their trust in him.

Can a woman forget her sucking child, that she should not have compassion on the son of her womb? Yea, they may forget, yet will I not forget thee. Behold, I have graven thee upon the palms of my hands; thy walls are continually before me (Isaiah 49:15–16).

Objection #4: My Body, My Choice

This argument is simply not scientifically accurate. The unborn has its own DNA, its own blood type, its own organs, its limbs, its own finger prints, etc. In every sense, the body of the unborn has a separate body from the mother.

Yes, it is completely dependent upon the mother, but as we said earlier, *that only increases the moral responsibility* upon the mother to protect and provide; not to treat it as a choice but a precious life.

I am staggered that this is an argument used to support abortion. Surely this should support the pro-life view. If a newborn needed an incubator to sustain its life, would we argue let's just terminate the baby because it cannot survive outside of it?

Surely this argument is more symptomatic of the selfishness of our society rather than anything else? I remember as a child being told to share my toys when other children came into our home. Why did my mother do this? To teach me not to be selfish. The 'my body, my choice' argument is simply a selfish expression to please self and no one else.

Abortion is a decision from which there is no way back. It can never be undone. The guilt and misery of many women who have had abortions is a strong human and moral argument against it.

The Biblical argument against this point is that our bodies are ultimately not our own but belong to the God who made and gave them to us. We are stewards of a precious gift of God and are responsible to him for how we manage such a stewardship.

So then every one of us shall give account of himself to God (Romans 14:12).

Objection #5: Fatal Foetal Abnormality

David Quinn, writing in the *Irish Independent* in 2016, states that:

It [fatal foetal abnormality] is an extremely imprecise term, so imprecise that it is probably impossible to properly define legally. It is, therefore, potentially highly misleading and should not have a role in this debate.[6]

In November 2016 *TheJournal.ie* ran a story which told of a couple who went to the UK for a termination and it reported:

> They say that their child has been diagnosed with Edwards syndrome, which could mean their child will only live for minutes or hours.[7]

The fact is that up to a quarter of children born with this condition can live up to a year and more. No doctor can tell a parent that their child will only live for a few minutes. Many of us have experienced the guesswork of doctors with people who are outside of the womb, never mind those who are inside.

Notice above the term 'which could mean'. That covers a very wide range of possibilities indeed. For example, I might say, 'your baby could live to six months or six years or sixty years' etc. Be careful of the 'could mean' phrase.

That being said, if a child was only to live for a few hours, would that not be a very precious few hours? I must come back again to the mindset of our society which seems to say in effect, 'it's not worth the bother' or something like that. Have we become so self-centred that we think of things on this level and not the immense and incalculable value of human life?

Conclusion

Most of the arguments used for supporting abortion are a smokescreen for the opinions of those who are pushing this agenda. Many of these people believe in abortion on demand. There are some who are pushing for abortion even up to birth in some countries. Some are even suggesting termination after birth.

You are probably thinking, we would never go that far. Do you remember the story of the frog who slowly boiled to death? Let us beware that we do not, as a society, go little by little into the realms where we thought we would never go. Did the population of the UK in 1967 think they would be voting for almost 200,000 abortions per year?

The Word of God declares:

> Righteousness exalteth a nation: but sin is a reproach to any people. The king's favour is toward a wise servant: but his wrath is against him that causeth shame (Proverbs 14:34–35).

Do we want a nation blessed by the righteous God, or do we want to break off all restraint and just do what we want? Look around you and see the trends in society. This is all as a result of forsaking the Word of God. Where will all this lead to? Scripture reminds us that:

> [T]hem that honour me I will honour, and they that despise me shall be lightly esteemed (1 Samuel 2:30).

Always remember that right is always right and wrong is always wrong. If this evil practice is allowed into our nation, it will not cease to be evil. What a responsibility is ours before God and to all further generations.

A GOSPEL PROMISE

Before we finish, I must deal with a very important question: is there forgiveness for those who have had an abortion? The simple and wonderful answer is yes! The gospel message of Jesus Christ declares to us that there is abundant forgiveness for all who truly repent of their sins and trust in the Lord Jesus for the salvation of their souls. God does not treat us as our sins deserve when we come to him in true and genuine remorse for all the sins that we have committed.

Hear what the Scripture says to those who have sought the forgiveness of God in the gospel of Jesus Christ:

> He hath not dealt with us after our sins; nor rewarded us according to our iniquities.
> As far as the east is from the west, so far hath he removed our transgressions from us (Psalm 103:10, 12).

A PERSONAL NOTE

I was born in England in 1968, a year after the abortion legislation was passed there. I am glad that I was not one of the first victims of such laws. May God Almighty save us from such things and lead us as a nation so that we will love him, his law, and the lives of all our children.

DECISION TIME

When the time comes to vote on this issue, we as a nation will literally hold the lives of future generations in our hands. What an ominous responsibility is ours. God help us as we make our choice: to save life or end it.

REFERENCES

BBC (2013) 'History: Omagh Bomb', *BBC News*, www.bbc.co.uk/history/events/omagh_
bomb.

Brooke, Chris (2002) 'Rapist Freed as "No Danger" Struck Again', *Daily Mail*, 3 June.

Campbell, Denis (2016) 'Abortion Rate in England and Wales Hits Five-Year High', *The Guardian*, 17 May.

Hilmar Eitzen, Kurt (1936) 'Zehn Knüppel wider die Judenknechte', *Unser Wille und Weg*, Vol. 6, pp. 309–310.

Levatino, Anthony (2016) 'D & E Abortion: Second Trimester', *Abortion Procedures: What You Need to Know*, www.abortionprocedures.com/#1466802057745-21666a85-9db0.

Quinn, David (2016) '"Fatal Foetal Abnormality" Is a Loaded and Misleading Term', *Irish Independent*, 8 July.

TheJournal.ie (2016) 'A Couple Are Live-Tweeting Their Trip to the UK for an Abortion Due to a Fatal Foetal Abnormality', *TheJournal.ie*, 10 November, www.thejournal.ie/abortion-live-tweeting-trip-3073742-Nov2016/.

ENDNOTES

[1]   Hilmar Eitzen (1936).
[2]   Campbell (2016).
[3]   Brooke (2002).
[4]   Levatino (2016).
[5]   BBC (2013).
[6]   Quinn (2016).
[7]   *TheJournal.ie* (2016).